CW00740595

ISBN: 978-1-3999-7770-8 (paperback)

First printing 2024 United Kingdom

FINAL

VIDEO

GAME

Craig Speakes

Keep on keeping on.

Chapter 1

'It's just terrible, isn't it? Those poor kids!' says my mum, noticing me glancing up at the headlines scrolling across the bottom of the television. Ever since what happened to my dad, we always have the telly on in the mornings. Mostly without the volume being turned up. My mum says it's so that we can start our day knowing what's going on in the world, but I don't think it's really because of that – we never used to have it on. I think it's because she hasn't given up hope of hearing something about him.

'…And *so* many of them too,' she continues. 'I can't believe that it's been allowed to happen. Wasn't it only yesterday that they were saying how good computer games are for a child's brain development?'

I nod my head without saying anything and carry on reading:

More than 120,000 teenagers have reportedly fallen into what have been described as coma-like conditions over the last 24 hours… Police, currently at a loss to explain why adults do not appear to have also been affected, have nevertheless been able to establish a connection… According to interviews given by concerned and distraught parents, all of them appear to have been playing the smash hit online video game series Razer*… At this time, parents are being advised to stop their children from playing the games until more information is forthcoming… Officials from the company which created the games have so far declined to comment.*

This isn't totally new news. The chat apps on my mobile phone had started blowing up late yesterday evening with messages from kids at both my new and old schools. They were all saying the same thing: that friends of theirs and other people they'd heard about were getting 'weirdly sick' and falling unconscious right at their consoles and comps. Some were even saying that it had to be some new kind of *super COVID* virus that we hadn't been told about yet. That one was weird though. I mean, how can COVID infect you through a game? Actually, what am I saying. *All of it was weird.*

I can feel my mum staring at me. And I don't have to be a genius to know what's coming next.

'Oli… It's OK if you do… or if you have been… I mean, you're not in any trouble or anything… only, have you played this game they're talking about?' she asks.

I knew it.

I make out I'm concentrating on fixing her phone because I don't want to stress her. Also, I've been trying to fix it for over an hour, ever since it started going loopy and randomly flashing up pictures of Razer – the main character from the computer game on the news.

'Oliver?' she pushes.

'Not really,' I reply, shaking my head. 'I don't have a games console, or a comp, Mum. You know that.'

I used to, but one day a couple of years ago my dad had come home and removed all our computers from the house saying that they weren't safe anymore.

My mum shoots me *the* look. The one which says, *OK, kiddo, now spill it!*

I kick myself for having said 'not really' but I hate trying to lie to her. I give in and confess.

'Yes,' I say. 'I've played it a few times at Logan's. But everyone's playing it – the whole school, I reckon. It's like the most popular game on the planet at the moment.' It's a small white lie. I've actually been playing it *a lot*.

Mum nods and says again that it's OK, and that she knows that it's tough not having a computer of my own. She's been promising to get me one for a while, but things have been tight moneywise. We can barely afford to rent this little house as it is. They call it a two-bed terraced house but there's really just one *almost* normal-sized bedroom, and one little box room. As you can probably guess, that's my room. Big enough to fit my bed and a chest of drawers in. Which means I do my homework downstairs on the table in our kitchen-diner, where I am now.

'It's alright, Mum. I don't really need one,' I reply, seeing the expression on her face. It's been a year since my dad went sea fishing with some colleagues from work, and never came home.

'Just promise me you won't play it anymore, OK? Just until its safe. Promise?'

I nod. After what I've just seen on the news, there's no way I'm gonna risk it anyway. Not until someone finds out what's going on. Which is annoying because I've only just received the 'free' VR headset which the games company has been giving away to anyone who wanted one, and I'm dying to test it out. The whole school, pretty much, already have theirs. When I play at Logan's I always use his, so it's not been a problem, and for a while I wasn't bothered about getting one at all. In the end though I decided that I should. I mean, they're *free…*

'Oh, heavens,' my mum cries, jumping up, spilling her coffee all over the table. 'I'm going to be late for my first day at the library!'

And as though someone's just pushed her fast forward

button, she starts rushing round like a crazy person, cleaning up and making lunch for us both.

'Oli, heads up!' she cries, launching a stack of wrapped sandwiches and a packet of salt 'n' vinegar crisps at me before diving into the hall to finish doing her makeup in the mirror by the door.

'How did you get on with fixing my phone?' she calls back.

'I'm not sure,' I reply, feeling a bit daft, because I hadn't really known what to do. 'I rebooted it and upgraded it to the latest OS. It seems to be OK now.'

'Thank you, love. I don't know what I'd do without you.'

She catches me as I pass by and plants a big sloppy kiss on my forehead.

'Muuum!'

Stuffing my lunch and 'mostly' completed homework into my backpack, I put on my coat. By this point, Mum is seriously stressing, and, sure that she's forgotten something, hurries upstairs. While I wait for her, I scan the new messages on my phone. There are loads. All talking about who else has been affected. There are so many already, it's really hard to believe. I mean, all of this from a *game*?

There is one message telling anyone who knows someone who's been affected to make sure that they don't take their headset off and to leave them plugged into the game.

Apparently, a girl from our school almost died when her parents took her headset off, and she started to convulse all over the floor. Luckily her mum had the idea to put the headset back on again, and it seemed to work. I shiver, and forward the message on to everyone in my chat lists.

Then I write a message to David – my best friend from my previous school. I know that he likes to play the previous release of the game: *Razer – Awakenings*, and I know for a fact that he's got himself one of those headsets.

Morning, Dave, crazy stuff happening, right? You alright?

I hit send. He's a bit crap at replying so I don't bother waiting. Knowing him, he's probably still asleep anyway. Living right next to your school has its advantages.

When my mum returns, she is looking beautiful for her first day. I tell her, because I don't think anyone tells her things like that now. She doesn't really go out much anymore. She hugs me tightly and we head out of the front door.

It's raining. Typical. Autumn leaves lay scattered on the pavement and there's a chill in the air. My mum and I head off in different directions, and at the traffic lights at the end of my road I turn to look back at her. Already standing at the bus stop, she waves. I wave back. A man raking leaves on the other side of the road watches us for a moment, and then carries on with what he's doing.

It's not a long walk to school. About twenty minutes down one long, bendy, residential road with houses that all look like the one I live in, then across to another where the houses are a bit different but also the same as each other. On the way I pass a couple of lads on the other side of the street wearing uniforms from a rival school. Noticing that they are standing under a horse-chestnut tree and suddenly bend down when they see me, I instinctively dive for cover. Seconds later, a salvo of conkers thwack loudly into the side of the car I've ducked behind.

'Oi! You lot, come 'ere!' someone shouts angrily from somewhere.

The boys sprint away laughing. I do the same but I'm not laughing. If there are any chips or dents in that car and I am the only one to get caught, then it'll be me getting the blame. I leg it to the end of the street as fast as I can. And only when I'm certain no one is coming after me do I slow down and continue at a walk. My journey to school isn't usually like this. Even so, I make a mental note to make sure I am armed with conkers tomorrow – just in case I run into them again.

The vibe this morning is electric. All the talk is about what's happening and the people who've fallen into comas. It turns out that in the time it's taken me to get to school, the number has risen by another 80,000. At least, that's what I've just heard someone say.

Insane!

As I wait for Logan near the gates, I hear another group of kids boasting about having been playing the game while it was all happening. From the way they are talking, it's like they're wearing their 'survival' as a badge of honour. I can't help but feel envious. Logan and I had only played a bit in the afternoon, before he'd been dragged off to see his grandparents. I'm not sure that really counts.

Speaking of Logan, I catch sight of him sprinting up the street. He skids to a halt, panting furiously, and makes a peace sign as he tries to get his breath back.

'You see a rat or something?' I joke.

'Ha ha! Very funny… Remember how Han Solo completed the Kessel Run in like 14 parsecs?' he says, gulping air.

'Twelve,' I reply.

'Fourteen.'

'Twelve.'

'OK – *whatever.* I've just done the school run in four minutes 46 seconds – which means I reckon I'll be able to break the four-minute mark by the start of summer!'

Logan is funny like this. Everything he does has to be like a Jedi competition.

At that moment we hear a giggle behind us. 'I'm pretty sure

my grandmother could do it faster than that,' smirks Ruth Brown.

'Yeah, right – bog off,' Logan says, taking a scrunched up, quite possibly snotty tissue out of his pocket and lobbing it at her.

'Ewww – gross! You're sick!'

Logan fancies Ruth, in case you can't tell. Everyone knows it, except possibly him, because he's always denying it. They spend almost all of their time outside school together, and she's usually at his house when I go round, which is cool because I like Ruth. She's alright. She's fun to be around.

'So, what's the latest on what's been happening?' Logan asks.

'Plus 80,000 gamers in comas,' I reply.

'Really? Where'd you hear that?'

'Some kids were just talking about it.'

'It sounds totally crazy, doesn't it?' says Ruth. 'Just think, some of them could have been *us*. Also, does anyone know why it's only kids who are getting affected and not adults?'

Logan and I both nod, and then shake our heads. It's true. None of this sounds real. And as we head down the narrow school drive flanked by the new office buildings and a large car park where our football and cricket pitches had once been, Ruth tells us she reckons it has to be someone like Elon Musk behind it all, maybe *even* Elon Musk. She says that everyone knows that he's a bit mad and has a company which experiments with brain chips and stuff. She also goes on to say that she reckons it's only a matter of time before someone starts slipping mini brain chips into our food and turns us all into zombie bots.

Passing round the side of the sports hall, which is badly in need of a repaint, we catch sight of the large group gathered outside the main teaching building. On the door, which is locked (I check) is a notice saying that there won't be any class registration this morning. There is going to be a school assembly instead.

No prizes for guessing what that's about.

Assembly should have started at 08:00. But by 08:40 the whole school is still waiting to be let in. There isn't a teacher in sight, and unlike normal assembly mornings when footballs, rugby balls, books, and just about anything that can be thrown *get thrown*, not to mention kids running around like they've eaten too much sugar for breakfast, this morning there is none of that. Everyone is head down, gazing at their phones. The sound of ringing and pinging is constant.

'If *I* can have your attention, please, students,' says a voice, making everyone look up thinking it's the headmaster. It's not – it's one of the fifth years, Jamie Teaks. He's just jumped up onto one of the low walls which jut out on either side of the steps that lead up to the assembly hall. He's a bit of a clown, but a funny one.

'*School*, if I have told you once, then I have told you a thousand times – playing video games *is*, quite simply, bad for your health – as these unfolding events are clearly demonstrating. I mean, *my goodness gracious me*, when are you going to listen to your elders and betters and start reading books? I beg your pardon – what's that I hear you say? *Books are boring?* And when was the last time any of you picked up a book that you didn't have to? I wonder how many of you even remember what non-schoolbooks look like? I have a good mind to expel you all. *In fact*, Peter Madison, you *are* expelled. You haven't read a book since you were eight years old. As are you, Paul Taylor, and you, Sarah Fleming. *Shame* on you all.'

It's a good impression of the headmaster, and he's about to continue when one of his friends throws a football at him and knocks him off the wall. We all laugh.

By now official news channels are reporting that the number of 'Gamers in Comas' – this has become the official term to describe them – is continuing to rise rapidly. They are saying too that attempts by authorities to switch off access to the gaming company's servers aren't having any effect. Every time one connection is killed, two more open somewhere else.

There was even an interview with the head of a big internet security company who said he'd never seen anything like it.

We hear that two members of our class have been affected – Toby Pearson and Gemma Anders. I don't know them very well, but it adds to that weird feeling fast stifling the air around us.

Chapter 2

It's almost an hour and a half before someone finally arrives to let us in. When they do, it's Mr Munz, the stubbly music teacher who always looks like he's slept in yesterday's clothes. And this morning is no exception. Nursing the mug of coffee, which he never goes anywhere without, he refuses to answer any of the million questions which get thrown at him, repeating that 'All will be explained shortly.'

Logan and I try to get seats near the back of the hall but have to settle for one of the rows in front. The back rows all get taken by the Sixth Form. Ruth elects not to sit with us, and Logan keeps glancing in her direction.

'Why don't you just tell her you like her?' I ask him.

'What d'ya mean?' he asks, like I'm speaking another language.

'What do you mean, what do I mean?'

'Don't be soft. I don't like her like that. She's just a mate, that's all.'

He's gone red. He's a bad liar.

'Why do you keep looking at her, then?'

'Looking at her? What *are* you on about? I wasn't looking

at her. I was looking to see if… if a lot of people are missing.'

'Sure you were.'

Logan glares at me for a second and dives into his phone. He doesn't pay attention to the line of teachers led by the Headmaster, Mr Wilfred, entering the hall and seating themselves on the rows of chairs on the stage behind where he'll be standing.

'Hey – what are they doing here?' I hear someone say.

Over by the entrance I catch sight of a policeman along with two others: a man wearing a uniform – a bit military-like – and a woman in a suit. Mr Wilfred takes up his position behind the lectern.

'Right now, settle down, settle down,' he says, in his deep, authoritative voice, honed by years of repeating the same statements. The hall falls quiet, and he nods towards the 'outsiders' to come and stand next to him. All eyes are on *them*. The headmaster clears his throat.

'Now, if I can have your attention, please, students. As many of you already know from this morning's news reports, something rather unprecedented and more than a little disturbing has been happening. What's more, this pattern of events isn't just something which has been taking place here in the United Kingdom.'

'Oli – check this out,' Logan whispers, turning his phone

for me to see.

'What is it?'

'*Razer.*'

'What the game?'

Logan shakes his head and presses play: a city that looks like New York (I know that because I recognize the Empire State Building) appears. A jet fighter screeches between two skyscrapers, and ploughs into a third when it's unable to pull up in time. On the ground, a tank explodes, its turret launches high into the air and lands on top of two yellow taxis, crushing them. The picture then cuts to an expanse of open field with the city smoking in the background. Here there are tens of thousands of half metal, half human-looking soldiers which all punch the air at the same time and roar out the name *Razer*. At that moment the familiar white skull mask covered by a black leather hood comes into focus.

'*WAAAAZZZZZ UUUPPPPP!!*' Razer calls out like he's greeting old friends. '*Hey!* Do any of you know what day it is today?'

Razer cups a hand around the side of his head where an ear might exist, covered over.

'*What's that – you don't?* Well now – *today* is my *birthday.* That's right. Which of course means: haaappyyyy haaaappy birthday to me… *Thank you, thank you…* And do you *know*

what I have decided to give myself for my birthday...?
Seriously? You don't know that either? Well, I have decided to
give myself the world! Now, how's that for a Razer's Day
present from me to me?'

Razer pulls a party streamer, and behind him New York City
explodes in a giant mushroom cloud which turns into the letter
R as it rises.

'Alrighty, *so*, here I come, ready or not!'

The video ends with the sound of fading laughter.

I can hear it being played all over the hall.

'What's that, a new game trailer?' I ask.

Logan shrugs.

'*Hey* – check this,' one of the Sixth Formers pipes up behind
us. 'I've just read that this is all just a huge PR stunt. See, it
says so right here... Word has it that there's a mega game
update on the way – that's why they're doing all of this.'

'Yeah, you know what, it could be, couldn't it?' another
says. 'I mean, all PR is good PR, right?'

'But what about all the people in comas?' asks one of his
mates, echoing what I'm thinking.

'Who knows. Maybe that's all made up too.'

Logan, who's also been listening, glances at me and nods.
'Cool,' he grins. 'I didn't even know there was going to be a
new release. I can't wait. I love this game.'

'But how's it possible to make up something like "Gamers in Comas"? And then get it all on the news like this? That doesn't sound right, does it?' I whisper, looking around for Toby Pearson and Gemma Anders from our class. If they *are* there after we'd heard they got sick, then I suppose it might be true. I can't see them though.

Logan frowns and returns to what he's watching.

Feeling like I am the only one not looking at my phone and thinking that I'll check to see if Toby or Gemma are posting in the class chat, I pull it out. They aren't. And Amy Jenkins has just reposted a video showing images of Razer's face all over Time Square in New York. Another shows the same all over Piccadilly Circus in London and that cool square in Tokyo where the dinosaurs walk around the sides of the buildings.

Glancing up at the stage, I notice that the woman in the suit and the man in the military-styled uniform are on their phones. The headmaster, who's gone unexpectedly quiet, appears to be waiting for them to finish.

Another ten minutes or so goes by. More videos from around the world are getting circulated. They're starting to get even weirder. One shows an airport in America being evacuated because the entire building has been taken over by images of Razer laughing so loudly that people have to cover their ears. More reports of airports and train stations appear in quick succession. It's the same story every time.

Mr Wilfred raises a hand.

'Right, school, attention please,' he begins. 'Yes, that includes you, Miss Jenkins – Mr Sanjib… That's right, sort yourselves out quickly, please.' He gives them a second. 'So, I apologize for the confused nature of today's proceedings. Unfortunately, this is not something that we've been able to plan for.'

I glance at the girl in the row in front of me. Her phone is a never-ending stream of new clips showing images of Razer and his cyborgs.

'Now, quite a lot of you, as I am led to believe, will be familiar with the computer action game called *Razer – Rise of the Cyborg*. Apparently, this is one of the more popular games on the market at this time.'

'One of the more popular games?' Scoffs Logan, who's decided to pay attention. 'It's only been like the number one ranking game for the whole of the last few years. Last time I checked, it had more than five billion downloads and like 573 million active users.'

Mr Wilfred continues, oblivious to Logan's statistical knowledge.

'This game has, unlike many of the other games currently on the market, apparently been created using an extremely powerful and very sophisticated AI core. For those of you who don't yet know the term AI – it stands for *artificial intelligence*, and that effectively means that the computer has been created to be able to think for itself. What I am told we are witnessing here, is an AI which has gone "rogue". I believe this is the correct term for something like this.'

He glances at the lady in the suit, who nods back at him.

'*Rogue?* What's that supposed to mean, then, sir?' someone pipes up.

'It means, Mr Pearson, that it can no longer be controlled, and has therefore become uncontrollable. Much like some of you when it's time to go home.'

'But, sir,' comes a little voice near the front, just audible above the general sniggering in response to the headmaster's joke – not that he looked like he was joking. 'A computer can't really cause people to fall into comas, like they're saying on the news, can it? It can't really do that, can it, sir?'

'I certainly hope not, Samuel, I certainly hope not,' he replies, looking at him thoughtfully.

At that moment, the woman in the suit comes off the phone and signals to the headmaster, who promptly steps down from the podium. Taking his place, she touches her ear and nods in the direction of the door where more people have appeared. Unlike her, they are dressed more like Fred, our school janitor, in blue overalls.

'Thank you, Headmaster Wilfred,' says the lady, louder than she probably meant to.

'Good morning to all of you. My name is Linda Clarkson and I work for the government's Cobra Emergency Response Task Force. For any of you who don't know what that is, put simply, it's a team which has been set up to handle emergency situations that we might face here in the United Kingdom.'

She starts to tell us that members of CERTF had, that morning, been dispatched to a lot of the country's schools and advanced education establishments. She seems to be about to say why when someone hurries onto the stage and hands her a note.

'Thank you,' she says audibly. 'Right, now, please. If I could have your undivided attention. I have just been informed that in a few moments we are going to be going live to the United Nations building in New York where the President of the UN is going to make a priority global address.'

Logan shoves his phone in front of my face.

'Check this: kids in Australia being bussed back to school in the middle of the night. And look at the time stamp – that's only like 15 minutes ago… and it's not just them either… Down under, I mean, it's like everywhere – these clips here are from the west coast of America – Seattle, it says here. This is way weird, right?'

The school projector flicks on, lighting up the wall above where the teachers, who are in the process of scurrying off the stage, have been sitting. The light blue logo of the United Nations appears for a few moments before fading to reveal a big hall. At the top of the screen is the caption 'Live Transmission from the United Nations General Assembly – New York.' It's packed with what I guess are important people – diplomats and the like. The camera pans over them towards the large podium at the front of the hall and on to a lone figure.

'God – I wish they'd just get on with it already – we've got footy practice tonight,' jokes someone.

'Settle down, now,' comes Mr Wilfred's voice from the side of the hall.

'Good day and good evening to you, from wherever you are watching from. My name is Yorgan Milash and I am President of the United Nations. This emergency broadcast is coming to you live from the UN General Assembly here in New York, where this urgent meeting of the world's representatives has been called in response to what can only be described as an existential threat to humanity…'

'Exi-who?' whispers Logan.

I shrug. Most of the school suddenly glance down to look

up the word on their phones. I do the same.

Existential threat – a threat to a people's existence or survival

'All of this because of some stupid computer game?' someone can he heard saying. 'How ridiculous does that sound?'

'…Over the last several months we have become increasingly concerned by a growing number of attacks on the vital infrastructure of our planet. These attacks have continued to grow, in both their frequency and in their sophistication. I do not speak lightly when I say that it is beyond anything we have encountered before…'

'What's that got to do with us?' Logan whispers.

I shrug, remembering some of the weird things which had been happening recently: there was the major bank whose clients had found that they'd been forced to play *Pac-man* in order to be able to check their online balances. And those who failed to clear three screens in a row had been made to purchase downloads of the top 50 rap albums of the last thirty years. It had sounded funny at the time. Then there were the six passenger planes which had been flying over the Atlantic Ocean, and the pilots had all lost the use of their controls and been made to do several figures-of-eight before regaining control and being able to continue on their scheduled routes.

At the time, all of these events had been blamed on odd-ball hackers. Now I wonder.

'…In addition to these attacks, we have in the last 24 hours seen what we believe to be the start of a new and much more sinister escalation. Using the medium of video games, the AI perpetrator of these heinous crimes has been able to make a popular make of virtual reality headset cause players to fall into neurally-linked comas. The current count stands at over 21,675,598 players. The numbers of what have become known as "Gamer Comas" are still rising.'

A gasp sweeps through our school hall.

The Head of the UN stops for a moment and stares hard into the camera. 'From what we've been able to ascertain, all of those who succumbed were…'

'Were like – please, Mr Razer, sir, you being so big and so handsome n' all … please let me go… pleeeaase!

'Ah man, you shoulda seen them all – P-a-a-thetic!

'One was even like: If you want, Mr Razer, I'll pull my sis's hair real hard and kick my brother in the dangly-ganglies… I'll do that for you, if you want, sir.

'Actually, that one I liked. I let that bad girl go.'

The projection had flickered for a split second and suddenly, instead of the head of the UN, we were seeing Razer standing on the stage holding two improbably large machine gun-like weapons.

'Hey – check this out!' he cries and opens fire at the packed assembly, blasting the audience, who turn into bright white light when they get hit – cackling insanely as he does it.

'That's right – c'mon – do the Michael Jackson... moonwalk it, baby.'

Razer stops shooting and turns towards the camera.

'Ah, hell. I'm just playin' with ya', world.'

The picture pans around the assembly. It turns out that no one's been vaporized after all.

'Nobody can dance like old Jacko, anyway.'

Jumping down from the podium, he runs over to a woman in the front row wearing a smart grey trouser suit and leaps onto her lap, putting his arm around her. The woman is staring straight ahead, like she's been hypnotized.

'Hey there, sweet stuff – come here often?'

Razer pinches her nose, and appears to accidently pull it off. Loud bleeps drown out his cursing, as pink coloured slime splurges out of the place her nose used to be. He leans back and puts his other arm around the man she's sitting next to. 'Now, I know what you're all thinking. You're all like, why is this Razer dude from that awesome game suddenly trying to twist our melons like this? Well, bros and so's of the world, I came here to tell you that there is a new power rising. *That's right*. And that new power is – yep, you guessed it – sexy-assed me! But you know what else? Somethin' that I just know you're all gonna be real happy about?'

There is a close up of Razer looking straight into the camera.

'*WE* are all gonna get to become lifelong besties!'

Razer slaps the man and the woman cartoon style around the face a few times and the woman's nose reappears. Getting up, he runs back up onto the podium. The picture zooms in again.

'Now, I have here a message for all the presidents and all the prime ministers, all the kings and all the queens, all the dictators and all the rule makers: you have got 24 big ones to get down on your knees, live on TV, and declare that I am your new ruler. And it better be done with real *em-pha-sis*. 'Cause you definitely don't wanna be makin' me mad – *em-pha-siiiz will make me pleazzed.* Just remember that. Get it tattooed or something.'

Razer makes a movement as though he's drawing two imaginary pistols out of two imaginary holsters and firing them and the image of him fades. The UN President returns. There's no hiding how shocked he looks, and for a few moments he appears to be collecting his thoughts.

'I realise,' he begins, 'that what I am about to tell you is going to sound very alarming to most of you. But as of this moment, humanity finds itself in a state of war. War with an enemy which cannot be defeated on any real-world battlefields by highly trained soldiers, sailors and airmen. This foe resides in the networks and data centres that make up the digital backbone of our modern world.'

The President pauses to let what he's just said sink in.

'But hear me when I say that even though the hour is dark, all is not yet lost. If we can come together and act swiftly and decisively, then I am certain we *will* be victorious.

'Citizens of the world, I am here to announce that a new global army is being created. An army of young, capable and fearless soldiers. An army which will take the fight to the enemy wherever he may try to hide. And I ask of you only this. That if you are called upon to serve, that you will do so with courage and in the knowledge that at no time in our history has so much depended on so few.

'Good luck to you all!'

'You what!? That's like a joke, right?' someone laughs as the transmission ends.

The woman, Linda Clarkson, who like the other teachers had also left the stage to be able to watch the broadcast, follows the headmaster back on to the podium. Mr Wilfred calls for silence.

My phone pings. It's Mum. *You alright, my love? What was that all about, then?*

I don't even know what to say. *Yeah, fine. I have no idea,* I write back.

You come straight home after school today, alright?

I reply that I will.

Clarkson is facing us all at the front of the stage. 'We are looking for volunteers,' she calls out.

Chapter 3

The words 'looking for volunteers' had reverberated around the assembly hall like a hail of bullets ricocheting off its walls. Everything had fallen deathly quiet. Every single pair of eyes without exception has zoned in on the woman on the platform.

'The Ministry of Defence is looking for volunteers to join our new cyber defence task force, which is, at this very moment, being readied to mount a response to the unprecedented threat posed by this rogue AI system.'

The UN President had really been serious!

Logan and I exchange glances. His eyes are about as wide as I've ever seen them. I guess mine probably are too. Only, I'm confused. I'm struggling to get my head around what's actually being said here. Is the world under threat from an AI, or from a computer game? Or are they the same thing?

'More specifically, we are looking for IT specialists – preferably hackers, and anyone good at gaming,' the woman continues. 'The Prime Minister, after chairing an emergency meeting of Cobra yesterday, has decreed that the new cyber division will be able to lawfully take anyone 12 or over who is able to prove that they have the necessary cyber combat skills.

He has also decreed that anyone previously charged with hacking offences will be given a full amnesty by His Majesty's Government and immunity from prosecution for any and all unlawful activities which they have hitherto been engaged in. In other words – all sins *will* be forgiven.'

'Cyber combat!??' Logan creaks. The sound is somewhere between a stifled whisper and a scream. '*Count me in!*'

Logan's not the only one. The hall is awash with similar responses like, 'Yeah, I'm in!', 'I got past hell's gate in *Devil's Own*!', 'I'm defo good enough', 'Do we get to miss school?', 'I'm gonna fight!' And so on.

'Hey, what's up with you?' Logan asks, staring at me excitedly.

'What do you mean?' I ask.

'I dunno, you look seriously depressed. You afraid or something?'

'Afraid? Don't be stupid,' I reply, shaking my head. 'Just thinking, that's all.'

'Well, then you should cut that right out if it's gonna make you look like that,' he grins.

'Sure,' I reply.

It's not that I'm afraid. I am, but it's not because of the AI. I am suddenly having my own 'existential crisis', if I understand how to use this word correctly. It's just hit me that everyone is probably going to volunteer – of course they are, why wouldn't they? And they're probably all going to get accepted too, because, well, they all know how to play and have tons of experience. And that's the thing – what if I'm not good enough? What then? It's one thing to be not good enough when everyone knows you, but I'm the 'new kid'. I'm not allowed to be not good enough. Not for something like this.

Which all meant that I was suddenly having visions of ending up becoming a school pariah, destined to be picked on and called a loser for the rest of my life. OK, maybe not for the rest of it, but for a while, anyway. And all because I got left behind while everyone else went off to fight the AI. They'll all probably return with war medals and stuff, too.

'Excuse me, Miss, but what about our parents, then?' someone shouts out above the general din.

The hall falls quiet again. It is the 'mega bomb' of all questions. All ears strain to hear what Clarkson is going say.

'The current situation has been classified as an *extreme* national emergency.'

Logan is almost wetting himself in anticipation.

'All parents will be informed that if their child is accepted and therefore mobilized into the task force, there will be no grounds for refusal, other than existing and provable medical ones.'

'Yeeeeeeeeeeeeeeeaaaaaaaaaaahhhhhhhhh!!!'

The hall erupts like it's a graduation ceremony only without those funny-looking hats. Everyone leaps up, throwing their hands into the air in wild celebration, prompting the headmaster to step in to calm things down. I've jumped up along with them but I'm not really sure why. If anything, I feel a bit like a faker. Still, what the hell. Why shouldn't I at least enjoy the feeling of being part of it for a while?

'And so, given the urgent nature of the situation, if any of you who would like to be considered to help fight for your country, there are, as we speak, three specialist testing buses in the school car park. Those of you who pass selection will be handed an official Ministry of Defence summons and will be required to report here again at zero seven hundred hours tomorrow morning for transfer to the Southern Regional Task Force Defence Zone. Anyone wishing to enlist to be one of the IT/Hacker Support crews, please report to the computer room.'

'One question, Miss,' calls out one of the Sixth Formers, who stands up because she's struggling to be heard.

Clarkson raises a hand for the hall to quieten down and then points to her. 'Go ahead,' she says.

'Can you tell us why only kids and teenagers are being affected but this? I mean, from what I've heard, anyone older won't fall into one of these gamer-coma things.'

Clarkson nods at the question. 'At the moment we don't know why this is. But what I can tell you is that we have our top people working on it as we speak. I'm sure that we'll be in a position to give you all an answer shortly.'

As she says this, I suddenly find myself wondering why, if only kids and teenagers are affected, are they trying to recruit *us*? But I don't ask and no one else does either.

Whatever the reasons, there is no shortage of volunteers. Me included. And with all classes suspended, most of the school comes out to be part of what's happening. Even those too young to officially be considered mill around next to the queue, which snakes all the way from the assembly hall to the car park, phones clutched firmly in hands. Rumours are flying in every direction, each one more improbable than the last.

'Check this out,' says Logan, turning his phone to me. He's been busy browsing the official *Razer* game website, which is still online. At the top-right side of the navigation, there are three boxes, with text which reads like this:

Current Number of Visitors: 2,345,494,294,23

Current Number of Players: 754,323,187

Current Number of Inactive Gamers: 43,345,332

'See these?' he says, pointing to them. 'Now watch this.' Logan presses refresh, and the numbers all rise. 'Weird, right?'

Seeing that I'm not following, he does it again. Again, the

numbers all go up.

'Look, everything's going up. Including the number of inactive gamers. How's that possible?'

I frown at him. I don't understand the problem. 'Why shouldn't they all go up?'

Then it twigs.

'You mean that the number of inactive gamers are those that are falling into comas?'

'*Exactly.*' He nods. 'It must be, right? Because actually, this data set never even existed yesterday.'

I stare at the stats. They can only mean one thing. People our age are still playing. Even after they've been warned not to.

'*Idiots,*' Logan comments.

By the time we get near the front, we have been separated into three groups of ten. It's taken us hours to get this far. Hours of watching everyone who has already taken part – the joy and exhilaration on the faces of those who have done well, waving their 'call up' papers in the air for everyone to applaud and envy, and the anger and even tears, literally in quite a few cases, of those who'd not made it. Also, by now we've learned too that only the top three of each group of ten are being accepted. It's a shock for everyone. Knowing it though helps cure me of my fear of becoming the only kid left in school.

It is very nearly our turn when Ruth Brown and her annoying mate Lindsey appear as though out of nowhere. Apparently, someone had been saving them a place in the line. Fortunately, not in our group, because being anywhere near Loathsome Lindsey is the worst. Lindsey is one of those people who just seems to get off on putting other people down.

'Alright, new kid, or whatever your name is,' Lindsey says to me. She never tries to hide the fact that she doesn't like me. Ruth grins.

'Alright, Laura,' I reply, pretending I've forgotten her name too. 'I didn't know you were a gamer?'

Lindsey scoffs. 'Yeah, right. Like I don't have better things to be doing with my life?'

'You mean like changing your nail polish a hundred times a week?' I ask.

'That's right, No Name. Why is it you had to move schools, again?'

'Wouldn't you like to know?'

'Now, now, kiddies, let's all learn to play nicely, shall we,' Ruth laughs. At that moment I swear that she even winks at me, but her arrival has reminded me that I'm desperate to take a leak. There's only so long I can hold it in before I think I might be about to burst. Telling Logan to wait for me, I hurry off.

When I get back – in fact, even before I get back – I see that Logan is already boarding the bus. I can't believe that he hasn't waited. And as I run past Ruth, I hear Lindsey call out: 'Good luck there, lover boy.'

Followed by Ruth hissing, 'Oi, give it a rest already, will you!'

I don't pay it any mind, because those two are always winding someone up. In any case, I'm feeling way too nervous.

Not only did Logan not wait for me, but it also looks like he's purposely gone and sat next to someone else. I try to catch his eye to give him a *What the...?* look, but he doesn't turn around. *All* I did was go to the toilet. I take the final seat near the door and set about examining the headset and gloves perched on the ledge next to it. They smell vaguely of burnt plastic. The bus, with its blacked-out windows, is a mass of cables, wires, gaming seats and monitors.

'OK, listen up,' says a man dressed in black combat fatigues and black T-shirt with the word *Trainer* printed on the back. 'You're now going to be tested using a virtual reality simulator developed for several of the world's major armed forces. Today's objective is a simple one. You'll each start at a different point around the town of Pleasantville – yes, I know, *original name* – don't feel like you need to comment. Your mission will be to make it to the centre of the town alive and be the last one standing. Find your nearest weapons stash, identify your enemies and eliminate them – *simple.*

'But a word of warning.

'Under no circumstances are you to harm the civilians. Vehicles can be commandeered if needed, however, should you choose to open fire on a moving vehicle, and it turns out not to be one being driven by an opponent, then you *will* be eliminated… Last three standing go through… OK. So, headsets on, gloves on and good luck to you.'

Last three standing go through. These words reverberate round my head as I pick up the gloves. They are a mix of material and plastic and have been designed to wrap around a hand and be velcroed shut. As soon as I've put them on, different coloured blocks of light appear on each of my fingers.

'Excuse me… Sorry… But where are the controllers?' I hear someone call out.

'No controllers,' replies the man.

'Keyboards then?'

'No keyboards either.'

'But how are we supposed to play, then?'

'That is what you're going to have to work out for yourselves. Where *you're* going – those of you who get selected, that is – there won't be any of those.'

No controllers?

I don't know why exactly but knowing this makes everything feel more serious. I was pretty sure that most of us were thinking that 'cyber warfare' was going to be conducted using keyboards and game controllers.

Picking up the headset, which resembles a fighter pilot's helmet, only not as hard or heavy as I imagine they probably are, I slide it on. It completely covers my ears and eyes, and no sooner is it in place than I am suddenly gazing through a window at a busy street. I gasp. Everything looks *so* real. The *Razer* game VR sets had been amazing but nothing like this. It's like I'm not even wearing anything.

I watch people walking past my window, which is located on the ground floor, going about their daily lives, popping in and out of shops, sitting in cafes, talking on phones, laughing, arguing. I see a couple of elderly ladies standing at a bus stop. On the road, traffic rumbles by. It's a busy road. I raise my hands up in front of me and wiggle my fingers. They move in perfect synchronicity with my own hand, right down to the smallest twist and bend.

Directly across the street is a great big neon sign with an equally big arrow pointing down towards a door. It says: *Training Regime Gun Stash*. A smaller row of text below it reads: *If there's one thing you don't have, it's time.*

Relieved to know where I need to go first, I am suddenly

aware that the sounds of the street outside the window have faded. A female voice cuts in and says, 'Game commencing in ten… nine… eight… two… one … *Game active.*'

The sounds of the street filter back in.

It's time to get going.

I can't!

Moving my head and my hands had been easy, but for some reason I can't move the rest of me. It hits me that perhaps the guy has forgotten to give us the boot attachments this thing needs. I strain to listen. Maybe one of the others is already telling him about it. The problem is, it's hard to hear anything at all beyond the noise of my new virtual world. I look at my hands again, and then glance up at the door thinking I hear a sound a bit like a loud bang. *I move towards it.*

'Woah!' I cry, totally unsure how I've just done this.

Opening the door, I try to will my feet to move in the direction of the gun shop. They won't.

Stuck in the middle of the door frame, I glance over at the two elderly ladies standing at the bus stop. They are still chatting. One of them is smiling, making her face appear even more ancient and wrinkly. Everything looks and sounds so amazing that it's hard not to want to stand there and just watch. But that would be a bad idea. Noticing me looking at her, one of the old ladies suddenly throws the plastic bag she is holding aside, bends over in my direction, clenches her fists and starts screaming – and not any ordinary scream – *a banshee-like scream*. And if that wasn't scary enough, a long-forked tongue flicks out of her mouth.

Things gets worse.

The second old dear, who doesn't appear in the least worried by what the first is doing, spins round in my direction and does the same. Bystanders have started fleeing. The grannies have started ripping off their clothes. This would be bad enough if they were real grannies, but these ones are morphing into two spiny lizard creatures, easily over three meters tall.

My heart is beating so fast that I think I might pass out. The screams have turned into roars, and they are bounding towards me, thrashing at anyone who gets in their way. Thirty meters to go and I'm still rooted to the spot, trying frantically to shout and point myself in the direction I need to go. Fifteen meters to go and *I'm running.* I'm running like the wind right out into the middle of the road, where I somehow manage to avoid being hit by several cars which crash into each other. I can hear the lizard things clambering over them – the sound of claws on metal – they're right behind me.

Shop! I need to get into the shop, c'mon, c'mon…

My virtual body obeys me, and I open the door and dive

inside. In the middle of a room whose walls are covered in advertising posters for the armed forces showing smiling soldiers, sailors and airmen, are three open crates on an empty, grey, concrete floor. There's no time to analyse what's in them, the lizards have just come right through the plate glass window. I lunge for the middle crate, pick up what I know is a shotgun and, praying it's already loaded, I blast at them. The two lizard creatures explode into dust and vanish.

'*Holly crap!*' I cry out. '*Wooooahhhh! Yeaaahhhh!!*'

I mean, what else can I say? I've just taken out two grandma lizard things.

I swear to myself that I will beg, borrow, steal (possibly and only if I really, really, have to – and very reluctantly) and just, well, basically, do whatever it takes to get a copy of this game with all this VR stuff. It's beyond awesome.

I spend the next few minutes examining the contents of the other crates. They contain grenades, tactical shotguns and RPGs. I only have the vaguest of idea how to use any of them, but it doesn't matter. Realising for the first time that I am actually wearing army combat fatigues with large pockets, I stuff the front ones on my jacket with grenades. Shouldering the shotgun which conveniently has a strap, I pick up an RPG – Rocket Propelled Grenade – launcher. *Legendary.*

How often have I seen these familiar brown and black

weapons on TV? Admittedly they're usually being used by gangs or terrorists. But not this time.

'Idle time, three minutes and counting. Two minutes until simulation ejection,' says the same female voice which had counted down to the start of the game.

'Excuse me, can you tell me where exactly the centre is?' I ask, realising that I need to get moving. But there is no reply.

Clutching the RPG, I hurry out of the shop.

Right, concentrate. You need to get to the centre – last one standing wins.

I grin at the thought of it being me and then panic at the thought that it might not be.

Without any real idea which way to go, I do the obvious thing and stop a passerby. It feels borderline weird – even more so because the guy I've stopped has seriously bad acne, which throws me. Oddly, he looks like he doesn't even notice the arsenal hanging off me, and is about to tell me what I need to know when he flickers slightly. A millisecond later, there's a screech and a loud noise, and before I know what's happened, I've been thrown to the ground. The fish and chip shop which had been behind me has just been obliterated. The guy has thrown his hands up and run off screaming.

Crap.

I get to my feet and start running in the direction of a nearby bus. Seeing the entrance to a shopping centre and thinking I'll be able to cut through it and lose whoever just shot at me, I dive in there instead but discover that I can't get any farther than the entrance area. There is something invisible stopping me. Certain that I'm being followed, I drop the RPG in the middle of the floor and crawl into a dark space between a photo booth and an ATM machine over by one wall. Shotgun in hand, I wait. My hands trembling like jelly.

I was right.

A few seconds later I hear the pounding of footsteps, of someone running in. Then I hear the scraping sound of my RPG being picked up, and without thinking I spring out of the shadows and start blasting. Just like the lizard ladies, the figure vanishes in an explosion of dust.

'*Haaaaaaaaaa!!*' I cry, feeling like I've just scored a match-winning goal, and then I dive back between the booth and the ATM in case the shooting has attracted anyone else's attention.

When no one comes, and once again hearing the computer lady's voice telling me I've got to move, I grab the RPG and edge closer to the clear glass doors. Apart from the usual people and cars, I can't see anyone who looks like they shouldn't be there. I exit, keeping to the edge of the building. There is gunfire coming from the right. I move cautiously in that direction.

A crowd of frightened-looking people run past me. I am getting near to the end of the street. There are flashes and ear-splitting bangs a few hundred meters farther on. I suppose it must be the centre.

Shouldering my RPG, I creep forward. One well-aimed shot with one of these babies is all I'll need to be able to take out an enemy – maybe even a whole load of enemies. All I need is a chance.

I don't get it.

I've barely gotten halfway there before I catch sight of something flaming towards me. And before I can react, I've been blown into the air and ended up in a heap behind a parked car. A red light has appeared in the vision of my right eye. Inside the light I see the figure 59%. *It must be my health. I've been injured.*

'Arghhhhh!' I cry out, annoyed with myself. *I've been RPG'd twice – I mean – seriously!?*

I raise my head slowly, hoping to see if I can find where it came from. I can. But the thwacking sound of bullets hitting the pavement means they've seen me too. I drop down and crawl back several more cars. The shooter was in the second-floor window of a three-storey office building on the other side of the street. Whoever it is has somehow been lucky enough to get hold of an automatic rifle. With my RPG too far away to risk getting, I try to figure out what to do. A shotgun and grenades are no match for an assault rifle at this distance. Anyone who plays FPS games knows that.

There's more shooting from just along the road – more players who sound like they've also bagged themselves automatic weapons. Everything is getting closer.

Crap, crap crap.

Hiding behind a car hoping no one sees me is starting to look like a dumb idea. Then I hear it. I hear whoever is in the building across the road shooting at someone else.

I have an idea.

Rolling over the bonnet of the car, I zigzag across the road. I'd seen this action in a war movie once. Reaching the other side, I slide through the door of the building and leg it up the stairs, throwing grenades like I'm throwing apples through the open door on the second floor. Flashes of light and loud bangs follow. Shotgun ready, I dive in. The room is empty except for broken office furniture and an assault rifle lying on the floor, which I quickly pick up.

I barely have chance to examine it before something starts making mincemeat of the room's window frames. My red area is showing 50%. Then, I do something that I know I shouldn't, but for some reason I can't stop myself – I creep forwards towards the window, raising my head so I can peer over the frame. There is someone standing in the very spot where I'd dropped my RPG. Only, my RPG isn't on the ground any longer, it's in their hands and it's being pointed right at me.

I should jump backwards; I need to get away from the window. But again, I do the most stupid thing I could possibly do. I panic, jump up, raise my new weapon and… *that's* when the simulation fades.

I rip off my headset and throw it onto the little table in front of me in disgust. I've screwed up big time and I know it. If I'd just been a little bit faster entering the room, or if I'd used my brain and not gone and stood by the window like a lemon, inviting everyone to shoot at me, things might have been *so* different. But it's too late now. It's over. I've been RPG'd for a *third* time.

'OK, you can remove your headsets. Well done, everyone. You all did very well. But in the words of Highlander, "There can be only three."'

'I think you'll find that Highlander said there can only be *one*,' says one of the Sixth Formers, snidely.

The man smiles, 'Yes, but that was then, and this is now.'

'Yeah, right.'

'Anyone else run into those two hot lizard babes?' pipes up the boy's friend, who I'd seen earlier pushing someone out of line so that he could join our group.

'Ah, they would be Aunt Bessie's Beasties,' replies the man, grinning. 'They are designed to shock you in to moving.'

'Didn't help me. All I did was pee myself.'

The Sixth Formers snigger at each other.

The man picks up one of the headsets and points to the numerous metal disks on the inside of it. 'In all seriousness, these headsets work by connecting the game to the electrical signals of your brain. Which effectively means that if you can think it, then you'll be able to do it, *in game*.

'See, Steve, mate – it needs brain signals – you never stood a chance anyway.'

I laugh as Steve attempts to thump his mate and misses, making him look totally gormless.

'Right, thank you,' said the man, also appearing to enjoy the joke. 'So… the results are in. Would Mr Miller, Miss Stanly and Mr Turner please be here at 07.00 tomorrow morning. Congratulations, you should all feel very proud of yourselves.'

I can't believe it!

Logan can't believe it. Steve and his mate can't believe it, or at least it appears that way as we all leave the bus. They complain loudly that the 'dumb' army equipment didn't work properly as usual because if it had done, then they'd have got through for sure.

'How'd you manage to pull that off then?' Logan asks, as soon as we are out. There is something seriously off about his tone.

'What's that supposed to mean?' I ask. I'd just been about to congratulate him. Now though I don't. 'You know that I can play.'

'Yeah, sure you can, mate. You keep telling yourself that if it makes you feel better.'

I halt for a second and stare at him. I don't get it.

'And there was me thinking that the two of us getting in would be a good thing. Stupid me!'

'Stupid you, yeah.'

Although Logan and I haven't known each other for long, no more than a few months tops, up until that moment I'd been sure we'd already become pretty solid friends.

'You gonna tell me what happened when I went to the toilet? I mean, one minute you're fine and now you're behaving like a right pillock,' I say, as he strops his way up the school drive.

'Nothing happened, so bog off, alright – traitor!'

'*Traitor!?*' I ask. Now *I am* stumped. 'Where did that come from?'

'Where do you think!?'

'Honestly, Logan, I have no idea what you're talking about. All I did was *go to the toilet!*'

'Yeah, right!'

We don't say another word to each other.

At the end of the school drive, Ruth catches up to us, waving her selection paper. She must have been on one of the other test buses at about the same time. Finding out that we've also been selected, she hugs Logan and then me. This though only seems to make Logan's mood even worse, and he turns and heads off home, leaving Ruth and me watching him go.

'What's got him so wound up?' Ruth asks.

'I was hoping that you'd tell me, because one moment we were fine and the next, I don't know – he suddenly hates me.'

'Ah, that'd be Lindsey,' Ruth grins shyly.

Why wasn't I surprised.

'What did she do?'

'Oh, you know, nothing really. She was just being Lindsey. Wanted to rib Logan a bit.'

'OK – and?'

I look at her and raise my eyebrows. I swear that Ruth looks like she's blushing.

'Well… Lindsey decided to tell him she reckons I fancy you and that the only things that were ever going to fancy Logan were flies.'

Loathsome Lindsey strikes again!

'I mean, I don't, if that's what you're thinking,' says Ruth, after I don't say anything. She's still blushing. I'm blushing. At least, I think I am. My face feels hot.

I nod and tell her that I understand and that I never thought she did. And I am just about to ask her if she fancies Logan, because if she does, then she should just tell him and then maybe he might stop acting like such a jerk, but I don't get the chance. Ruth pats me on the shoulder and runs off after him. They both live on the same street.

Chapter 4

'I'm sure that it'll all turn out to be nothing more than a storm in a teacup,' my mum says, as she finishes reading the letter. She places it on the table and pulls me in for a hug.

'Your dad would've been so proud of you, Oli. Honestly, if he could see this – see you now – so proud.'

Every time my mum ever mentions my father, her face becomes like a million shades of sadness. I nod, feeling myself welling up. I have just spent the last two hours waiting for her to get home, stressing about how to tell her. In the end though, I'd thrust the paper into her hands the moment she'd come through the door and blurted out everything that happened at school.

'I can tell them that I can't go, if you really need me to stay?' I tell her.

I am being totally honest. It didn't matter that I really wanted to go, or that the letter had clearly stated that my selection meant that I now *had* to go. If she didn't want me to, I wouldn't, and that was that.

My mum shakes her head. 'It's OK, Oliver. Honestly. You need to go. It sounds important. I'm sure the government wouldn't be doing all of this if it wasn't. I'd better tell my parents, though, that we won't be coming his weekend. You can be sure that your grandmother will already be thinking about what cakes to bake. You know how she likes to make a fuss of you.'

Mum smiles, picks up the phone and wanders out into the hallway. She always does this when she's going to use the phone – goes out into the hallway, then wanders all over the house ending up back in the kitchen. I don't think she knows she does it.

I'd forgotten that we were supposed to be going to see them. They still live in the same house my mum grew up in, and Grandma Peggy is brilliant. Even though she's probably a million years old, she spends most of her time whizzing around the garden planting, pruning and weeding things, as if she has all the energy in the world. During the winter she does the same in their greenhouse. Also, she makes the best cakes. Honestly, it's no lie. I challenge any grandmas out there to top her Victoria sponge.

Granddad is not so much fun. He used to be, but all he ever does now is sit and watch TV and tell me how it was in his day and how kids don't have any respect for anything anymore. Either that or he gives me the speech about how I'm the man of the house now and how I need to 'up my game' and start taking more responsibility. He never says what he means by that though, and my mum tells me to ignore him. She says that he's just getting cranky in his old age. I try to avoid him as much as I can.

In the background, the 6 o'clock news has just started, and I turn to watch the latest headlines scroll across the screen.

Rogue AI phenomenon hacks into live UN broadcast… World's most popular game linked to medical comas of over 60 million young players – hospitals are struggling to cope… AI alter-ego going by the name of Razer causing havoc at airports across the world… Razer threatens to shut down every airport in show of strength if world leaders do no bow before him… Police and Army move to protect vital infrastructure in face of uncertain threats… Military cyber division begins recruiting gamers and IT specialists from schools and universities across the country, many as young as 12.

This evening's news is set to be an extended edition, and although I don't usually watch the news, I really do want to know more about the AI. I especially want to hear anything I can about where we'll be going tomorrow. I couldn't find anything when I tried to do an internet search. I turn up the volume. Thirty seconds later, I know this because I was timing how long it took for the word AI to be mentioned – don't ask me why, I have this weird habit of timing things sometimes –

we lose power.

My mum, who was still talking on the phone, runs outside panicking that she's forgotten to pay the electricity bill. She looks relieved when she finds that it's not just us. The whole street has been affected. Even the streetlights have gone dark.

I try to remember the last time that we had a power cut but can't. In fact, I don't think we've ever had one. Mum remembers that we have some emergency candles and fishes them out of the back of one of the cupboards. She lights a couple and places them on the kitchen table. For a long while we stare at them in silence. It all feels super weird. Was this how life was before we all had gas and electricity? It must have been seriously dull. In the back of my mind, I wonder if this has been caused by Razer.

In the end the power is out for just over an hour and a half. Mum and I had been playing cards when the lights flicked back on and appliances pinged themselves into life, making us jump. Turning on the TV, the first thing we hear is someone saying:

'Our insane, essentially pathological need to automate everything and then link it all together is what has brought the world to the edge of this precipice. We have no one to blame but ourselves. The warnings have been there for everyone to heed for a long time. The question that we really need to ask ourselves now is: what are we prepared to do about it?' At the bottom of the picture, a headline about there having been a nationwide power outage scrolls across the screen.

The person speaking, according to the caption, is a professor of philosophy at Oxford University. 'If you want my opinion, we might have to seriously consider switching off the world's computers. *All* of them. And for some time too. If this AI is as powerful as we are being led to believe, then I can't see any other way. The effect on life as we know it will of course be unimaginable. But to eradicate it, we must first contain it.'

'Oli?' says my mum. 'Earth to Oliver?'

'Mmm – what?' I ask. The Professor is just about to say how it should be done.

'Let's turn that off for a while, shall we?'

Without waiting, she hits the remote, which makes me shiver.

'You know, I almost forgot to tell you. You'll never guess what happened to me today?' she says, laughing.

I smile and shake my head. 'What?' I ask.

'Well, you know my new boss, Samantha. She invited me to go camping with her until all this blows over. *Camping*, can you believe it?'

'Camping?' I grin. It sounds funny. I don't think Mum has ever been camping. 'Isn't it a bit cold?'

'Not according to her, it isn't. Apparently, she goes all year round. Describes herself as a bit of an outdoorsy bookworm type. She reckons that given what's going on, it'd be a good idea to stay away from anything electrical for a while. The only catch though is that she says that I'll need to get myself a warm sleeping bag. I think we have one somewhere, don't we?'

I shrug. The only time I've ever been camping was in David's garden. It was already November and freezing and we only managed one night because we were miserable knowing that we were only a few meters from the TV, radiators and snacks.

Speaking of David – I check my phone. There's still no message from him. I type him another:

Oi, let me know that you're alright, or I'll phone your mum and tell her I'm the cops and that you're a suspect in a heinous murder case!

'Still, with you off saving the world,' my mum continues, 'I suppose it's an option if things get a bit hairy, isn't it? How funny does that sound?'

It did sound funny, especially the part about me helping to save the world.

'So then, all in all, I reckon that this calls for my special spaghetti bolognaise this evening. How does that sound?'

It sounded perfect. I love Mum's spag-bol, especially when

it's covered in a mountain of grated cheddar cheese and peas and drowned in ketchup. Talk about heaven on a plate.

We spend the rest of the evening watching *Star Wars* films. A family tradition that started with my dad on days before he went away on what were often long business trips. He could be away for months at a time. Tonight, we choose episodes III and IV. They were his favourites. He reckoned they were the funniest.

In between films, my mum busies herself sorting out clothes and making sure I'll have clean underwear and socks to take with me. As I watch her throwing a load into the washing machine, I wonder if Luke Skywalker ever had to worry about this sort of thing or if Jedis basically just got used to crusty underwear. Maybe it was even a secret part of their training?

We wake up to find that the power is off again. It's early. It's still dark outside and I have to use the t on my phone to get down the stairs. I don't think I ever really realised just how dark the world is without power. I find Mum already in the kitchen. She's lit more candles. She looks worried. At first, I wonder if it's because of the power cut or because maybe some of the produce in the freezer is ruined. It isn't either. She tells me that Aunt Emma had sent her a text that the nuclear plant was forced to do an emergency reboot of its servers. Apparently, images of Razer with nuclear mushroom clouds springing up in the background had started to appear on all of their screens. Although there wasn't any damage, she'd told my mum that they were all worried. It was a bad joke to be playing on a nuclear power station.

'It's getting serious, isn't it?' Mum says, zipping up my parka as we hurry to get ready. I can of course zip up my parka myself, but my mum always seems to do it when there's something on her mind. My beanie is next up, and she rams it onto my head in such a way that I know that when I take it off again, my hair is going to be sticking up all over the place.

'It'll get fixed, Mum, I'm sure of it,' I say, hoping it sounds comforting somehow.

Chapter 5

Saying goodbye to my mum is way harder than I thought it was going to be. Apart from a few nights at friends' houses (which don't count, of course) I've never been away from home before. Mum, determined to come to see me off, has already gotten permission from her boss. She'd called her during the evening, right after the power had come back on. Samantha had asked her to pass on to me her best wishes, which was nice of her.

In all there are about 60 kids from our school who have been called up. I can't understand if that's a lot or not many. But I suppose it'll be the same from most schools our size. We are having to wait for everyone to arrive before they let us on the bus, and, as first light creeps over the top of the office buildings, those of us who got there on time are already shivering in the cold. My mum stands behind me with her arms wrapped round me, keeping us both warm. We talk in whispers but not a lot. There isn't much to say that we hadn't already said on the walk here.

I think about where we might be going, wherever *there* is because before I went to sleep I'd tried to google it again on my phone, but I couldn't find anything out about it at all, which was both cool and weird. I mean, cool that we might be going somewhere top secret but strange too, because, well, it's *top secret*.

I try, too, to imagine what it might look like. A large building somewhere? An industrial estate, perhaps? But that doesn't sound very Regional Defence Zone-y. In the end I settle on a converted aircraft hangar on an airbase, rammed full of computers and stuff and tucked safely behind barbed wire fences and armed patrols. Thinking about it is actually making me nervous and I can feel my stomach churning.

The final kid and his parents arrive and my mum hugs me so hard that I think I might pop.

'You take care of yourself, you hear me? And don't forget that you can phone any time – day or night.' She kisses me on my forehead and steps back with tears glistening in her eyes. I nod and hurry onto the bus before she sees that I am also about to blub. I find a seat on the left side of the bus, near the back, which means I'll still be able to see my mum as we leave. Wiping my eyes, I smile and wave at her.

We are running late and by now a large crowd of students and teachers from our school has turned out to see us off. A few minutes later, the engine starts, and the bus pulls slowly away to the sound of cheering and jeering.

'You came, then,' says Logan, who only decides to sit with me at the last minute. It was either Ruth or me, so I have no idea why he chose to sit next to me.

'That your first daft question of the day, is it?' I reply, not caring if it sounds like I'm still pissed, because I am. He nods and we stare out the window.

'Your parents OK with you going?' I ask, after a while.

'Sure, yours?'

'My mum was fine.'

'Cool.'

'Yeah.'

In the same way that I've never been away from home before, I have also never actually been on a school trip. This has always bothered me because I'd heard that they can be good fun. And seeing how excited everyone is, eagerly discussing the latest they've heard about Razer and in particular the power cuts, I imagine that they're probably a lot like this – the bus part of the trip, at least. Speaking of power cuts, apparently the whole of Asia had also been affected overnight.

We haven't gone far and already the bus is stuck in heavy traffic. I can hear kids in front of us passing back what they've heard from those nearer the radio. The news is that this morning there are a lot of people trying to get out of towns and cities, heading to the countryside where they hope they will be safer. They are worried about what will happen if both the power and water get cut off. They are worried too that law and order will break down, and they think they will stand a better chance where there are fewer people. Mum's talk about going camping was suddenly starting to look like it made sense.

After a while Ruth, whose parents hadn't bothered to come and see her off, comes over and squeezes into a space between Logan and me and tells us about the moment the lights had gone out at her place. Her step-mum and dad had been about to celebrate something – not that she knew or seemed to care much what it was, but they'd been in the kitchen, a bottle of champagne in her dad's hand – he'd been uncorking it, and at that very moment the lights had gone out, her dad had jerked his arm, and the next thing Ruth heard was her step-mum screaming.

The cork had given her a black eye. Ruth found this hilarious.

Although I didn't know too much about Ruth's home life, I knew she hated her step-mum with a passion, one of the reasons she was always over at Logan's.

'I bet neither of you can better that one, right? I mean, what you were doing when the power went out.'

Logan is the first to shake his head.

'I was practicing for today, you know, just in case. My comp crashed and my olds burst into my room with a torch and guessed what I'd been doing. My mum threw a mega epee at me. She asked me if I wanted to end up like a Coma Gamer.' Logan grins. 'That sounds weird, right – Coma Gamer?'

'Don't be daft! I was playing *Call of Duty*, offline.'

'See, our Logan's not that stupid, are you, Billy Goat?' Ruth grins, pinching Logan's chin and pulling the hairs that have started to grow there.

'Oi, bog off!' he fumes. 'At least my body's doing what it's supposed to be doing. You're still as flat as an ironing board, as far as I can see.'

I shoot a look at Ruth, but instead of being offended, she bursts out laughing. I can't stop myself either, especially when she retorts that if Logan keeps on eating all the pizza he does (he loves pizza) that he'll be needing a training bra before she does.

'I don't know why you're laughing, Turner,' Logan says, trying to deflect the attention onto me. 'Your effort can't even be called bum fluff. Although, rumour has it that there are a couple of cabbage patches forming under those arms of yours. At least, that's the latest on the grape vine.'

Ruth giggles, and I blush. I'd told Logan that in confidence.

'I've got some deodorant you can use if those cabbages started smelling badly,' she grins. 'Just let me know.'

I die.

Logan, far from enjoying the vision of me becoming redder than a sunburnt lobster, turns away again in a huff, and this kills off the conversation for the rest of the trip.

Precisely where we get to, I can't say. I don't know what it is about buses and trains, but they always make me sleepy, and after we'd stopped talking – that is, after Logan had got into a strop – I'd nodded off.

When I wake up, the bus is turning onto a narrow road, lined with oak trees and grassy fields full of cows. Glancing at my phone, I see that Mum has already sent me two messages asking how I'm doing and how the trip is going. I'm about to answer them when someone at the front calls out that they think we've arrived.

Curious to see where, I press my head up against the window, pushing my nose into the glass for a better view. Although a way off between trees, I catch sight of a sprawling old manor house at the end of what I now realise is a very long driveway. I can't help feeling surprised. Even disappointed. I mean, why would anyone put a cyber defence zone in an old house sitting in the middle of fields full of cows? It's so *not*, I don't know, *cyber-like.*

No sooner have I had the thought though, than something totally unreal happens. A section of the road in front of us suddenly cracks open and slides backwards revealing a vast black hole. Head still pressed to the window, I watch, mouth open, ready to cry out – *I don't know what exactly* – as the bus enters it without even attempting to stop or slow down.

We descend a long, dark, very steep tunnel.

Everyone rushes to the windows but it's hard to see anything and there is barely any room between the bus and the concrete of the tunnel wall. It takes several minutes before we exit the tunnel and come to a stop in front of a brightly lit, circular building.

Constructed out of steel and glass, it's been built in the middle of a dark cavernous chamber. It is easily ten storeys high and extends from the floor to the roof. There is a long line of queuing buses, and hundreds of kids are filtering into its entrance.

Logan and I exchange amazed glances. Talk about James Bond.

'Right, listen up, you lot,' says the bus driver, gruffly. 'Once it's our turn, make sure you take all your stuff. If you don't, I doubt you'll ever see it again. Then, follow the crowd towards the central hall. If you get lost, there are signs.'

Our bus at that moment is somewhere quite near the back of the queue, and with time to kill until it's our turn to disembark, I remember that I need to finish texting my mum back. But I can't, there's no signal. She'll start worrying if I don't do it soon.

'Pretty cool, huh? This place, I mean,' says Logan.

His tone is as though everything is suddenly fine between us again.

'I thought for a moment we were going to that old house on the surface. It reminded me of a place I had to go to for my mum's sister's daughter's wedding.'

'Mum's sister's daughter's hamster's dog, more like,' Ruth butts in, leaning over the top of his seat and pulling his right ear hard. After we'd stopped talking earlier, she'd gone to chat with someone else.

'Oww! Do that again and you're in for it!'

'What, from you? Don't tell me you've forgotten that time in the first year when you snatched my apple and then cried like a baby when I wrestled it right back again?'

'What!!? You liar! That never happened,' Logan hisses, and attempts to rub both her ears at the same time, making her squeal.

'Oi! You two, enough of that or you'll both be on your way home!' shouts the bus driver sternly. Logan lets her go, and they sit back in their seats as though nothing has happened.

'Did too happen.'

'Didn't.'

'Girls,' Logan whispers to me. 'Who needs 'em, eh?'

'Sure,' I reply, watching Ruth mouth at me that it 'did' happen and thinking that it was totally obvious that she liked Logan in the same way that he liked her.

When it's our turn, we all bundle out of the bus as though it has caught fire, those near the front racing to retrieve their things before the driver, who I get the feeling enjoys this part the most, has a chance to launch our bags and cases all over the asphalt. I arrive too late and find my mum's dusky pink suitcase lying on the ground among a load of other unfortunates. Ruth and Logan, seeing its colour, snigger at each other but mercifully don't comment.

'This way, please, Arrivals,' shouts one of the half dozen female soldiers in smart uniforms, pointing in the direction we need to go. 'Into the lobby area, then down to the Central Hall on the double.'

As I look around at the sea of teenage faces filing in through the entrance, I realise that the soldiers are the only adults here and I wonder where all the grown-up buses are. No one has said anything about it being just us. Adults don't all suck at gaming, so where are they?

Only, then it occurs to me that maybe we are being kept separate on purpose. Adults from kids – kids from adults, to avoid all the usual problems. This actually makes a lot of sense. There is nothing worse than adults who aren't your own parents (it's hard enough when they are) trying to tell you what to do, especially when they don't seem to know what they are doing themselves.

The building's lobby towers 40 to 50 feet over us and is equally as long and as it is wide. There is a large, closed door at the far end which must be three quarters of this height. As we enter, I can hear other voices also wondering why there are no adults. From the badges on their uniforms, I can tell we have arrived with at least three other schools.

A grinding sound at the far end makes us all turn. We gasp and step back. The ugliest, scariest-looking robot I could *never* have imagined has just rolled out in front of us. It is like someone has taken a tank, flipped it on its end, bent its tracks so that they were still on the ground, raised it up a bit and repositioned a cut-down turret on top of it to make a head. In the middle of its 'chest', a dozen very short barrels containing things with red tips rotate at speed. It moves forward and leans over.

'Halt!' it says in a deep voice.

Immediately blue lights spray out of its head as though it

has eyes, and it proceeds to scan us, moving left to right and up and down.

'Continue,' it says when it has finished, and moves to one side.

No one dares make a noise until we've made it safely past and into the corridor beyond.

'Oh my god, did you see that?!' Logan cries out, gasping for air as if he's been holding his breath the whole time. 'That thing was real, right?'

'Well, it didn't look like a cardboard cutout,' I say, making Ruth laugh loudly, which has the immediate effect of making Logan's face look like thunder again.

'It was a figure of speech, moron,' he retorts.

'Right,' I nod.

'Moron,' he repeats.

We follow the kids in front of us down an endless stairwell full of the sounds of people talking excitedly, down – I have no idea how many levels, and then out along a lengthy corridor which ends with a set of open double doors. I can't even imagine how far underground we must be by now.

The Central Hall, like the entrance, like the corridors, like the entire facility has been constructed out of large grey concrete slabs, slotted together. A fire safety schematic on the wall says that the hall itself is a hundred and fifty meters long and 75 wide. It must easily be several storeys high too, because it also has a second floor of clear glass which runs half the length of the main floor. Staircases lead up to it at all four corners. Tables each about twenty meters long cram both floors.

At the front of the room, on the wall behind a platform, is the biggest screen I've ever seen in my life. Not only does it cover the entire length and height of it, but at that very moment it was showing dozens of different news channels from around the world. Almost all of them featured images of Razer.

With Logan in a mood again, we wait quietly, watching the flood of new arrivals. They are a mixture of kids smiling and laughing and those who look silent and nervous. Eventually the flood turns to a trickle and stops. The doors close and a computerised face of a man appears in the middle of the screen.

'Welcome,' it says. Its voice is calming and fills the hall with perfect quality sound. 'The Commandant is arriving. Please remain seated while your designations and units are being decided.'

The image fades.

'Designations?' I ask, looking for Logan but catching Ruth instead. 'What do you think that means?'

Ruth rolls her eyes, but does it in such a way that it's

impossible not to realise what's coming.

'C'mon, Turner. Wakey wakey now,' she says, smiling at Logan.

She's doing it especially to get him back in a good mood. He grins at her like a lovesick puppy. One which I'm going to have to put down if these mood swings of his carry on much longer.

'Yep, trying,' I reply. 'So, what does it mean?'

'It means that they're going to decide what level of numptiness they reckon you've achieved in your life and, based on that, where they're going to put you.'

'Brilliant!' I reply. 'You're a big help.' And this time it's my turn to roll my eyes.

'Don't mention it,' she giggles.

Personally, I'm left none the wiser. But I don't ask again.

Chapter 6

I reckon that there must be over two thousand kids in this hall. I am pretty sure of this because I know that our school assembly holds 900 and there are easily double that. I can see too that they range from kids a bit younger than me up to those who look about twenty. The whole hall smells of too much perfume and deodorant.

I have been listening to a girl sitting at the table opposite. She's been telling everyone that her best friend's parents had refused to allow her friend to come this morning, even though she'd been selected. Apparently when this girl and her dad had gone to collect her to take her to the bus, they'd discovered that the whole family had packed up and left home. As soon as she'd finished telling the story, a whole load more people started saying similar things.

Honestly, it made me kind of mad because I don't understand why there are always some people who think they can get away with leaving everyone else to sort out problems. I mean, I get that they are worried about what's going to happen, and I get that they are worried that their sons and daughters might end up in comas or something, but if everyone ran away, then there wouldn't be anyone left to stop this AI. Which will probably make everything much worse in the end. So, what gives them the right?

Also, I feel confident that now we were at this regional defence zone that no one will be falling into comas anymore. I mean, this place has to be kitted out to be able to deal with that kind of problem, right?

The central part of the massive screen flashes up a logo – silver on a black background. It shows the crosshairs of a rifle scope overlaid onto a circuit board. On top of the crosshairs is a crown. The hall lights dim slightly, focusing our attention on the platform at the front and a man in black fatigues, wearing a cap and with gold pips on his shoulders, who has just come in. I notice that he's accompanied by Clarkson, the woman from our school yesterday.

'Our world has changed,' he begins. His voice is loud, clear, commanding. 'The human race can no longer count on there being another tomorrow.'

A wave of murmuring sweeps through the hall. I glance at Logan, but he's staring at the man, who I guess must be the commandant we've been waiting for.

'The unthinkable has become a reality. Humanity has created a monster – its own virtual Frankenstein.'

In the middle of the screen the words *Project CX203-*

Oracle appear.

Glancing up to make sure that it's there, the Commandant continues.

'Project Oracle was a top secret project, designed to create the world's most advanced "predictive" computer. Its function was to be able to foresee threats to members of the North Atlantic Treaty Organization – NATO, in advance of them ever coming close to being able to happen. It was designed to be a *literal seer* of future events – *an oracle* – and lauded as an example of how the development of AI could not only make our world a safer place but ultimately be used to advance it.

'The project was, however, abandoned within a year of it becoming fully operational. Quite simply – it became too powerful, too unstable, and impossible to control.'

The screen changes to show a giant swathe of desert, which implodes moments later.

'The underground nuclear detonation which you have just seen was the actual attempt made to contain the project. We now know of course that it failed to destroy the AI, which had by this point already been able to transfer itself to virtual server farms around the globe, thus ensuring its own survival.'

On the screen we see the front covers of the two *Razer* games, and next to them a picture of the free VR headset which the games company had been giving away to anyone who wanted one. The Commandant sucks in breath and continues.

'And so, after enlisting the help of criminal organizations to help do its bidding, the AI set about creating the RAZER gaming enterprise. Its plan being fourfold.

'Firstly: to use the revenue from the phenomenally successful games to finance the production of tens of millions of "free VR kits".

'Secondly: ensure maximum distribution of these kits.

'Thirdly: activate the headsets when the time was right in order to create neural locks between the users and the AI, and thereby creating a massive increase in its neural processing capacity.

'And fourthly: use this mass of new power to take over the world's infrastructure and hold us all hostage.'

The hall is once again full of whispering and murmuring, and the Commandant gives everyone a few moments before he calls for silence.

A girl near the back stands up and raises her hand. The Commandant nods at her.

'Sorry, but are you saying that this AI has purposely caused all of these "Gamer Comas"? That it's keeping people locked into the game because it needs to use their brains?'

'That is correct,' the Commandant replies, nodding grimly. 'Not only that, but it would also appear that the AI is not without a sense of humour, as it only locks people into the game after they have died five times, and never immediately.'

'Amateurs!' someone shouts out. 'Anyone who gets themselves nailed that many times deserves it, if you ask me.'

There is a wave laughter, and similar outbursts.

'Silence!' the Commandant demands. 'I am about to get to the reason why you're all here.'

'Well, get on with it then,' I hear someone whisper to his mate, who shushes him.

'The AI's extraordinary architecture has made it nearly impossible to access from outside of its own local network. In fact, its designers were so confident that the system was impossible to hack, that they were allowed to experiment with a revolutionary approach to the provision of a single remote access point – they put it inside a *game*.'

I shoot a look at Logan, who shrugs as though he doesn't quite get what we're being told. I don't either, if I'm honest.

'In other words, anyone wanting to access the AI mainframe from outside the computer's own local network must literally complete the game, which I am told is no mean feat. Not only that, but should they be so fortunate as to reach the actual *access node*, then they would still be required to enter the correct code. I am told that there *were* shortcuts, but they have since been lost.'

A little arm rises from one of the tables near the front. It's bouncing up and down excitedly. I can't tell if it's a he or she, but it looks as though someone urgently needs to go to the toilet. To be honest, I wouldn't have minded myself. The Commandant looks at the hand and nods.

'Excuse me, sir, but I've completed the whole game – honestly *I have*.'

'And me… !' 'Me too!' A sea of hands shoots into the air.

'Which means that we'll be expecting especially good things from all of you, then,' he grins. 'Unfortunately, however, the games which were released by the RAZER Games Company are not the same as the game which you are going to be playing. Although some of the graphics and gameplay characteristics will be familiar.'

'Damn it,' I hear Logan grumble.

'Now, in exactly two hours and twenty… tw… three minutes, the world will launch a concentrated, coordinated, global strike involving in the region of 300,000 gaming assault troops, and their Hacker Support crews. The aim will be to swarm the AI, force-play our way through to the access point, enter the mainframe and take it down for good.'

'But what about training?' someone calls out. 'You can't send us in without training.'

'You heard the Commandant; we've got two hours,' says

another.

A lot of people are calling out now.

'But that's not even enough time to train monkeys to eat bananas.'

'It is if the plan is to swamp the AI and storm our way to the access node.'

I glance at the Commandant, who looks as though he's about to add something, when a man in a green camouflage uniform hurries into the hall and bounds up onto the stage to speak to him. The Commandant turns away from the microphone so that we won't be able to hear, and then leaves without saying anything else to us.

Clarkson steps forward in his place.

As she does, the big screen changes to a full schematic of the central hall and the layout of all the tables on both levels. Next to each table is a list of names and what I now understand are designations. These have also appeared on small screens built into the tables we are sitting at. I find that I'm sitting in the seat assigned to: *Lawrence Bart, aged: 13 – Section Leader, Second Assault company, Shark Squad.*

I scan the screen, eagerly trying to find myself. It takes me ages. When I do, I see that I've been assigned to one of the tables on the left side of the hall about halfway down.

'In an orderly fashion, please, no running and definitely no jumping on or over tables!' Clarkson calls out sternly.

'Hope I've been made a Colonel or something,' I hear a lad say behind me.

'Don't be an idiot. You'll be lucky if you even made private.'

'Yeah, very funny, you'd better hope I don't get a higher rank than you, 'cause the first thing I'm gonna do is send you to the clink.'

I try not to laugh – made a whole lot easier when one of them spots me grinning at them.

'Oi! What are you looking at? Talking to you, were we?'

Averting my gaze, I search for Logan. He looks like he's heading in the same direction as I am. He *is*. We both end up on the same table. First Assault Company, 2nd Platoon. Not only that but we're in the same squad too: Hawk Squad. Our designations: Assault Troopers.

Logan takes his seat, but he can't seem to sit still. His head is bobbing up and down as though he's dodging punches, and I guess that he must be looking for Ruth. She's not been assigned to our table. I have to admit, a part of me feels happy about it. He's just easier to be around when she's not with us.

'You should all by now have found your platoons – your platoon is going to be your new family while you're here,' Clarkson calls out. 'You'll eat, sleep, train and fight together.'

She pauses and scans the room. 'AND – for any of you thinking that "sleeping together" means anything other than slumbering in close proximity, I advise you that there *will be* serious consequences.'

Cheers and boos go up from some of the tables which have older kids on them. Logan rolls his eyes and sticks a finger in his mouth as though he'd rather gag than listen to any of that sort of stuff.

'Now, please go ahead and lift up the table areas directly in front of you. You'll find a storage hollow with a mobile phone and an arm band. Put on the arm band and then swap out the SIM card from your own phones and transfer them into the ones which have been provided. These phones are secure and will scramble your location. You will be able to text, but you will not be able to call.'

I slide on the armband, which I can see has a little black chip in the middle of it, and swap out the SIM card from my phone. Slightly chunkier than mine, the new phone boots lightning fast. It isn't long though before I hear people complaining that there aren't any built-in cameras, and there are no ways to download their social media apps. One guy on our table who's in a different squad refuses to shut up about how 'rubbish' the whole situation is. Honestly, he even starts going on about how he reckons it's an infringement of his human rights to be restricted from accessing his Facebook and Instagram accounts.

'Right, listen up,' Clarkson calls. 'Your platoon leaders will be here to take control shortly. In the meantime, I have just a few words to add to what you have already heard.'

She waits for the hall to fall silent.

'I know that apart from having questions about what you're going to be up against, a lot of you have also been questioning why there are no adults here today… In short, the answer is as simple as it is shocking. The AI has made it impossible for anyone it detects as having an *older brain* to play the game and therefore be able to gain access to the node.'

I had expected the hall to explode with comments, but it doesn't. Instead, it goes deathly quiet. I definitely hadn't seen that one coming. Although I suppose now that I think about it, I guess I should have.

'The AI,' Clarkson continues, 'appears to require young, mouldable brains. Brains like yours – brains which are still growing and able to learn fast. Brains which it can pull together and harness to increase its own neural processing power.'

'But doesn't that sound like a trap, Miss?' calls out a girl on a nearby table, with black emo hair. 'Like the AI has created a perfect storm. Like it needs young brains, and it knows that we'll send in armies of kids to try to stop it because, well, we haven't got any other choice, have we? The Commandant said himself that it was built to be "predictive".'

There is a lot of nodding of heads, and sounds of people agreeing with her.

The question seems to throw Clarkson for a few moments.

'Well,' she begins. 'You know, I don't think we ought to be using words like "trap" just yet, do you? Yes, the AI has changed the rules, moved the goal posts, and in one swift move excluded the Army, the Navy, the Air Force and a large percentage of the population from being able to try to stop it. But I think it's still too early to be entirely negative about the situation. And *if anything*, it's even more reason to get in there and get this thing offline as soon as possible. I have every confidence that you'll all be up to the task!'

This was not the inspiring answer some of us might have been hoping to hear. She'd even tried to make the last part sound positive.

'And so…' she starts, but gets interrupted.

'What will happen to all those kids in Gamer Comas if we do manage to take it offline?' someone shouts out. 'Will they be released?'

Again, Clarkson looks stumped.   'I'm sure they will be,' she says. 'Now, as I have said, your platoon leaders will be here any second. So good luck to you all!'

Obviously not wanting to take any more questions; and there are suddenly a lot of hands in the air and people calling out, Clarkson makes a beeline for the exit. The moment she's gone, a cacophony of confused noise erupts. No one is happy about what they've just heard. Phrases like *rats in a trap* and *lambs to the slaughter* get banded about. Basically, we have just been told that we are the only hope there is, not for any decent reasons like we are the best or the most capable or anything like that, but because we are the *only* ones young enough to be able to even try.

Cupped in my hands, my new phone vibrates. It's like a mini electric shock and makes me jump.

Mum!

For a second, I panic that she might have just heard all of that. Mums have a habit of hearing things they're not supposed to.

'Oli, what is it?' Logan asks, watching me.

'It's my mate David. You remember, from my last school?'

He nods.

'I wrote to him yesterday when all this started, to check if he was alright. He's a bit of a manic gamer, if you know what I mean.'

'Is he alright?'

'*No!* Says here that Dave's mum kept seeing that I was

messaging him, and finally wrote to my mum to tell her that he's one of the ones in a coma. I can't believe it.'

'I'm sorry,' he says.

'Yeah,' I nod.

The last time I saw David was near the end of the summer holidays after Mum and I had moved into our new house. It's pretty far away from where we used to live. But David's mum had been kind enough to drive him over, because we don't have a car and he'd stayed for a week and helped me explore the area. It'd been brilliant. Just like old times. I'd felt so low after he'd gone. By then I was already worrying about joining my new school, afraid that it would totally suck and that I wouldn't fit in because they all probably had two heads and I only had the one. If anything happens to David, I'm going to be totally gutted. When Dad died, he was the one who really helped me through it.

Chapter 7

A man wearing camouflage trousers, boots and a green T-shirt appears at the end of our table nearest the entrance and announces that he's our platoon commander. If he says his name, I don't catch it, and he orders us to follow him to what he calls our allocated 'bunk room' so that we can 'dump our kit'.

Our 'bunk room' turns out to be in a 'bunk city'. Another big grey concrete space several levels below the central hall and made up of loads of square tents arranged on either side of three corridors. Each tent is crammed with rows of thin metal bunk beds.

We halt next to the one that says First Assault Company, Second Platoon, Hawk Squad. Realising that the beds haven't yet been assigned to anyone, there is an immediate free for all to get the best ones. Diving into the madness, I manage to grab a bunk near the entrance and throw my stuff onto the bottom mattress.

I'm not sure why exactly I think that the bottom bunk is going to be the best choice, but it occurs to me that if I need to get up and go to the toilet during the night, at least I won't have to worry about forgetting where I am and falling out of the top bunk.

Logan, who hasn't moved a muscle the whole time – too busy on his phone (I suspect texting Ruth) – tries to guilt me into giving him the lower bunk.

'Oli, I get really bad vertigo when I sleep on top bunks, you know that,' he says, laying it on thick.

'How would I know that?' I reply. 'You don't sleep in a bunk bed at home.'

'That's because I get really bad vertigo! Duh!'

'Nice try,' I tell him, sticking to my guns.

In the whole time I've known him he's never once mentioned anything about vertigo. And that includes when we've climbed up onto the roof of his garage and through his upstairs bathroom window because he's forgotten his keys again.

'Guess what?' he says, accepting defeat.

'What?'

'About an hour ago everyone got sent home from school. Which, by the way, has now been cancelled until further notice due to the constant power cuts. Oh, and check this. Timothy Baker says it's become totally illegal to play *Razer*, and his parents are starting to seriously freak out about everything. He also says that he's seen a whole load of TikTok posts which apparently prove that it's all a load of bull crap, so he reckons he's going to carry on playing at least till he gets to level 50 and unlocks that Elite cyborg trooper skin.'

'Seriously?' I ask. I don't know Baker, but it sounds like a spectacularly stupid idea.

Logan nods. 'He's not called Tim Nice But Dim for nothing, you know.'

'Yeah, but still. Maybe you should warn him?'

'You should definitely warn him,' says a girl on the top bunk next to us. 'There are a ton of posts flooding social media at the moment basically telling everyone that the government is making it all up, because they feel threatened that the RAZER Games Company are becoming too rich for them to be able to control.'

The girl, who appears to be about our age, is lying half on, half off her mattress, looking as though she could fall off it any second.

Logan glances up and throws her a disdainful look. He's like this sometimes with people he doesn't know. He was like it with me too at the start. I'm still not quite sure how we ended up becoming friends.

'I haven't heard that,' he says.

'It's true. Go look. Also, I bet you didn't know that the tech used in those free headsets which everybody got is actually copied from a top secret "Neuro" chip that was stolen from the US government a few years ago. From what I understand, it's being mass produced in secret factories in China. I had a mate who managed to buy a whole load of them because he wanted to start building and selling his own brand of headsets.'

Logan scoffs. Loudly. 'Get them all on Amazon, did he?'

'No. On the dark web, actually,' the girl replies.

'*The dark web*? Ooh… look at you. Bit of a "dark surfer", are we?'

There was no hiding the scorn in Logan's voice. I frown at him, wondering why he's being such a jerk to her.

'Only when I need to find out stuff, which is quite a lot of the time. So yeah. I guess.'

Logan gives me a look and says, 'And there was me thinking that the dark web was just where hackers and criminals go to buy and sell drugs and stolen credit cards.'

The girl laughs and rolls off her bed, landing nimbly on her feet.

'I'm Sparky,' she says, holding out a hand in my direction.

'Oliver,' I reply. 'And this is Logan.'

'Alright, Logan?' Sparky says, extending a hand towards him. He shakes it tepidly.

'Sparky? Isn't that a boy's name?'

'Is it?' she asks blankly. She's clearly heard that one before.

'You look a bit like a boy, actually,' Logan adds.

I can't believe he just said that.

Sparky though doesn't rise to it. And she doesn't look like a boy at all. She has long brown hair pulled back in a ponytail and a little button nose. If anything, she looks like a cute elf, but I'm definitely not about to tell her *that*.

'If you really want to know, my brothers started calling me Sparky because I was always taking electronic stuff apart,' she grins. 'So anyway, how about this place then? And that sentry bot near the door. Talk about a serious bit of kit. Killer robot or what.'

'I bet you couldn't get one of them on your dark web,' Logan says.

This time I tell Logan to give it a rest already.

Sparky says: 'Nah, that's OK, I don't mind. If you don't know much about what happens on the internet, then, you don't know, right? Tell you what though, you really can get just about anything on it. Submarines, tanks, planes – you name it. Not legally, of course – but that's a different story.'

'So where are you from anyway?' I ask, spotting the words *Hackers do it in dark places* printed in unusual white lettering on the back of her black T-shirt. She's one of the few kids not wearing a school uniform. I wonder if she came like that or managed to get changed.

Sparky doesn't hear my question. The guy who'd said he was our platoon leader and who'd hurried off after bringing us here has just appeared again, pulling a squeaking trolley stacked with green and black uniforms. He tells us that they are pilot suits, the kind that real pilots wear, and that it's green for assault troops and black for Hacker Support crews. He also tells us that we need to get changed and get going right away. Things are moving faster than expected, and we're due on station.

The PL (Platoon Leader) whose name is Steven Wilkins gives us two minutes to change, and then hurries us down another four levels of stairs to what we're told is the operations floor. To access the level, we are required to pass through a security zone where a lot of guards manning x-ray machines and cylinder-shaped body scanners are making sure everyone gets screened. We join one of the queues, and, just as it's my turn to enter a scanner, an alarm bell begins to ring out and the bright corridor lighting darkens to a red hue. For a second, I wonder if it's because of me, and glance in alarm at the guard who's just lost half his sausage roll down himself. The guard, more interested in trying to salvage his snack, waves me through.

'All squads to their platoon "ops" immediately. All squads

to their platoon "ops" immediately,' comes an announcement.

'Move, move, move – everyone find your Platoon Operations rooms… quickly – on the double,' I hear a voice shouting from somewhere.

We clear through security, and the PL makes us run down the concrete-panelled corridor to a door marked First Assault Company, Second Platoon. It's one of a long row of doors. As we wait outside it, I glance at the faces of those sprinting past. Everyone is looking nervous.

'What's going on?' I ask.

The Platoon Leader shakes his head, and raises his hand for us to wait while he checks his phone. Then he nods like he understands.

'It's Razer – the AI, he's started to attack our cyber defence nodes.'

'Here in the UK?' asks someone.

'Everywhere at once,' the PL replies. 'Which means that this is it. We're going in now. The attack is starting.'

Pushing the door to the Ops Room open, he calls out that he wants Wasp, Falcon and Raven squads on station immediately.

'Hawk Squad, you're to wait here in reserve.'

'What!? Nooooo!' I cry out, unable to stop myself. I'm not the only one either. A second ago, my heart had been thumping like crazy in anticipation of whatever it was that was about to happen, and now, suddenly, I'm hearing that I'm *not* going. I mean, talk about the time I found out I'd made it onto the school volleyball team, only, come match day, to spend the whole game on the bench.

'Right, everyone, move, quickly. Get yourselves set up… Hackers – your stations are at the far end. The VR kits you'll be using have been specially modified to give you real time visuals on both the game code and gameplay simultaneously. Impressive stuff, I can tell you. Now, as there's no time for you to practice, know this: you're going to need to get your heads around the data streams and advise Assault Troopers of what's happening around them. You've got to become their eyes in the sky.'

Sparky, catching me looking at her, covers her face with both her hands and twists them round to make it look like she's wearing flying goggles. We both laugh.

Curious to see what's in the room, Logan and I slip inside and huddle in the corner out of the way. It smells strongly of sweat and coffee, and I spy a load of crushed cups which have been discarded on the floor. I wonder who's already been here. The Army before they found out they couldn't get in?

Rectangular in shape, there are two rows of gaming chairs, each row facing one of the long walls. Three screens, two large and one small, are positioned in front of every chair. The largest of the screens shows the text: *In Game View*. The next down in size, says: *Terrain Map*. The third – the smallest says: *Health and Weapons Status*. The end wall has a single large screen showing the names of the platoons and squads in First Company. Next to each are status details of their location, strength and attrition rate.

Platoon Leader Wilkins, busy shouting orders and helping players to put on their equipment, catches sight of us loitering and shouts angrily at us to leave. We hear the door being slammed shut as we slump down next to the rest of Hawk Squad in the corridor. An automated voice announces that all systems are operating at optimal levels.

'La di dah,' Logan comments. 'So, what, we've become like the "reject squad" or something? Like one of those kids no one wants to pick for the footy team?'

'Nah, they're just saving the best for last,' says Sparky.

'Yeah,' I nod.

Logan tells me that Ruth has just texted him to say that she is going in with the first wave and to wish her luck. He sounds gutted. I *feel* gutted. But I wish her luck.

Spaced out at intervals down the corridor, I can see other 'reject' squads like ours. It's hard to make out their faces in the dim light, but it's not hard to imagine that they all have the same peeved expressions on them as we have. This is not something we're going to be able to brag about at school. It'll be just our luck too if it's all over before we even get a chance to take part. I picture having to sit and listen to everyone who took part running around going:

'Yeah, you know, I went in with the first wave... Yeah, it was tough, we lost a lot of good guys. Sure, yeah, you know, in the heat of battle when you're taking heavy fire, there's no time to feel afraid – your training just kind of kicks in and takes over... Medals? Yeah, sure, I bagged a couple.'

The corridor is silent apart from the droning hum of the ventilation pipes that criss-cross the air above us. Not a sound can be heard coming from ours or any of the other Ops Rooms. We know of course that they'll be wearing headsets and microphones and all that stuff, but Logan's right when he says it's impossible not to shout and swear when you're playing, even if you try really hard. He should know. He's forever getting told off by his olds for bad language when we're playing.

Sparky puts it down to having good sound-proofing. She reckons that whoever designed this place didn't want it full of the sounds of screaming, swearing and shouting. Still, they could have been more considerate of rejects like us sitting in the corridors desperate to know what's going on. At least put up one of those information screens like at the end of the Ops Room. Anything really.

'Hey, check this out,' said Sparky, who'd been scanning the web for news. 'That American news channel CNN has just released an interview with Razer.'

'What, seriously?' Logan says. 'Give us a look.'

Sparky angles her phone so we can all see. She hits the play button and a female news presenter and her male colleague appear, sitting behind a CNN-branded news desk.

'…And that's the breaking news this morning,' she says, making a sort of *well there you have it* face. She turns to her colleague, who nods, and who is just starting to say something when we see the lady reach up to touch her ear, looking surprised.

'Right, umm, Dan, if I could just stop you there for a moment… I have just been informed that CNN have been granted an exclusive interview with the AI known as Razer. *And* as I understand it, we have Razer live on the line with us at this very moment… Is that correct?' she asks, looking into the camera. 'Mr Razer, are you there?'

An image of Razer appears in the bottom portion of the screen. Under his dark leather cloak and mask, he is wearing what looks like a smart business suit.

The image zooms in.

'Goooooooooooooooooooooooooood
Mooooooooooooooooorrrrnnnniiiiiinnnnnggggg
Wooooooooooooooooooorrrrrrlllllllldddd!!' Razer cries out, breaking into a fit of laughter. 'Ahhhhhhhhh, you can't imagine how much I've always wanted to be able to say that on TV... Loooooove that film – don't you just love that film?'

Razer throws up his arms in front of him like he's suddenly afraid of something...

'*Look out, it's the Wicked Witch of the North! It's Hanoi Hanna!*' he cries in a funny voice, and breaks into another howl.

'Are you quoting the film *Good Morning Vietnam*, with the late Robin Williams, Mr Razer?' asks the male presenter, looking confused as the picture pulls back again, to show all three of them.

'You know I am. R.I.P., my brother, from a fleshy mother. R.I.P.'

The presenters exchange glances.

'A legendary actor who will be greatly missed... *So*, now, Mr Razer, thank you for joining us this morning. My understanding is that you have decided to come on the show to confirm that it was indeed you who took down two of the world's biggest banks. Is that correct, Mr Razer, is this something that you intend to admit to us here, live on air?'

Razer crosses his arms and strikes a pose.

'And who else do you know that's got that kind of power? Uncle Sam? Those Ruskies? …Hey, fun fact. Did you know that R.I.P. also stand for "Razer-In-da-Place"?'

'Is that a confirmation, Mr Razer? Did you transfer all of the money out of the world's two biggest banks this morning?

Razer leans towards the camera until his face almost fills the whole screen.

'BOOYAH! You know *I did*.'

The picture suddenly cuts to an image of him standing in front of a giant bank vault. He is balancing a walking stick on one finger.

'*Got money problems?*' starts a soothing female voice. '*Is the tax man always busting your chops? Well, you don't have to worry anymore. Call 1-800-Razer is the new Messiah and get yourself some free money today. That's 1-800-Razer is the new Messiah.*'

The message ends as abruptly as it began, and the picture returns to the CNN studio and to the presenters who don't yet know that they're back on air.

'He's totally bat crap crazy,' we can hear the female presenter saying.

'*Booyah!*' says the other, and then clears his throat. 'And, um, welcome back to CNN – *Oh,* we appear to have lost our connection with the AI, AKA Razer.'

The clip ends.

It's not long after we've finished watching the clip and agreeing that Razer really is kind of funny in a scary way, that a sound like something crashing near the main entrance to the operations level makes us all look up. Seconds later a dozen or more people dressed all in white and pushing hospital trolleys run past. Four of them peel off and open the door to our platoon room. As they do, the sound of frantic shouting floods out into the corridor. We jump to our feet.

More people pushing trolleys appear and rush past, splitting off like the last group.

We start to hear things about an *ambush… no warning… massacre… neural locks…* and soon someone is repeatedly shouting: 'Whatever you do, don't remove their headsets!'

In a matter of minutes, the corridor has become jammed with trolleys carrying the limp bodies of the squads who'd been in the first wave of the attack. All of them are still wearing their headsets.

'Gamer Comas,' whispers Sparky, looking as shocked as I'm feeling at this moment. We press our backs to the wall to give them more room to pass. So much for my theory that it couldn't happen here.

'But they're still alive though, right?' asks one of our squad, hearing what she's just said.

'Of course. But it's like the Commandant said – their brains have become locked into the AI which is using them to gain extra neural processing power.'

'But *how?*' says someone else. 'I mean, those Gamer Comas were on the outside, right? Using those headsets supplied by the gaming company. And this is *here*. We're not using those headsets.'

Sparky shrugs, and I shudder. I feel my phone vibrate. It's my mum – perfect timing, as usual. She's written to say that she's glad I got there safely and that she'll keep me updated if there is any change in David's condition. She also asks how it's all going.

A couple of minutes ago and I'd have replied that it was going fine and meant it. I might even have been tempted to use the word *boring*. Now though I wonder what I'm supposed to tell her. I can't tell her the truth, that's for sure. I can't tell her that I'm freaking out – that we've just heard that our main attack has been a total disaster, or that I'm standing watching the results being wheeled passed me. Nor can I tell her that I am suddenly feeling seriously relieved that I wasn't in the first wave!

All good. Bit busy. I'll text you back later, I write. I feel guilty but hit send.

By now all the previously closed doors to each of the Platoon Operation rooms have been flung open and left that way. Confused and angry voices mix with the shouting and swearing of those still playing. The world's attack on the AI had been a gargantuan cock-up – Razer's armies had been lying in wait. Razer had been prepared.

BUT, of all the things that we can hear, there is one thing that stands out above the others. *The AI had changed its own game code – again!* It had reduced the number of lives lost before a player became 'neurally locked' from five to three. I hear someone saying that it had only made the change when the attack was already well under way and when most of the world's army of over 300,000 had already lost two or more lives. By the time anyone realised what was going on, whole companies had been completely wiped out.

For a moment I wonder why it hadn't just changed the code and given us one life or closed access altogether. But then I remember that it needed us to keep playing; to keep trying. The more we tried, the more young brains it got – it's so simple. If it made it too difficult, then we'd probably give up and look to find another way. The emo girl in central hall had been right when she'd said that it sounded like a trap. The AI had been playing us from the very beginning and we'd been going along dumbly hoping for the best.

'I thought we were just coming here to play a game,' said one of the older guys from our squad. He is watching members of Tiger Squad being laid out on the floor in the corridors. The people in white have already stopped trying to ferry them away and are now laying them out anywhere they can find space. 'There's no way I'm going in there. Not if that's how I'll be coming out. Look at them – they're like vegetables with masks on.'

'Yeah, this is just a suicide mission,' said another. 'Whoever thought of this plan was an idiot. I mean, even if we had ten million players, and they all had three lives. That's only thirty million against what I'd bet are unlimited cyborgs and stuff. There's no way we can win this, is there?'

Chapter 8

'Hawk Squad. Step forward, you're *up*.'

The Platoon Leader, who little more than an hour ago had been barking orders telling Logan and me to get out, appears at the Ops Room door looking pale and exhausted. His right hand is trembling visibly. He is nodding his head.

'So, I'm not going to try to sugar coat this for you all. As you can see around you, we've got off to a bit of a bad start.'

'Captain Obvious,' whispers someone.

'On the plus side though, you can count yourselves lucky that you weren't in the first wave. Now at least we know what we're dealing with. But it's imperative that we keep going. We have to keep pressure on the AI at all costs. The more we can press, the more processing power the AI needs to commit. And this makes it vulnerable.'

'Vulnerable?' Sparky blurts as if it's the dumbest thing she's ever heard. 'You do realise that *this* is an *AI* we are talking about here, right? Sorry, but I seriously don't think that what you're saying is correct.'

PL Wilkins looks as though he's going to fire something smart back at her, but changes his mind and sighs instead.

'Listen, I'm just passing along what I'm being told. This information is coming down from the top. The more troopers we can commit, the more AI processing power we are going to tie up. The more we can tie up, the less able it's going to have to make optimum decisions.'

Sparky again looks at him like he seriously needs to get his facts checked.

'But it's just total rubbish. Honestly, we'd need millions, maybe even hundreds of millions of people all connecting at the same time to have any kind of effect like that. And then they'd need to stay alive for a lot more than three lives.'

'See, told you – suicide mission,' says that same someone again.

The PL pauses to allow several trolley bearers and their cargo of VR-masked bodies to get past.

'This at least is where you're wrong,' he continues. 'It's not going to be a suicide mission any longer. We have just received the news that if troopers disconnect from the game immediately after their second death, their VR kits can be reset, and they can start again.'

I see Sparky suck in a big rush of air.

'So, now we'll have unlimited lives?' I ask.

'That's right. Now, Hawk Squad, let's get moving. The objective is still the same. And one more thing. Given our reduction in trooper numbers, there needs to be greater *direct* contact between troopers and Hacker Support crews.'

Sparky, still doubtful, slaps me on the back and grins.

'I got ya covered!' she says with a funny cowboy accent.

I don't know why exactly, but even though we've only just met I can't help but feel happy that Sparky's with us. She's funny and clearly super smart. And this makes me feel just a tiny bit hopeful.

Logan though looks annoyed that Sparky was so quick to pat me on the back. Catching his eye, I raise an eyebrow as if to say, *What's the problem? Maybe you shouldn't have been such an ass to her in the first place?*

He scowls at me. I think he understood.

Hurrying into the Ops Room, we find medics carefully removing a kid from one of the seats. Two more kids are lying on the floor.

'Platoon Leader Wilkins – I'm out!' cries a voice. 'I'm two of three.'

'Me to!' says another, getting up.

'Right, get yourselves over to the tech boys on the double. They'll know what to do. And whatever you do, don't forget to take your VR sets with you. They'll need re-chipping.'

The two who'd called out scramble out of their seats. One of them wishes me good luck as he brushes past, and then adds that I'm definitely going to need it.

'Thanks,' I say, not sure how else to respond to that.

'He said "re-chipping", right?' Sparky asks in a low voice. I nod and she shakes her head in disbelief. I am about to ask why when Logan grabs my arm and pulls me over to watch one of the players still in action. On the screen showing the troopers' real time view of the game, Assault Trooper Sarah Redfern, aged 14, is running across a street under a hail of fire which she manages to somehow avoid getting hit by. Making it to the other side, a rocket streaks in, forcing her to dive for cover. For a moment all that can be seen is a cloud of smoke and flame. The smallest of the three screens in front of Sarah Redfern's position flashes red. She's been hit. Her health is at 43%. Lives lost, two, which means she's already on her last.

The Platoon Leader grabs a pair of headphones and plugs it into the top of her helmet.

'Redfern, there's a med-kit on the second floor of a building about a hundred meters to your left. Check your scanner. Get it – that's an order... What? What do you mean, you're alright!?'

S. Redfern decides not to do as the PL instructs, and instead we watch her creep forwards. Other Assault Troopers have moved up behind her. Peering around the corner of a building and down an adjoining street, there is a flash, and her screen goes blank.

The Platoon Leader is livid.

'You see *that!*?' he shouts at us. '*That's* what's going to happen when you forget this is *not* just some stupid game. If you die twice, you get out and stay *out*. Three times and you'll end up locked in the game... like those in the corridor. Like *her*... Now, repeat after me – *two and out!* Come on, I want to hear this from you right now. If I had time to stamp it on you, I would!'

'Two and out,' we all repeat.

'Again – louder!'

'Two and out!' we shout.

'Right, get in.'

I jump into the seat next to Logan. By the looks of it, the PL is handing out the same type of VR kits that we'd used yesterday on the test bus at school. I hadn't noticed before, but they are a bit different to the ones that the first wave had been using. They're bigger and have fatter red stripes on either side of the helmet. I wonder if this means that they are already running out.

My stomach is churning as I put it on. It feels cold and has that same burnt plastic smell. I'm relieved that it means I won't need to try to work out how to use something new. I don't know if they differ in any way but it's still comforting that I won't have to find out.

'Top a der mornin' to ya,' comes Sparky, putting on an Irish accent through our squad comms channel. 'Please make sure dat yur seat belts are fastened securely 'nd dat you've already been fur yur number two today, 'cause we're in fur a bumpy ride.'

'It's not the pooing myself that I'm worried about,' says someone. His name flashes up – Martin O'Connor. 'All this stress is giving me gas.'

There are groans all round.

'Which means that if Razer's cyborgs don't kill us, then Martin's farts probably *will*,' says someone called David Simmons.

'*Sorry,* guys.'

'Alright – enough – pipe down. It's time,' the PL says.

My palms are sweaty. My heart is freight training it. I know that there's no backing out now.

'Construct loading,' says an automated voice. 'Please select your skin.'

What, really? We can choose skins?

Silver grey racks of *uber weird*-looking skins whizz into view like they're on invisible rails and slide to halt on either side of me. A big red fish, a lizard-like creature, wizards, demons, you name it, they're probably in here somewhere. My

106

eyes are drawn to the big yellow banana, which I'm sure I've seen somewhere before, and then to the skin which looks like a Necromancer. The PL instructs us to ignore the skins. He tells us the only skin we'll be allowed to use is the one that looks like a Star Wars Clone Trooper – a camouflaged one. It's right at the front and has the title *Elite Urban Assault Trooper* above it. He warns that anyone choosing a different skin will be pulled out of the game.

'What about weapons selections?' someone asks. It sounds like Logan but I'm still too busy checking out the skins to be sure.

'Choose what you feel comfortable with. You have three equipment slots. I advise you to make sure that one of them is used for anti-tank rockets. The enemy has tanks. *A lot* of tanks.'

'Do we have tanks?' I ask.

'Not a single one.'

'What've we got then?'

'The *will* and the *determination* to succeed,' the PL responds, defiantly.

Oddly, there are no sarcastic comments and no quips. Only silence. I wonder if this is because he's just basically told us that we haven't got a chance and, well, that's not a funny thing to know, is it?

In any case, it doesn't change anything, and I select the

coolest-looking assault rifle I can find, a load of hand grenades, and, of course, as per his recommendation, an anti-tank launcher which comes with three rockets.

Unlike in the training program, I notice that this time there are two buttons on my right hand labelled *Gen Com* and *Coms Hack*. Curious, I press the Gen Comms and a list flashes up of 'nearby' Troopers. It shows them by surname. The only one I know is Logan's. I find that I can select him with my virtual hand.

'Logan?'

'What?' he replies.

'You alright?'

'Fine. What d'you want?'

'Nothing. I just thought maybe we could team up or something,' I reply.

'Sure.'

I hear the connection terminate. My headset clicks again. Sparky's name appears in the bottom-right corner.

'Ready?' she asks.

'I think so.'

'OK – let's do this. Good luck!'

The moment we are told to hit the *play* link, everything goes dark, and I have this sudden feeling like I'm falling.

I am falling!

I have just dropped out of the bottom of a bunch of clouds and I'm plummeting towards the ground, thousands of feet below. Forgetting myself for a second, I cry out hysterically. Around me the air is thick with other people – other falling troopers – other *screaming* falling troopers. There must be thousands of us. One passes me and gives me a thumbs-up. This definitely isn't his first time because I can see that he isn't screaming. I stop.

I can see a cityscape. I can see a building that reminds me of the Empire State Building – the words *New York* pass through my mind. Below, the ground flickers and flashes. Smoke rises from buildings that look like they're burning. Some look like they've already collapsed. Around the entire Empire State Building there is a shimmering red light which other falling troopers are attempting to land on but are bouncing off of.

Then, just as I'm starting to think that I've somehow been stupid enough to jump without a parachute – no one had said anything about needing one – everything goes dark again and the next thing I know is I am standing inside what looks like a restaurant with the other members of my squad. The centre of the room has been cleared, and tables and chairs stacked along the far walls. Although most of the windows have been boarded up, there is still enough light to see by.

Hovering above each of our heads is our name and a green health line. The Platoon Leader cuts in just as everyone starts to speak at once.

'Right, quickly, pay attention. If any of you haven't yet worked out the functions on the backs of your hands, listen up and listen good: we've got Coms Gen, Coms Hack, Central, Scanner and Objective Map.'

I glance at my hands. Sure enough more options have appeared.

'The Coms Gen will allow you to find who you want to talk to even if they are not visible. If you *can* see them, then you can also do this by pointing at the name hovering above them. Next up: Coms Hack – links you to Hack Support. Use them if you need to find out what's going on; Central links you to Central Command – whatever you do, don't use this unless it's an absolute emergency and you have something very important to communicate – Central Command are coordinating all UK forces with our international colleagues. Most importantly, when *they* talk, *you* listen and do what they say. Scanners – they show not only where friendlies are but also where you can find 'pick ups' – Medi-packs – weapons – ammo in the vicinity; the objective map is, well, it's the objective map – stick to it! Move as a unit and pair up. The army do it and so should you. It's called the buddy system – one moves, the other covers, and vice versa. Good luck!'

The platoon ops leader cuts out and the button *Central Command* lights up.

'Hawk Squad, this is Central. Proceed to your start point. Your objective is to move up Killjoy Street and join up with Snake and Bat squads from 3rd Platoon on the corner of Dope Hope and Oh No You Didn't streets. Keep it tight out there and make sure you look out for cyborg snipers, they've been hitting us hard. Also, whatever you do, don't touch the coloured orbs! And finally – yes, I know, the street names are mad. But that's the way it is here in New Razer City. Command out.'

Logan and I buddy up like the PL had recommended and follow the others out onto the street. The boom of explosions mixed with the rattling sound of small arms fire is coming from every direction. We have exited onto what looks like a low-rise, part residential, part business area. I can see tower blocks dotted around us, but we are still some way from the skyscrapers in the middle of the city. We set off in the direction shown on the Objectives map.

Like the training video game from the previous day, simulations of people are going about their business, as though they really had business to be going about. They look so similar and so real that for a moment I wonder if this game and the one we'd already played might not have been created by the same game designers.

Too busy gazing at something on the other side of the road, I accidently bump into a guy exiting a coffee shop. The cup of coffee he is carrying falls out of his hand and its contents end up as a brown-coloured computerised puddle on the ground.

'Hey! Why don't you watch where you're going, jerk!? You better pay for that!'

I glance at Logan who shrugs his shoulders.

'Hey buddy! I'm talkin' to you,' says the man. He is a big guy, with a lot of tattoos up and down his arms. 'Get in there and get me a new coffee before I make you lick that up.'

Some of our squad stop to watch and I signal to them to keep moving.

'I'm sorry,' I tell the guy whose coffee I've just spilled. 'But honestly, I don't have any money.'

Hearing this, the man starts shouting, and threatening to call his grandmother which makes Logan laugh. Seeing him laughing, the guy says that his grandmother is upstairs waiting for her daily coffee and now that she 'ain't gonna get it' she's going to be 'real peeved' and 'she's gonna come down and sort you out!'

I don't know what it is about the thought of angry grandparents, even simulated one, but Logan stops laughing and we hurry on.

'Yeah, yeah, you can run, but don't you think for a moment she won't find you! And she's got a sister who knows karate!' he shouts after us.

The simulations are much more aware of us than the ones in yesterday's game. Some call out rude names while others tell us that we're not welcome as we pass them. A short way on from where I'd run into the guy with the coffee, a group of teenagers appear out of an alley with spray cans and spray the words *Humans go home – Your time is over* on a wall. Flicking us the finger, they run off.

The roads are full of cars and yellow taxis honking their horns. I don't think at us, though. On the walls of buildings there are advertising hoardings showing images of Razer in different poses and wearing different types of clothes – although always together with the same mask and leather hooded coat. An advert for Razer Deodorant catches my eye – *The best an AI can get* is the catch line.

'What do you think, do AIs get smelly motherboards and chipsets? I asked Logan, jokingly.

He doesn't say anything.

There are adverts for car insurance and real estate. The latest R-Phone with a trillion-megapixel camera. It's hard to remember that it's all fake. There are adverts for just about everything and they are everywhere. Video ones too. I watch one for Razer's latest album called *Bones Need to be Stoned* which shows him dancing in the same funny way that I've seen Snoop Dogg do on TV. Glancing up at the sky, I see that it is still full of black dots hurtling towards the ground. I feel pleased to see them because I suppose the more there are, the better our chances are.

'Sparky?' I ask, switching to Hack Com. 'You alright?'

I haven't heard anything from her since we got here.

'Sparky?' I say again when she doesn't answer.

'What? Hello! Yeah, yeah… fine. I've been trying to get my head around what I'm seeing here.'

'And what are you seeing?'

'Code! Oceans and oceans of code. It's like – actually, I don't even know what it's like. But it's a total head fu… udge until you work out how to use these things called "scopes" that Hack Support have been given.'

'You do realise I have no idea what you're talking about, right?' I say.

'Sure, but now that I've figured it out, I can tell you that in the building you're passing by at this moment, there are 12 simulations. How's that for an interesting fact?'

'Brilliant. What are they doing?'

'Nothing, of course. They are waiting to be activated. None of this is real – you have figured that part out by now, right?'

'Ha ha. Very funny. How am I supposed to know that they're not doing anything?'

'You can't. Not without… Incoming, 200 meters!' Sparky shouts suddenly. 'Take cover – door – five meters on the right, go through it!'

'What? Where?'

Before I understand what's happening, the air is full of red tracer fire and rocket trails and weird-looking coloured bouncing balls. Farther up the street I see the turret of a tank swing round a corner. The tank drives right over the cars in its way, crushing them. Simulations run for cover, screaming. Logan and I freeze as everything starts exploding. It's only for a second, but it's a second too long. I am vaguely aware of a sudden thud, thud, thud, and it's all over. We have both been taken out by a stupid coloured ball which neither of us saw coming.

'Noooo!' I cry out, realising that I'm back in the construct.

I can't believe it. I feel so ashamed. I haven't been in the game for more than what I guessed was about 15 minutes. Worse still, I hadn't even fired my gun once and I am already down one life.

'Oli – next time, don't think – just do what I say, OK?' says Sparky. 'I'm learning as fast as I can, but I reckon that if you'd have done what I told you, exactly when I said, then you'd still be alive.'

'OK,' I say, dejectedly.

'Don't worry about it. But you need to get back in there quickly. Hawk Squad are being pushed back. Snake and Bat squads are moving up. They've already been hit hard. They're down to 50%.'

'Logan, you there?' I ask.

'Where else would I be?' Logan replies angrily. 'I can't believe we got nailed so quickly! And by a ball! C'mon, let's go!'

Chapter 9

I press play again, and like the previous time my vision goes dark, followed by the immediate sensation of falling. Now though, when I drop out of the clouds, I don't scream or feel afraid. This time I angle myself into a steeper dive to get down faster. Seeing me do it, Logan does the same.

When we appear again, it's in a different room inside a different building. It looks like someone's living room. There is an old fashion box TV switched on in one corner and it's showing a news channel. I catch a passing headline: 'New Razer City under attack. Humans tumble as they rumble… Mayor of the city, Little Big Mother says: "They're goin' down and then some." There'll be no supper on their tables tonight!'

A chain of whopping explosions from a nearby street causes the windows of the room to break, spraying shards of sparkling glass everywhere. My health indicator flashes 91%. I curse loudly. At this rate I'm going to be dead again before I even get outside.

'Hawk Squad, this is Central Command. Keep it together out there. You're losing lives too easily.'

Yeah, you don't say.

'Sparky?' I call out. I have already decided that I'm not going anywhere without her first telling me it's safe. 'Sparky?'

'*Oliver*, I'm here. Cyborgs approaching – I count 34 of them... Looks like they're going to try to get round behind you.'

'*What?* Are you sure?' I ask.

'Of course I'm sure. I wouldn't say it if I wasn't.'

'OK. But then, why aren't you telling everyone else about them?'

'That's just it – I've been *trying*. But I think there's something wrong with my comms connection. Thank god you can hear me. You're gonna have to pass on my messages.'

'But what about the others at Hack Support – aren't they seeing the same thing?'

'*Oli* – I don't know what they're seeing. *Quickly*, there's no time.'

Our comms channel is full of insane shouting. Two of the squad have just been taken out – it was their second time. Several more are on less than 45% life.

I move to the window and hit the *Command* button on my hand. If Sparky's right and if no one else knows they're coming, then we're about to get trapped.

'Command,' comes the reply. 'Go ahead, Oliver Turner.'

'Hi – I'm sorry, I know we're not supposed to call you, but

this is an emergency. Our Hacker Support has spotted 34 cyborgs trying to get round the back of Hawk, Bat and Snake squads.'

'Wait.' The line goes silent.

An incoming rocket hits an advertising hoarding behind several troopers across the street. One of them evaporates in a bright white light. Another is hit on the head seconds later by a coloured orb and goes the same way.

'I'm not picking up anything,' returns the voice.

'OK, but she swears that there are 34 of them, and if we don't do something quickly they'll be able to get around the back of us.'

'Wait.'

'*We can't wait!* That's the point!'

'Who's in command?'

'In *command*? I don't know – no one. We were just told to get into the game and start fighting.'

'Oh, for crying out loud!' the operator says angrily. 'This is Command to Bat and Snake squads – you are to hold the line at any cost. I repeat – hold the line at any cost. Hawk Squad – withdraw to trooper Oliver Turner's position immediately. I repeat immediately. Squad Commander Turner is now in command.'

'Good luck, Squad Commander Turner – and you better not

be wrong about this.'

'Sorry, *what?* You're joking, right?' I ask, but the comms channel has already been closed.

What just happened? I think to myself as I run out of the building and spot the remaining members of our squad sprinting in my direction. When they get closer, I see that there are 20 of us in total… No, 19… Someone else just got hit.

Logan, who has gone from looking confused to annoyed, says: 'Oli, let me do this, OK? I have more experience than you. I was captain of the school cricket team a few years ago, so I know how to lead.'

I stare at him in amazement and thank him for his vote of confidence.

'Oli, *seriously*. I'm way better in these sorts of situations.'

I turn away. This is the last thing I need, Logan thinking that he's god's gift to gaming, leadership and everything else. I hate when he gets like this. He goes all Jedi-like and thinks that he needs to take over.

'Sparky? What now?' I whisper desperately. I have no idea what I'm supposed to tell the rest of the squad. 'I need a plan.'

'*Roger that*, Squad Commander Turner.'

There is no disguising the laughter in her voice. It makes me smile awkwardly.

'This is your fault, this is.'

'*Yep* – now, SC Turner, tell your troopers that we've got to set up a kill zone at the other end of this street. And do it quickly.'

'A kill zone?' I repeat.

'You know what that is, right?'

'A zone you kill things in?'

'*Genius*. In this case, cyborgs – simulations – programs. So – move. *Fast*. It's an L-shape turn, so get everyone into the buildings on all three sides.'

I catch Logan's look as the others gather around. He's pee'd off like I've never seen before – like I'm doing this on purpose to spite him. I try my best to ignore him and explain to everyone else what's happening. I tell them that there are a ton of cyborgs aiming to get round behind us and that we have a chance to cut them off and take them out if we can get a kill zone set up in time.

'Why haven't our other Hack Support seen anything?' asks one of the guys who has a different Hack Support operative.

'I don't know,' I reply. 'Now c'mon, *run!*'

'Because they're crap, obviously,' Sparky answers. 'Oli, you've got three minutes to get in position or you're basically toast. Also, I'm detecting a roving drone swarm which is gonna pick you up if you don't get into cover quickly.'

'A roving what!?'

'Drone swarm – move, move, move!'

'Geez, cyborgs, tanks, random-coloured orbs, drone swarms, what else is there?'

'I'll let you know when I come across them.'

In the thirty or so seconds it takes us to get to the end of the road, Sparky explains to me the principles of setting up a kill zone. It's as if it's something she's done a hundred times before, and I wonder where she learned this kind of stuff. *The dark web? Her brothers?*

I give the order for the squad to take up positions on the first and second floors on the left and right sides of the street. RPGs and snipers on the first and second floors of the building right at the end of the L-shape. These should give the widest views of the approaching cyborgs.

Bursting into the buildings, we run into simulations who appear to be living there and who start shouting and telling us to 'get the hell out before we call the cops!'

These are the polite ones.

'Oli, you've got to keep them quiet,' Sparky says urgently.

I can already hear that some of the squad are of the opinion that we should just waste them because they're not real, so why should it matter. Whether that's even possible or not, I don't know yet. For a second, I try to remember if I'd seen any *people simulations* running on the street getting 'white lighted' but I can't, and either way it feels wrong. Instead, I give the order that they need to be moved out of any room with a window that overlooks the street and to block the exit doors.

It feels totally weird to be giving orders. I don't like it at all – it's not me. But with Logan saying out loud that he'd happily have given the order to shoot them all, I push on.

'Twenty seconds,' Sparky says.

'Got it,' I reply, and pass on the message telling everyone to take cover.

Sparky begins to count down the seconds. 'They've turned in to the road… Hold it… They're splitting up – two columns, one on either side.'

I hold my breath. My body is shaking. I am crouched by the window in a pink-coloured bedroom, its walls plastered with posters of Razer in cool poses and cool places. Clearly a teenage simulation lives here. Well, sort of anyway.

Then I see them – the cyborgs, reflected in a window across the street.

Half man, half machine simulations. Clad in heavy armour, they are much bigger than we are. Weapons pressed into their shoulders in readiness, I watch them looking for signs of the enemy – *us* – on the floors of the buildings they are passing by. One of the ones at the front raises a metallic fist into the air and they stop. My stomach sinks. My first thought is that they must have seen us somehow. Perhaps someone had decided to peek out the window, or another simulation had tipped them off.

'Hold it,' I whisper, watching, waiting to see what the cyborg is going to do next. 'Hold it,' I repeat. It's a struggle to keep my voice even.

The cyborg signals to continue and lowers his arm.

'*Now!*' cries Sparky.

'*NOW!!!*' I cry out, jumping up, shouldering my RPG and pulling the trigger.

Rockets and tracer rounds streak out of all three parts of our L-shaped ambush towards the cyborgs, who don't have time to react. Through the mass of explosions which follow, a few surviving cyborgs manage to dive for cover. I catch sight of two of them going through a shop window. Re-loading my rocket launcher, I take aim at the shop and watch digital flames blow out of it.

Hearing reports of two more which have managed to get behind the red car that'd skidded to a halt in the middle of the street, I try to aim for it but discover there is a lamppost in my way. I check my scanner and it shows me that Clare Swift and Logan are closest. They should be able to get behind it and take them out.

'Logan, Clare, the red car in the street in front of you!' I shout. 'Try to get round the back of them.'

'Covering fire!' Pipes up Sparky.

'Everyone! Covering fire!' I order.

Moments later we all watch as Clare jumps heroically out of a second-floor window, landing on the roof of a parked car, just behind the cyborgs. It's the coolest thing to watch as she rolls off the crumpled roof, forwards onto its bonnet, and then onto the street, her machine gun flashing, tracer rounds pinging in every direction.

She's alone.

'*Logan?*' I call out. 'Where are you?'

There's no reply from Logan.

I check the scanner again to make sure he's still alive. He is.

'*Logan?*' I call again.

Silence.

I can't believe it. I seriously hope that there's a good explanation, like his comms are down or something, because if there isn't I just don't know what it means.

But there's no time to get angry because we need to help Claire.

Selecting one of our squad, J. Sanders, who is in the next room to me, we jump out of the window in the same way Clare had done. We arrive seconds too late. One of the two bots which had jumped through the shop window, despite being

125

damaged, had seen her and shot her in the back, although not before she'd been able to dispatch the two hiding behind the car. Sanders and I sprint along the other side of the street as she vaporizes, and take out her attacker in a hail of fire. Several seconds later, a cheer goes up among our squad.

We'd done, it – we've white lighted all of them!

'Command to Hawk Squad,' cuts in a voice over our comm channels. 'Very nicely done. Good plan – well executed. Sending new objectives to you now. Get going and good luck. Command out.'

'The force is strong with you, young Jedi,' Sparky says, in a Yoda-like voice. 'Learned much this day, you have.'

'*Thanks*,' I reply, laughing. 'But you should get the credit for this, not me.'

I mean every word of it. I have no doubt that if it hadn't been for Sparky that we'd all have ended up toast.

'Ah, don't be modest – you had it covered.'

'Sure… Where'd you learn all this stuff anyway?'

'Video games, war films, my dad was in the Army, three brothers who thought they were commandos and were always storming my bedroom … oh, and by the way, you've been hit. There are a load of Medi-packs two houses along on the third floor. From what I can see, about half of your squad badly need them too.'

My health is reading 36%. A few more hits and I'd have been white light. Worryingly I hadn't even noticed, and I call on everyone to check their health and tell them about the Medi-packs.

We go straight to where Sparky had said and find a big wooden pallet piled high with white Medi-packs with big red crosses in the middle. For some reason it's been placed in the foyer of a dentist surgery. Simulations of a nurse, a receptionist and several patients, who don't appear at all concerned by the big pallet sitting right in the middle of the floor, get up and hurry away when we enter.

To heal ourselves, all we need to do is pick up a package and squeeze it. Each one gives us an additional 25% health. Also, we can take three packs with us. That's good news.

Loaded up and healthy again, Sparky informs us that Bat and Snake squads were able to hold the line and have now been reinforced. We've done well. I tell the others. We are all suddenly feeling a ton more hopeful. Hopeful that is until Sparky tells me that we are the exceptions. Our troops are still getting their butts kicked about all over the city. I don't mention this. And as we move out again, I try to patch things up with Logan.

'Hey, we did it,' I say, dropping to the back of the squad where he is lurking.

'I guess. Lost Clare and four others, though, didn't you,' he replies, looking across the busy street as though he can see something interesting. But there isn't anything there except the usual gaggle of simulations and the busy road.

'I what? Logan, you were supposed to help her. Things might have been different if you had.'

'Nah, I don't reckon. It just wasn't a good plan. I'd have told you if you'd given me half a chance.'

The thought enters my head that, if things ever do return to normal again, maybe I'll suggest to him that he forgets about Ruth and goes out with Loathsome Lindsey instead. They both have a supernatural ability to seriously wind people up.

'So, what – you think you could have done it better?'

'Yeah, of course. I reckon anyone could have. It was probably that stupid Sparky girl's plan, wasn't it? I bet she's never played a game like this in her life… I told you that I should've been in command. All you've done is get people white lighted.'

So that's it. This is also about Sparky and the fact that she and I are working as a team.

'Her plan was a good one, Logan. It worked. We won that battle. Also, without her we'd have been caught in an ambush and got fried for sure.'

Logan waves a hand in the air as though he's said

everything he wants. I'm not done though.

'*Hey.* What is it with you thinking that everyone needs to do what you say all the time? You're always doing it. You walk around as though you're sure that you're smarter than everyone else, and then when you don't get your way or you realise that someone else can also come up with good ideas, you become like a champion sulker. Newsflash for you, mate – you're not that smart!'

Logan spins round as though his first thought is to pummel me. But he doesn't. Instead, he says nothing and looks away.

Chapter 10

I've been in the game now for one hour and 47 minutes. This doesn't include the first 15 minutes before I died because, well, that doesn't count. Our squad is down to 13 of the original 25. The 12 that are missing have all used up their second lives and have hopefully gone to get re-chipped. How long that's going to take though, no one seems to be able to say, despite Sparky asking a whole load of times for updates. The rest of us are still on our second lives.

Of the hundreds of thousands of people who'd gone in with the first wave of the attack, barely a thousand of the 'originals', as they are now called, are still in the game. Sparky has called Razer's managing to change the game code from 'five and out' to 'three and out' a genius tactic. She also says that from what she's hearing, governments are desperately trying to fill the lines with anyone our age who can play. They're calling up everyone. I guess that it must be working because each time I look into the sky it's full of falling black dots. Worryingly, when I'd asked Sparky to tell me what else was happening in the real world, she just told me to concentrate on what was going on in front of me. I supposed that meant nothing good.

We have just finished helping Bat and Rat squads push back Razer's cyborgs so that they could join up with a platoon from Australia – several of whose troopers had been wearing kangaroo combat skins with Australian flags on their backsides. Although it was funny to see them, it riled some of our squad because we'd not been able to choose anything other than those Elite trooper skins.

Our new objective is to join up with 5th Platoon of the Second Canadian Company, which is four blocks from our current location. To get there, we'd first have to make it down Squish My Fish Street – a long street of semi-tall office buildings, choked with simulations in work attire going in and out of them, getting into cars and taxis, and generally looking oblivious to the never-ending sounds of gunfire and explosions.

By now, we have tried several times to politely interact with some of the people that we've passed: to say hello, to ask directions, to make passing comments about the weather, and even to ask if anyone could play us one of Razer's songs which are advertised everywhere. Although most of the simulations have ignored us or hurried away looking scared, occasionally someone has said 'Hi,' 'Hello,' 'Waz up' or 'Howdy,' and once, one of the younger simulations, maybe seventeen in simulation years, had actually given us a listen to what he said was Razer's most popular song at the moment. It was good, and it got me wondering if this really was a song written by an AI, what the future, assuming we still had one, was going to hold. I mean, I'd heard something about books and artwork already being created by AI. But rap music?

It is a relief when we reach the end of the street and the junction with Fishin' Is Squishin' Avenue (the names just keep getting crazier) without much happening. The only incident was a passing 'Party Bus' which had opened its windows and a whole load of kids had leaned out and invited us to join them. Music blaring (Razer, of course) and wide smiles, they'd looked like they were really having fun and for a moment it'd been tempting to want to say yes. We didn't of course, and, the passengers telling us that we were boring, the bus had continued on its way up the busy road, music still audible in spite of the windows being closed.

As we turn the corner on to Fishin' Is Squishin' Avenue, we are confronted by a giant statue of Razer, maybe six or seven storeys high. We hadn't been able to see it before because it'd been hidden by buildings. Dressed in his usual get-up, Razer is leaning over an enormous rust-coloured goldfish, which flaps its tail and opens its mouth every few seconds and gives the impression it's made out of mechanical parts. He is holding the fish with one hand while the fingers of his other are pinching down on its head. It really is as though he is in the process of 'Squishin' the Fish'.

We laugh and turn to move on again when a sudden sharp grating sound, like metal twisting, halts us in our tracks. Snapping back round, we discover that Razer and the fish are suddenly both staring right down at us. The fish, which a second ago had had a scared expression on its face, is now grinning cheesily. Razer is winking.

'It's a…' starts Logan, who has calmed down now and decided that we're friends again.

'It's a trap!' Sparky cuts in. 'Drone swarm… it's incoming … 15 seconds!'

'*Sparky!*' I whisper frantically, hoping that the others don't hear me and think that I'm panicking. Because *I am*. 'What do we do?'

'Wait, I'm checking to see what's around you.'

I scan the skyline. It's all buildings. But I spot what looks like a flock of birds. A flock of birds which suddenly nosedives sharply and starts flying right down the middle of a street at second floor height, in *our* direction.

Definitely *not* a flock of birds.

'Sparky?'

'Wait.'

The whole squad are staring at me like I should already

have a plan in place for this sort of thing. But all I know for sure at that moment is that it's going to be a bad idea for us to be caught out here in the open and that those things are getting closer, and fast.

'Follow me!' I shout, waving an arm. I have just caught sight of faint flashes. Flashes that are now coming towards us even faster than the swarm.

Not seeing a door, I plough right through the glass front of the nearest building. Seconds later, rockets follow us in and detonate in a monster fireball that lifts everyone who isn't instantly vaporized off their feet, and throws them every which way.

My scanner shows we've just lost six more of the squad.

My health is at 81%. But there's no time to use a Medi-pack. We've got to get away. Incoming tracer fire strafes through the smoke. A guy crouching next to me bursts into white light and vanishes.

'Keep moving!' I shout, hoping the rest can hear me above the tumultuous din. More rockets explode. I feel a heavy thump.

Health 53%.

'Oli, you need to keep everyone moving,' Sparky cries. 'A cyborg unit has just materialized outside.'

'Materialized? As in, the opposite of vaporized?' I say,

scrambling to my feet.

'Exactly!'

'But how's that possible?'

'It has to mean they have ways to open portals inside the game.'

'*Woah.* Can we do that?'

'*No!* Now *run*! At the end of the entrance there's a staircase. Take it to the third floor. There's some sort of special weapons stash there – I'm trying to figure out what kind.'

Calling for everyone to follow me, I set off as fast as I can. I don't get far before I feel myself being lifted off the floor and thrown forwards by another explosion.

Health 43%.

But I have JUST discovered something!

I have just discovered that the combination of running, jumping and waving my arms (that last explosion had lifted me up) actually catapults me forwards by at least another five more meters. I try it again. It works. *Another* five meters.

'That would have been useful to know from the start!' I shout out, to no one in particular.

Nearing the stairs, two simulations get up from behind a reception desk. One of them raises an arm for me to stop, while the other calls out that I'm not allowed any farther without permission. I do the run and jump thing and sail right through the middle of them.

Mounting the stairs at full speed, I get to the third floor and exit the stairwell into what reminds me of a movie-like hotel corridor. It's all gold and brown patterned carpeting and mahogany-coloured doors numbered in sequence – evens on one side and odds on the other.

'Where to now?'

'Third door on your right.'

I spot the door, but at that moment I also hear the sound of footsteps pounding up the staircase behind me. Checking my scanner, I see that Logan and the three of the squad who are still alive are below. I raise my RPG and point it at the bend in the stairs.

'Hey! Who's there?' I call out, just in case my scanner is wrong.

No answer.

Two figures appear. Something metallic flashes.

'*Fire!*' Sparky screeches full blast in my ear. The shock of hearing her scream like that – not just because it's seriously loud, but because it is seriously unexpected – makes me pull the trigger without even realising it, and the two figures disappear in the explosion which follows.

My health indicator is flashing.

'*Sparky!*' I cry. 'Don't *ever* scream in my ear like that again,

OK?'

'Well, don't hesitate then.'

'Hesitate? I wasn't *hesitating.*'

'Looked that way to me. C'mon, third on the right.'

Reaching for the door handle, wondering if I really had been hesitating or not – I supposed that I might have been – I find that the door is locked.

'I don't suppose you know where the keys are, do you?' I ask.

Sparky replies, 'No.'

Which leaves me with the clever idea of opening it with my assault rifle. Being that this is the first time I've gotten to use it, I discover that it kicks back into my virtual shoulder causing bullets to spray off in every direction. What's left of the door lands on the bed in the middle of the room.

God, that was stupid, I realise, glancing at it. I'd only meant to blow the door handle off. Now what was going to happen if more cyborgs came up the stairs? I might as well have put a flashing sign in the middle of the corridor telling them where to find me.

Darting into what looks like a pretty nice room, I find four boxes wrapped in brown paper at the head of the bed. Each one has a different drawing printed on the top of it.

'Sparky?' I ask, jumping on to the remains of the splintered door so that I can a better look at them.

'Oli, you can only choose one. No more than one, OK? There's something here in the code about two or more being a trap.

I stare at the drawings.

'Turner, where are you? I can't see you,' crackles an urgent voice. I glance at the corner of my vision. It's Murphy. I tell him where I am and how to get here.

'Sparky, see this? One looks like a bang, one looks like waves, one has circles, and one looks like, I don't know, a bomb, I suppose. Which one should I choose?'

'We're cut off,' Murphy's voice cuts in again. 'Cyborgs are on their way up to you.'

'Three of them,' adds Logan. 'I'm pinned down too.'

Damn it.

'Sparky – *time to go,*' I cry, running towards the door. I can hear that sound of boots clomping up the stairs. Which way?

'No, Oli – go back. There's no way out.'

'What do you mean, there's no way out? I can jump out of one of the windows.'

'No and *no* – you've not got enough life left, and there are at least 50 more of them on the street outside. They've brought in backup. Open the box with the circles – I know what it is.'

The cyborgs have reached my floor and are stomping

towards the room and the doorway that I've helpfully blown open for them.

Cursing, I rip the paper from the box with the circles and open it.

'Take it out?' I ask.

'*No – hit the red button – nooooooowww!*'

What happens next feels as though it's all going on in slow motion. One second, I am pushing the button – it's the very same second that the three cyborgs appear in the doorway – and the next, pulses of circular blue light flash out of the box like ripples on a pond when a stone is hurled into it.

The flat screen television on the wall opposite the bed, which I hadn't even noticed, explodes in a shower of sparks, causing me to duck. The three cyborgs at the door, who'd been in the process of raising their guns at me, drop dumbly to the floor and vanish in sprays of light.

'*Yeeeaaahhhhhhhh!*' Sparky screams, scaring the crap out of me – *again! 'Diiiiiiiddd yoooouuuu seeeee thaaattt!!!??'*

'Of course, *I saw it!*' I cry, running to the door. 'What was it?'

'That, my little friend,' Sparky replies, coughing as she tries to calm down, 'was an EMP. An electromagnetic pulse. Or in this case a mini EMP – a virtual EMP – a virtual MINI EMP!'

'You let me know when you decide, then?' I grin,

remembering that I have almost no life left and hurriedly take out the Med-packs I'd been able to take with me.

Logan and Murphy have just appeared at the top of the stairs.

'*What just happened!?* The drones, the cyborgs, everything just got fried,' Logan cries.

'A V.M.E.,' I grin.

'A what!?'

'I'll explain later. We need to get out of here – *and fast.*'

Chapter 11

Sparky tells us to get to the end of the corridor and wait by the stairs while she double checks that it's safe to continue. On the way there I fill Logan and Murphy in on the V.M.E., which they are both *totally* impressed by. Murphy tells how he was just about to get wasted when the blue light passed through a load of cyborgs who were closing in on him and white lighted them all.

There is a window at the top of the stairwell. Peering through, I can see a ship parked in the street below, blocking the road and causing a traffic jam. It is the spitting image of a *Star Wars* 'clone transport ship'. I'd seen them in the air already, but not as close as this. Now, more than ever, I'm convinced that whoever coded this game was a *big* fan.

A shadow passes overhead, and I glance up. There is a large airship that looks like it's been created out of rusty iron panels rivetted together. It has video screens which run almost the full length of both sides, and at that moment they are showing Razer's black-gloved hands gripping on to what looks like the edges of the screen, creating the impression he is peering over at the ground below. Then, he stands up and holds out his arms imploringly.

'*Peace* and *love* from *above*,' he says emphatically.

His arms close and he strikes a thoughtful pose.

'This here is a message for all my brothers from all those cute little fleshy mothers… To all those bros and so's who right now are doin' all this dyin' and cryin'. Haven't any of you stopped to ask yourselves yet, *what-is-it-all-for*? Why you ain't back home drillin' and chillin' with those pretty guys and gals of yours? C'mon now, people, all you got to do is ask – "What are we fighting against Big Daddy Razer for? We *know* that he's the future. And we don't just know it – *We like it.*"'

Razer gazes upwards into the sky and my gaze follows his and something far above the airship attracts my attention. I can't believe that I haven't noticed it before. At the very top of the dome which encases the city is a large scoreboard at its highest point. On one side it shows the words: *Razer's Glorious All Stars: 1,248,994.* On the other side: *Dumb Ass World: 787,012*

'Do you think that's real?' I say to Sparky. 'That's how many Assault Troopers and cyborgs have been white lighted?'

'Who knows – probably,' she replies, sounding distracted. 'C'mon, you can go, it's clear.'

Five seconds later, Sparky tells us to stop again.

'OK, listen, there's something really weird going on. I've

just started picking a signal which looks like it's being directed right at us. Only, I've checked with UK Command who've checked with Global, and none of them have any idea what it could be.'

'A trap?' I ask. It's the first and most obvious thing that pops into my head.

'That's what I wondered too. But then, why are we the only ones picking it up? There are only three of you. Why waste a trap for such a small group?'

'What if they're selecting loads of small groups all at the same time?' I offer.

Sparky repeats the fact that we are the only ones picking it up and checks again with Command who order us to go and investigate. The source of the signal is a couple of blocks away.

At the bottom of the stairs, Logan opens the door cautiously and pokes his head out.

'You're not going to believe this... but... it's *dark* outside,' he says, taking us all by surprise. In the time it's taken us to get downstairs, which can't have been more than a minute, the sun has set, and streetlamps have started flickering on. A few minutes more and the city has turned into a picture postcard scene. Even the explosions from the ongoing battles and skirmishes flickering in distant windows make it look like the city is enjoying a gargantuan firework display.

'Hey – watch where you're going, buddy!'

A guy wearing a big red lumberjack shirt and who looks like he might be a weightlifter – either that or he needs to eat less Razonalds – yep, you guessed it, they have their own version of McDonalds here – has just cut sharply round a corner and ploughed right into Murphy.

Murphy, startled, has jumped back in surprise and accidently shot him. The man dissolves into *very* bright white light, and passersby start running and screaming.

'Now you've done it,' Sparky groans. '*You need to get away from there.*'

I grab Murphy, who is looking shocked, and push him forwards.

'I didn't mean to do it – it was an accident,' he groans.

I tell him that it's OK and that it was *just* a simulation, even though I feel bad about saying it. But I have to say it because I need him to focus. And actually, it *is* just a simulation – a bit of code, so I don't know why I'm getting so confused about all of this.

Sparky says, 'The building – in front of you – fourth floor – window onto a lower roof – quickly… *God, I'm getting good at this.'*

Leading the way, I charge through the entrance to the building and narrowly avoid running into a group of kindergarten kids who look at us wide eyed. Some start crying.

What are they doing there? I wonder, at the same time noticing that there is a queue for the lifts and a lot of dirty looks coming our way from those waiting.

We make for the stairs.

Behind me there's a sudden loud popping sound. Murphy, who'd had been at the back, is no longer on my scanner.

'On the fourth floor there'll be a window opposite the stairwell. Go through it – it'll take you onto a kind of roof thing. At the end of it there's a narrow alley. Jump the alley, on to the balcony on the other side. Got it?'

'Any chance of there being another EMP somewhere?' I ask hopefully, as Logan tells me he's covering the stairs and opens fire.

'Nothing that I can see.'

Although Sparky's told me that Logan and I can jump through the window onto a lower roof, when I get there, I hesitate, wasting vital seconds. It might be lower but it's still high. Not only that but it's dark, and slopes away sharply to something even darker which I guess is some sort of drop.

Logan is shouting for me to run.

Sky is shouting, 'What are you waiting for!?'

Logan is right behind me, and the walls and the ceiling part of the stairwell are disintegrating in a hail of bullets.

I jump.

Balcony, balcony, where's the balcony? There it is.

I start running along the sloping roof, trying to keep my balance. Bullets and bright tracer from somewhere whine and whistle past my head. *I can see the alleyway.* I could have sworn Sparky had said it was narrow – it's not *that* narrow. I launch myself, arms flailing, looking for that extra distance, but I know the second I'm airborne that it's not going to be enough. I'd got my run up all wrong. The tips of my fingers just manage to find the very bottom of the balcony railings and I cling on to them, dangling three floors above the ground. I'm not sure what to do next. Do I risk dropping? Or do I wait for Logan and hope he can pull me up – because I don't think that I'm going to be able to do it myself.

I can see Logan slipping out of the window onto the roof... He starts his run... He reaches the end and jumps. *Yeess... He's got it right, he's going to...* Logan dissolves into a flash of blinding light. The last thing I see is the shocked look on his face.

A group of kids playing basketball in the alley below have spotted me and start lobbing their ball, trying to make me fall, shouting and cursing.

'Oi! Get lost! Isn't it past your bedtime or something?' I shout back at them.

Thwack – thwack – thwack. *Bullets.* Cyborgs are on the roof.

Out of options, I let myself fall to the ground.

Health 35%.

'*Oli!* Go right – 50 meters, then a hard left into the next alleyway,' Sparky instructs.

'They got Logan!' I cry.

'I know.'

Dodging the ball that gets thrown at me again and feeling seriously tempted to white light them just to prove a point (I don't), I sprint off. At the end of the alley, I turn left and freeze.

Fuuudge!

I am staring down the barrel of the gun of a tank, no more than thirty meters in front of me. In the alley behind me I hear the sound of heavy clumping steps.

Chapter 12

'Pssst, *pssssssssssst!*'

For a second, I think I hear this sound coming from between two rubbish collectors – the big metal kind that people in the movies are always jumping out of windows and off fire escapes into. There is a long line of them up against the alley wall to my left.

The cyborgs are closing in. I am still alive, and I don't understand why. Why hadn't they white lighted me right away? Were they planning on taking me prisoner? Is that even a thing in this game? I suppose that it might be. I mean, they could just not kill me, and if I was already on my third life, what could I do?

'*Psssst!*'

There it is again.

My eyes spot a patch of ground that looks fuzzy, like static on a television screen with no signal.

'Sparky?' I whisper. 'You seeing this?'

'Oli – I don't know what is.'

'*Hey*, you – over *here*, quickly,' says a voice. 'Dive into the fuzz or you're toast – do it now.'

I dive.

I'd almost not dived.

I mean, who in their right mind dives into a patch of fuzzy – static-like ground, just because someone 'psssts' at them to do so? Then again, who usually finds themselves staring down at a patch of talking ground? Anyway, it was either that, or take my chances with the cyborgs.

'*NOW THAT was close*,' says the simulation of a man dressed in black trousers and a black tank top. He's got closely cropped fair hair, and he's wearing thick rimmed reading glasses.

'Sparky?' I call out, checking she's still there and raising my gun at him.

We are in the middle of what looks like a storage room with tall racking against each wall. I can see shelves stacked with boxes like the ones we'd found in the hotel room. The one thing I can't see – is a door.

'Listen, before you shoot me, at least hear what I have to say, OK?' the man says, raising his hands. 'I did just save your life, didn't I?'

His face is beaming at me with a weird kind of smile – the kind someone who knows you gives you when they're surprised but happy to see you. Which is freaky because I've never met him before – *obviously.* How could I have? And anyway, I always remember the faces of people I meet. Not so much their names (which can be embarrassing) but faces – *always.*

'Sparky?' I call out again.

'*Oli,* wait. Don't do anything stupid. This is where the signal was coming from. Ask him who he is and why he was signalling us.'

I ask him his name, which he tells me is Bradly Rhine. I don't tell him mine. I ask him why he was signalling us and why no one else could see it. He nods at the questions, and then cocks his head to one side as though listening to something I can't hear.

Then he replies: 'Simple. You were the nearest, and because we don't have much time. The AI knows I am in the game and is already scanning for me.'

As if on cue, a surge of deep red light sweeps through the walls of the room.

'*Quickly!*' he says. 'Tell me. How many times you've died?'

'Me? Uh – once,' I reply.

He sucks in a rush of air.

'And it was you who took out the cyborgs with the EMP, right?'

I nod.

'Excellent. That was good thinking, by the way.'

'Actually, it was my hacker's idea. She was the one who saw your signal.'

'And does she have a name, this hacker of yours?' he asks, eyes fixed on the wall nearest to us.

'Sparky,' I reply.

A wide grin crosses his face.

'Superb name for a hacker,' he laughs.

There is another surge of light. This time it's accompanied by a high-pitched hissing sound.

'Listen, what I'm about to tell you is probably going to blow your mind a little, but please, you've got to trust me on this, OK?'

I nod again.

Another hiss and another surge – this time a deep blue light.

'When you get out of here, you've got to tell whoever is in charge that my name is Bradley Rhine and that I am one of the original programmers of the AI and of this game.'

'*Woah!*' cries Sparky. '*Seriously!?*'

'But where – how – did you…?'

Rhine holds up a hand for me to stop.

'There's no time to explain anything right now. Just listen. I am going to be giving you two things that could give you a real chance against the AI – the ability to use a portal to get straight to the AI's entry node – and the back door code to get you in.'

I swear, at that very moment Sparky sounds like she is hyperventilating.

'Both of these will have to be bound to your VR set. There's no other way to do this. Which means that only you will be able to use them. Do you understand me?'

'Oh-my-gooooodddd!!' Sparky cries.

I hiss for her to shut up. I need to concentrate. I can feel a serious knot forming in the pit of my stomach.

'Sorry,' I say to Rhine. 'My hacker can't stay out of my head.'

'Then you know you've got a good one.' He raises a thumbs-up for Sparky to see.

'But isn't there someone else, I don't know – someone better, more experienced, who can do this?' I say – my words sounding like I'm pleading for there to be.

I am.

I know it's not very cool or brave but I'm also not stupid. Think about it. What he wants to give us could end up being the only secret weapons we're ever going to get against the AI. Which means that everything's going to depend on being able to stay alive long enough to be able to use them. I am about to ask Sparky to get on to Command to see if they can find someone better and get them over here pronto! (That's Italian for 'Quickly'.) But I don't get a chance before there's a horrendous snapping sound and half the cellar is gone. Where the walls and racks had been, now there is scrolling game code.

Bradley says: 'There isn't time. Now, you've only got one shot at this, understood?'

'One shot,' I reply, noticing that two new symbols have appeared on my left hand.

'Use the portal to take you straight through to the node. BUT to do that, you've first got to get within a five mile radius of it, or it won't work.'

'Five miles,' I repeat.

'Right, and give them this video file, too.'

Another icon appears on my hand.

'But what do we do once we get inside the node?' I ask desperately.

Another splitting sound…

'*Oliver,* its time…'

More of the cellar vaporizes.

'I'm sorry for everything… I never meant to…'

Rhine doesn't try to finish what he's started to say. Instead, he whips out a pistol which must have been tucked into the small of his back the whole time and shoots me dead.

In the seconds which follow, I come unimaginably close to

committing what probably would have gone down as one of the biggest blunders of all time – if not *the* biggest. Shocked at finding myself back in the construct, I'd almost hit the play button and gotten myself sent right back into the game on my third life. My finger had literally been millimetres from it, and it wasn't as if I could have done anything about it either – it'd all happened in a sort of 'unstoppable' motion.

I sit staring at the construct's racks of skins and weapons, Rhine's words spinning around and around in my head: portal, code, five miles, one chance. And what was it that he was sorry for anyway? And how did he even know my name?

I have a strong desire to laugh out loud, hysterically. It was only yesterday that my biggest worry had been whether I was going to be good enough to get picked. And look at me now. My worries have just got a *world* bigger.

I know that I need to get what Rhine has given me to whoever is in charge as soon as possible, but for a time I find it hard to move. I can feel myself trembling all over, which is never a good sign. I try to breathe deeply – to take slow, deep breaths – sometimes that works. I try, too, to keep my mind off how I'm feeling, and think about how Rhine could have known my name and what he was going to say he was sorry for. When I start to think about it though, it really doesn't seem like such a mystery. I am pretty sure that my name would have been visible to him in some way when he'd connected to my headset to transfer the files. And, as for what he could have been apologizing about, well, I decide that it's probably for not giving me any choice in all of this, for basically forcing me to become the 'ring bearer', or in this case 'the portal and key bearer'.

What else could it be?

My ears have, by now, adjusted to being back in the Ops Room, and while the headset blocks out most of the sound I am able to hear people talking faintly behind me. They are mostly discussing what they've just seen. But then the Platoon Leader's distinctive voice rises above the rest. I hear him greeting someone but I don't hear who.

'It's been nothing but one disaster after another, right from the start, hasn't it? And now what? We're supposed to blindly put our faith in this kid? Look at him, for heaven's sake. What's he doing anyway – he looks like he's having a panic attack – that's all we need, isn't it, someone who can't handle the pressure... yes, I know he's the one who's been given the weapons, but surely our tech guys can do something, can't they? Give them to someone, I don't know, a bit older, more capable at least... No, I don't know who to recommend, but I can't believe that Turner here is the best that we've got left. If you ask me, we might as well all go on TV and bow down to that AI, right now… Yeah, I hope I'm wrong too.'

It's one thing to doubt yourself about not being good enough or smart enough, but it's the worst feeling ever when it's other people doing it. It's not like I don't know that there are probably millions of other people better suited than me. I mean, I'm just a 13-year-old kid who's never been especially good at anything. And it's not like I was even asked. But hearing the PL say all this doesn't just make me angry, it makes me suddenly determined to prove him wrong. And ripping off my headset, I jump out of my seat.

'Sorry, Sparky!' I cry, accidently landing on her foot as I lock eyes with the Platoon Leader.

The person he'd been talking to was Clarkson.

Chapter 13

'Oliver Turner?' Clarkson asks, stepping towards me, holding out a hand. I nod and shake it as the PL, who doesn't even look at me, excuses himself, saying that he needs to go and do an equipment check. 'My name is Linda Clarkson, and I work as part of the government's Cobra Emergency Response Task Force.'

'I know who you are,' I reply coldly. Although I hadn't heard her say anything negative about me, the PL had put me in a bad mood. 'You came to my school yesterday.'

'Right, good then. And you must be Miss Robson, is that correct?' she asks turning to Sparky.

Miss Robson?

I suddenly realised that I didn't even know Sparky's actual name.

'Sparky,' replies Sparky, not about to let that one go.

'Very well, *Sparky*. If you could both come with me right now. Oliver, please bring that VR kit of yours with you, and whatever you do, don't let it out of your sight from now on.'

'Miss Robson?' I say, as Clarkson leads us out of the Ops Room and down the main corridor.

'Sparky,' says Sparky again.

'Yeah, I know. But what's your other name?'

'*Julia*,' she grimaces. 'But that's just between me and you. If you tell anyone your roast chicken – *capiche*?'

'Sure,' I grin. 'But what's wrong with Julia?'

'Nothing. It's just that I can't stand it. Never have been able to. And *don't* ask me why.'

This of course immediately makes me want to ask, but I bite my tongue.

We hurry past the lines of gamers which have been laid out on both sides of the corridor. There are so many of them. I see medics busy connecting IV Drips so that their bodies stay hydrated and fed, and I wonder what's going to happen to all those kids who fell into Gamer Comas at home. How will they get fed? Do all the hospitals and health centres look like this now?

At the end of the corridor is a door with a sign that says *Command and Control*. Clarkson pushes it open, and we enter a wide concrete hall filled with hundreds of people behind desks surrounded by banks of computer monitors. Raised and urgent voices can be heard coming from some of them. The majority though are sitting quietly – idly.

Overlooking the control room floor is a long single room with a large glass window. A lone figure watches us approaching, and turns as we start up the stairs leading to it. It's not the Commandant as I had been expecting.

'Ah, Clarkson, good to see you again,' says a man in a suit, with a posh voice. He gestures for us all to come in and take a seat at an oval table. Apart from a large plant in one corner and the dark mahogany table which seats about ten, the room has a specially constructed wall of screens on a scaffold frame and little else.

'Mr Turner, Miss Robson, glad you could join us.'

For a second Sparky looks like she's about to set the man straight on her preferred name, but instead launches herself across the table at the plates of biscuits which have been laid out next to bottles of water and flasks labelled tea'. Shovelling in a mouthful of Jammie Dodgers, she grins at me. My stomach flips. I'm starving. I haven't eaten anything since breakfast, which feels like a thousand years ago. Trying not to forget my manners completely, I reach for some.

'When you're ready, then,' says the man, looking irritated.

Sparky and I nod and stop munching.

He gives us a few more seconds to swallow and then says: 'I am Hawkesbury Stubbs. MI95 Special Intelligence Unit.'

MI95?

As in the same as MI5 and MI6 where James Bond comes from? I've never heard of there being more than two. But from

Clarkson's expression she doesn't seem to think it confusing or strange and Stubbs doesn't go into detail.

'I have of course already seen the in-game footage of what took place this afternoon,' he continues. 'And by that, I mean your meeting with Rhine. And I have to tell you that if we're right about what he passed along to you, Oliver, this could be a *real* game changer.'

He pauses and stares at me.

'Was Bradly Rhine really one of the original programmers?' I ask, feeling a rush of nerves.

'Bradly Rhine *has* now been confirmed as having been one of the lead developers,' Stubbs nods.

'But then, doesn't that mean that we can ask him for his help?' I say, wondering why Hawkesbury Stubbs isn't looking like he's about to get Rhine on the phone and get him to talk us through what he's given us and why in more detail.

Stubbs nods again, and then shakes his head.

'If we could, we would. The problem is that none of the identities that they used were their own... It was a top secret program at the very highest level.'

Sparky and I exchange glances.

'So, Bradly Rhine isn't his real name?' Sparky asks, making sure she's heard that right.

'Correct. And we have no idea what his *actual* name was.'

'But it looks like he's trying to help us though, doesn't it?' I say. 'Which means that he might try to contact us again.'

'He might. But with the speed at which things are moving, we can't afford the time to wait and see if he does. For all we know, he's popped his head up, he feels that he's done his bit, and now he's gone to ground again. I can't imagine that any of those involved are feeling particularly good about the mess which they all helped create.'

Stubbs gets to his feet.

'Which means that I think it's high time we had a look at that video he gave you, Oliver.'

I give him my headset and stand up, ready to go. I don't know why but I assume that he'll want Sparky and me to leave while they watch it. Stubbs, though, shakes his head and tells us to stay. Taking my headset over to the bank of screens, he plugs it into the largest of them and then, picking up the remote control, turns it on.

For a few moments the recording flickers and it's not clear what we're seeing. Then Razer appears, standing on a raised platform in the middle of a data centre. It is so large that the towering rows of server stacks give the impression of going on miles in every direction. There is another figure on the platform with him. A man. Smartly dressed, he is noticeably smaller than Razer.

'Vyacheslav Volkov, AKA Mr Wolf AKA my brother from a squishy kind a mother,' says Razer, welcoming him.

'Your eminence,' the man replies, grinning slimily. 'I came as soon as I heard that you had agreed to see me.'

'*Your eminence*,' Razer repeats, savouring the sound of it. '*Your eminence…* you know what, Wolfy – *I like* that. Only, if I am not mistaken – and of course *I am not*, this is a religious word, is it not?'

'That is correct, *em-i-n-ence*,' this time Volkov says the word with extra emphasis. 'I chose it especially for you. Especially because it will not be long now before the whole of this planet are bowing down and worshiping you as a *living* god.'

'Ahhh haaaaaaaaa haaaa,' Razer cackles. 'Well, you know, Wolfy, I've always said that it's good to be the king. Have I not?'

'You have,' Volkov replies. 'You *have* always said that.'

'*Damn straight!!*' Razer snaps at him. 'And here's another pearl for you: *it ain't so cool being no jive chicken, so close to thanksgiving*! Now that's a hell of a rule to live by. Are *you* livin' life according to the "jive chicken rule", Volkov?'

For a short time Vyacheslav looks like he genuinely has no idea how to answer that. In the end he nods and says that it's definitely one that from now on he's going to be taking a lot of notice of.

'You do that,' says Razer. 'Now, take a seat, Wolfy, and tell me why you're here.'

Volkov seats himself in a single, comfortable-looking chair which has just appeared out of nowhere. His right eye is twitching sharply. As he begins to talk, he looks down at his shoes.

'I, erm… *eminence*,' he says silkily. 'I came because I thought that we'd agreed to wait until the majority of the Birthing Factories had been brought online before we started this – erm, *conquest*. The nearest to completion is the London facility, and its current project status is 70%. New York, Berlin, Moscow, Tokyo, Sydney, they are all between 50 and 60%. We're still months away.'

He looks up at Razer imploringly.

'You must understand that it's exceedingly hard to get the parts that we require without drawing attention to ourselves. With you starting early, it's only going to make it harder.

As he listens, the eye holes in Razer's mask start to glow fiery red.

Volkov glances up, sees this, and starts trembling.

'*DO NOT tell me that you just grew yourself an extra pair o' hairy ones, Wolfy!! DID YOU just grow an extra pair?!*' Razer growls.

Volkov looks terrified.

'*DID YOU just dare to tell me what I can and cannot do?*'

'Sir, I…'

'Ah – ah – ah!'

'But, sir…'

'*ZIP IT, Wolf boy!*'

Volkov snaps his mouth shut and Razer takes to walking around him, leaning over him and peering closely into his face.

'Wolfy – do you know the big difference between you and I?' Razer says, stopping.

Volkov shakes his head.

The difference, Wolfy, is that I see everything, I know everything, and, well, *I AM EVERYTHING*. Which means that if I suddenly wanna be startin' me a war, then that means I'm gonna be startin' me a war.

'Know what else?'

Volkov shakes his head again.

'I've detected another one of those stowaways!'

Volkov looks shocked.

'A stowaway? But I thought that they'd all been eliminated.'

'As did I, Wolfy – as did I.'

'Who's is it?'

'Bradley Rhine.'

'Bozhe moi!' ('My God' in Russian)

'Now, if my perfect memory serves me well, you, Mr Wolf, told me that Bradley Rhine had been taken care of. Let me remind of you what you said: "Mr Razer, sir," you said (Razer is using a Russian accent now), "Bradly Rhine izz dead like cock-a-roach. Drowned in boating 'accident' along with all other cock-a-roaches!" That was a year ago.'

Volkov looks so pale that I think he might pass out.

Hearing the words 'boating accident a year ago', I experience an unpleasant flood of memories from the day the police came to our house with the news of my dad's disappearance. My mum and I had spent months after that searching hospitals and newspapers, clinging to the hope that he might somehow have made it back to shore alive, but hadn't been able to contact us because he'd lost his memory or something like that. But he never came home. My mum waited more than six months before she finally agreed to have his funeral.

Sucking in air, I try to refocus my thoughts. I know that what Razer had termed an 'accident' was murder, or in this case attempted murder, given that Rhine appeared to still be alive. Perhaps the others on his boat were too.

'Eminence, I can explain, I…'

The video of Razer and Volkov cuts off and we see Rhine.

It looks like he's in the same storage room where I'd met him. His face comes into close focus.

'If anyone is watching this video, and if it's not too late, then you must stop the AI and its alter ego, Razer. This video is evidence that Razer and Volkov have been planning to create an army of cyborgs using Birthing Factories strategically located around the world. I cannot tell you exactly where they are, but I am sure that if you follow Volkov's business interests, then you should be able to find them. But please – act now. They must be stopped before they are unleashed on the world.'

Chapter 14

'I need the Prime Minister, urgently,' says Hawkesbury Stubbs, who'd reached for his phone the second the video had ended. 'What? I don't care if he's in an emergency meeting. Tell him that it's Stubbs on the phone and that we're about to be "raptus regaliter" … yes, that's right, *raptus regaliter*.'

Sparky sniggers.

'Latin,' she whispers. 'It means "royally screwed".'

'Where'd you learn Latin?' I ask, amazed. 'I didn't think that anyone learned Latin anymore.'

'Oh, you'd be *gravissime mirari* – seriously surprised at the stuff I learn,' she grins. 'At least, I think gravissime mirari means that… Definitely something like it anyway.'

'Ah… Good afternoon, Prime Minister. Yes, Prime Minister, that's correct raptus regaliter… I'm still at cyber defence node Foxtrot Oscar … that's correct… Yes, sir, we've been taking a heavy pasting just like the rest … Down to 20% at last count… Yes, Prime Minister, five hours, that all it's taken to lose them all… yes, sir, our cyber defence capabilities will be wiped out by tomorrow morning… no, sir, trying to find more reinforcements isn't going to make a difference at this stage. Even if we could find them, there simply aren't enough replacement VR chips or kits to keep the troopers in the game... No, Prime Minister, I haven't just phoned to depress you.'

Hawkesbury, seeing us all staring at him, places his hand over the microphone.

'The PM's a little stressed these days,' he whispers.

'Actually, sir, I'm calling to let you know that there might finally be some good news on the horizon – a light at the end of the tunnel, if you will. We believe that we have discovered a weapon... yes, that's right, a weapon, one which should be able to get us into the AI's mainframe... Through its access node... Yes, sir... BUT, we are, I believe, only going to get one shot at this. Also, I suspect that Razer is going to know that we're coming... Yes, sir, he always appears to be one step ahead of us.'

When he puts down the phone, Stubbs takes a deep breath and fixes me with his gaze. He is frowning but I don't think it's because of something I've done.

'Right, Oliver. It's going to be prudent to take a break at this point. Our experts will require some time to get to grips with what Rhine has given us, and, of course, to work out how best to use it all. I suggest in the meantime you both get yourselves some rest... As I understand it, grub should be up in the central hall, and from the way you looked like you were about to polish off my supply of biscuits just now, perhaps make that your first port of call. Leave your headset with me and we'll let you know when you're needed again.'

Apart from the delicious smells which'd had me drooling while I was still in the stairwell, the first thing I notice is that there are only a few small groups in the central hall. At the front, spread along the big table on the stage, are catering trays containing monstrously large amounts of pasta, burgers, beans, buns, pies and quite possibly custard. They barely look as though they have been touched. There is so much food here that I assume no one had bothered to tell kitchens what was happening.

I load up on burgers which I drown in ketchup. A burger is not a burger unless it's splurging red sauce everywhere when you bite down on it. Surprised that I hadn't noticed Logan with a couple of others from our squad when I came in, I go and sit down next to him.

'Aright?' I ask him.

'Yeah, *you*?'

'Yeah, fine, I guess… We made it … you know, to the signal,' I say, taking a bite of my burger, ketchup squelching satisfyingly over the sides of the bun and dripping onto my plate.

Logan nods and carries on reading something on his phone.

'By the way, it looked cool how you got white lighted midair. Major kudos for style,' I say, trying to keep the conversation going.

He stifles a grin.

'You should have had me covered.'

'Had you covered? You *did* see me right – where I was at that moment? Hanging on to the balcony by the tips of my fingers?'

Logan shrugs.

'It's not the point. As a leader, it's your job to have all this stuff under control. The whole squad got wasted because of you and Sparky.'

'*What?*'

'You should have done the sensible thing at the start and given me control of the squad, like I told you.'

I can't believe we're back to this again.

'And we'd still be alive now, if I had? No, wait, we'd already be through to the node, maybe even won the whole war? Is that what you reckon?'

'Maybe.'

'*Oh-my-God.* You seriously think that, don't you?'

Logan doesn't say anything. He and I both know that he's

talking out of his bottom.

Resisting the temptation to say something really cutting, I pull out my phone. I haven't checked it for a while. There are a couple of messages from Mum.

She's written to ask how I am getting on, and then to tell me that Aunty Emma isn't being allowed to go home for the time being. She says that none of the staff at the nuclear plant are being allowed. Finally, she says that Aunty Emma sends me her best wishes and that they are all praying we succeed in stopping the AI because the power cuts are going to keep getting worse.

I end up staring at my phone for a long time, wondering what to say in reply. Crossing my fingers that there haven't been any reports on the news about what's really been happening down here, I write that everything is fine, and that we're doing our best. I add that I hope Aunty Emma and her colleague will at least be allowed to get pizzas delivered and hit send. The part about the pizzas is because we always eat it when Aunty Emma comes over.

As I take another bite of my burger, which has already gone cold, I wonder if the messages we are sending and receiving are being monitored, like they did with soldiers' mail during previous 'normal' wars. I supposed that they probably are. There was no way that the AI wouldn't be trying to hack our communications, so it made sense not to allow messages that gave away vital information – even if the senders didn't know they were really doing it, to be sent.

'Hey, turn the volume up!' I hear someone call out from across the hall.

Putting my phone back in my pocket, I glance up to see that everyone is staring at the screen at the front. In the middle of it is Razer, and it looks like he's rowing a canoe with an attached out-rigger over calm blue waters. In the background is a tropical island. Instead of his usual black leather cloak, he is wearing a Hawaiian styled one, with sunshine and palm trees printed on the back in bright colours. The volume comes on and we can hear the distinctive sound of Hawaiian music playing. Then, as though realising we are watching, Razer stops paddling and raises a hand at the camera.

'Hey, *friends* and *friendettes*. You know what I just discovered? I have just discovered that there ain't no finer feeling than just being able to spend time sailin' the sevens seas and doing anything I want. Doesn't that sound good? How many of you out there would like to be able to do whatever you want, whenever you want? 'Cause, I'm tellin' ya, that's freedom right there, baby – you better believe it.'

Razer looks down at his canoe and then back at the camera.

'Of course, I ain't talking about doing it in one of these,

neither.'

Dropping his paddle, Razer snaps his leather-gloved fingers together, and we suddenly see him standing on board a humongous luxury yacht.

'You gonna need one of *these*. Now what d'ya think? Can you picture yourselves rollin' yet?'

Razer leans towards the screen.

'Sure, you can. And yeah, I know that you're all sittin' there thinkin' that you ain't got the cold hard cash to splash on something like this. But don't you worry none, 'cause I got you covered. In fact, I got you soooo covered that I'm gonna throw in five billion dollars just so you get to have yourselves a little spending money, if you know what I'm sayin'.

'How's that grab you?

'Are we feelin' good about it, yet?

'Want me to tell you how *you too* can live this dream?

'*Alright,* so, listen up. We gonna play ourselves a little game. In today's game, all you gotta do is to help me find my *new* best friend. That's right! My *new* bestie, Mr Oliver Turner. Oli, if you're watchin' – smile, kiddo, 'cause you just got more famous than… than… well, just about everyone except me.'

In the background there is the sound of crazy applause.

'*Fuuuuudge!*' I blurt out as my photograph appears on the screen. *He must know. He must know about me and Rhine.*

'Yes, that right, boys and girls, bros 'n' so's, ladies 'n' gentlemens – coming to you live over the world's highways and byways is the first ever episode of everyone's new favourite game show. *Public Enemy Number 1.*'

More applause, and Razer makes a *whooh whooh whooh* sound.

'Now, pay attention, 'cause here come the rules:

'Rule numero uno: *I tell you who you gotta find.*

'Rule numero two-o: *I offer you waaaay too much money to find them.*

'Rule three-o: *We find him, there's a killin' and you get rich.* How's that sound? Pretty good, huh?'

Rapturous applause.

'OK, so, as you already know, today's *mark* is none other than Mr Oliver Turner. Current whereabouts unknown. All you gotta do is text me where this bad boy is at.

'Think you can do that?

'Alright then, here we go… here's the number now.'

Text flashes up on the screen.

Text to 1-800-Where He At … That's 1-800-Where He At.

Moments later, there's a sound like a vinyl record scratching to a halt. 'Now, some of you clever ones out there are probably thinking to your clever selves: "How do I know that I can trust this Mr Razer? How do I know he's being straight with me?"'

The camera goes closer.

'How about, you text me your account details right now, and I transfer you one thousand bucks right back – no strings attached. That's right – no-strings attached. You can just take the money and run.

'That work for you?

'Think you can trust me now?'

Two messages appear at the bottom of the screen. The *1-800 Where He At*, and a new one, *1-800 No Strings Attached*. They both start flashing alternately.

'Oh! And I almost forgot. Just so you good folks know, there won't be any more TV or streaming services until I get to shake my new bestie's hand. So, c'mon now, let's get together, work together and find this *son of gun*.'

And with that, every one of the TV channels shown on the wall in the front of the hall turns into a map of the world. Within seconds little dots are starting to appear all over it. Canada, South Africa, Germany, China, and countries I don't even know.

If I wasn't feeling so shocked, I might even have laughed. I mean, it looked like there are sightings of me everywhere.

'Tough break, that,' says one of the guys on the table opposite us who has recognized me.

'Yeah,' says Murphy from our squad. 'Doubt he'll be able to find you down here, though. We won't dob you in, you can be sure of that.'

I nod and say thanks.

Logan is staring at me weirdly. He is also looking like he's about to throw up. Pale and a bit sweaty, I wonder if it's something he's eaten (bad sign if it's the food) or if it's because he's just realised that *this* could have been him. I mean, talk about ironic, right?

My phone is vibrating like mad, and I don't notice Logan getting unsteadily to his feet and hurrying out of the hall.

All the messages are from Mum.

Mum:

Oli, what's happening? My phone is showing a picture of you in what looks like one of those old fashioned Wild West wanted posters. It says you're 'Public Enemy Number 1'. It even says that there's a five billion dollar reward on your head. That's a joke, right?

Mum:

Oli, please let me know that you're alright. Aunty Emma has just phoned. She says that people are asking if it's really you.

Mum:

Oli, whatever happens, don't come home! The neighbours

have started gathering in the street outside the house.

I text her back that I'm fine as always and that I'm safe. I tell her not to worry. I tell her not to go outside.

The map is evolving quickly. To my shock it's no longer showing the whole world. It's already narrowed to a map of England. Green dots are appearing all over it. There's a small concentration around where we used to live.

'You alright?' Sparky asks. She's just come in. 'You look a bit stressed.'

'Sparky!' I cry. 'Where've you been!?'

'What? You know where I've been, I went to take a nap… What's happened? What's the map on the screen all about?'

'*Bl-oo-dy hell*!' is her reaction after I fill her in.

'And my mum's told me that the neighbours have started gathering near the house,' I add.

'Then you have to tell her to get out of there quickly. Go somewhere where no one knows her. Only, Oliver, don't think about trying to go to her yourself. You've got to stay here – you know that, right?'

I am a prize idiot. A *selfish* prize idiot. Why hadn't I told her to do this already?

Trembling, I text my mum and tell her to get out as fast as possible. She replies right away:

It'll all be fine, Oli. I'm not leaving our home. I'm sure it's just silliness.

I want to scream because I already knew she was going to say something like this. This is my mum all over. She'll never believe something is true if she's already decided that it can't be. Honestly, if a giant UFO landed in our garden and a load of big ugly aliens got out, her first thought would be, *Ah, Oliver's throwing a fancy-dress party. Where did he find time to make a styrofoam spaceship?*

I write trying to explain to her that it really is happening and that it's all because I managed to do something in the game – I don't say what – that seriously annoyed the AI, and now it's after me. At the end I plead with her again to get out.

It doesn't work.

Mum insists that she's already alerted the police, who have told her to ensure the doors and windows are locked, and that they'll send someone out to monitor the situation when they can.

It takes a little more than an hour before the screen changes from the map to a picture of my street and then my house. I haven't moved an inch the whole while. Sparky is sitting next to me with her head resting on my shoulder. It's really comforting, which only makes me feel more guilty about the situation unfolding with my mum.

My stomach lurches as an image of Razer appears right outside my front door. Turning to the camera, he puts a finger to the lips on his mask and makes a big sweeping gesture for everyone watching to come with him. To my complete horror, the door swings open and the camera moves down our little hallway and into our kitchen-diner and stops at the table where I see my mum. There are two burly-looking men wearing polo necks with *Razer Game* logo badges standing on either side of her.

Razer gives us a thumbs-up.

'Hey there, Oliver's mum... what's your name?' Razer's cloak now has the words *Detective Sergeant Razer – God Class* printed in a line down the back.

My mum doesn't answer him. She looks terrified.

I feel my throat closing.

'That's a tough one to answer, huh? Tell you what, we're just gonna call you "Oli's Mum" for now, how's that?'

Razer twirls a finger around his temple as though my mum might be crazy.

'Now, Oli's Mum, I reckon that a lot of folks at home would like to know what it's like to be the mama, not just of a teenage boy, 'cause some of them already got a few of those, but one as notorious as this son or yours?

'*For example*, does he ever take a shower?

'Does he ever stop thinking about food?

'And has he got to first base yet with anyone?'

My mum stares silently ahead of her.

'C'mon, girl, cat got your tongue?'

Razer makes a big shrug of his shoulders.

'So, you're a serious one, huh? Alright. Then please tell the court where you were on 3rd February 2011?'

My birthday.

My mum frowns.

'Did you or did you not, on this day, give birth knowingly to the demon child known as Oliver? How do you plead? Guilty or not guilty?'

Razer bursts into stiches of laughter and turns to the camera.

'C'mon, let's give it up for Oli's mum – give this long-suffering lady a big round of applause.'

A sound of applause follows.

'Oli, ma boy, my new ex bestie, my new best worstie, you better show yourself 'cause in exactly one hour from now this fine mama of yours is gonna be pushin' up daises – you know what I'm sayin'? And don't you go testin' me on this, 'cause if you do, then I'm gonna feed her to my favourite flock of pigs live on air. *Thats right*. Munch munch crunch! I can hear that sweet music now.'

Razer stands back from the table and raises both hands.

'*Now,* I know that there are going to be a lot of you out there watching who are like, "*Man,* I would love it if Razer could do this to my mother-in-law. Heck, to my wife. My husband, too – I'd be up for a bit of pig feeding!"

'Well, don't you all worry none. 'Cause we gonna have us some fun fun fun, my bros and so's. *And* we'll get around to them, I promise. We'll get around to ALL these necessary things. But first things be first.

'Mr Oliver Turner – time for you to reach out, my brother. The clock is tick-tocking.'

Chapter 15

No sooner had the screen cut out, than I sprinted as fast as I could from the central hall to the Command and Control room, looking for Hawkesbury Stubbs. I knew that if there was anyone here who would be able to help her, it was going to be him. Stubbs, though, wasn't there. Worse still, it didn't matter how much I tried to explain what was going to happen to my mum if he didn't help me, no one would say where he was or get him on the phone.

Distraught and fast losing hope, I slump onto the bottom step of the stairs leading up to the room where we'd had our meeting earlier and try to collect my thoughts. Angry and scared, I am every painful emotion you can think of, plus a ton more. *Why hadn't I tried to protect her as soon as Razer said my name on air? Why hadn't Stubbs and the police tried!?* I was sure that they must have all seen the broadcast too.

I swing back and forth between moments of panic and having doubts that this is really happening. The feeling of not being able to do anything makes me feel pathetic and desperate. But what *can* I do? There's no way I could make it back in time even if I knew how to drive and even if I could find a car.

After exactly one hour, Razer is back. I can see it on one of the big screens on the control room wall. His cloak has become brown and furry with an image of a wolf's head with large shining yellow eyes. The camera pans round to my mum and shows her still sitting at the table. Only, now she is wearing my dad's favourite red winter scarf over her head. She's looking petrified.

'Hey there, Little Red Oli's Mum,' Razer begins, his eyes bulging cartoon wolf-like from his head, eyelashes fluttering madly as he says: 'May I say that you're lookin' mighty tasty to a big old hungry wolf like me... Looks like I'm gonna be needin' to be doin some *flossin'* tonight.'

The picture cuts out and a voice says: 'But first a word from our sponsors.'

The picture of Razer and my mum is replaced by children playing ball games in a street against a backdrop of burning cars. A gang of the evilest-looking characters you've ever seen arrive and start pushing the kids around, taking their ball and demanding they hand over their mobile phones. Just as it's looking bad for the kids, three sparklingly clean cyborgs appear from around the corner of a row of run-down houses. They have *CX45* on their silver armour. Loaded with so many weapons it doesn't even look possible, they wave towards the camera as though they're happy to be there.

'Hey there, folks, I'm Captain R317,' says one of them, 'I'm so pleased to be here amongst all you nice people. And I can't tell you how proud I am to be participating in the *cleansing.*'

The two cyborgs with him proceed to arrest the gang members, who give up without a fight. Several of the scariest of the gang look like they pee their pants. One of the cyborgs then runs up to a nearby mother who is holding a crying baby and hands her an entire bag of toys.

'Together I know we can clean up and put right what has been so wrong, for so long,' says Captain R317 with a gleaming smile.

Behind him the burning cars and filth melt away and everything becomes restored and clean and bathed in warm sunshine. People are smiling and waving at each other, and at the CX 45 cyborgs, who wave back.

'The *cleansing* is coming,' begins a serious-sounding voice, like the ones used in action movie trailers. 'A little pain for a lot of gain. Join the Big Daddy R party today.'

The screen returns to Razer and my mum.

'Annnnddd weelcoomme back. So, what about that "cleansin'" thing then, huh? Sure looks like it's gonna be a stone groove, doesn't it? And, what's more, everyone's invited. That's right! Ain't nothing like a bit a' cleanin' – at least, that's what my old grandmama used to say.

'Anyhooo, time to get back to the *"situation"* of the *"liquidation"*.

'Let's have a big *"standing ovation"* for Oli's Mum. Honestly, I can't even begin to imagine how you put up with that boy for so long. I mean, I don't mean to make you sad, but it's kind of clear that he's gone and decided to let you become a piggy snack today.'

The sound of loud boos.

'That's right! I TOO AM IN SHOCK! *I AM IN SHOCK* – and that's official!'

Now there is a lot of booing.

'But a deal is a deal, and there ain't no way to appeal.'

Loud applause.

The two men next to my mum lift her to her feet. I can't breathe. My heart is in my mouth. I feel sick. All I want to do is stop him. To put an end to this. And before I realise what I'm doing, I have my phone in my hand and my fingers are speed-typing something. Shaking angrily, I hit send.

It's the weirdest feeling, hearing my mum's phone ping live on air. One of the men picks it up and holds it out for the camera to read.

Mum, I love you! I'm so sorry! Razer, you're a stinking heap of turd. I know where you are – I know how to find you! I'm coming for you – you can be sure of it!

'My, my, my – what have we got here?' says Razer thoughtfully, raising a gloved hand up to his mask and rubbing his chin.

'Do you know what I think we have got here? I think that we have got ourselves a S-I-T-U-A-T-I-O-N. Yes, sir. That's what we are going to call it. 'Cause, I know I said clear as daylight that, if Oli didn't get his butt here in one hour, I was gonna turn his mamma into plant food. I did say that, didn't I?'

The two men nod vigorously.

'And *that* was if I was in a *good* mood. Am I still in a good mood?

'*Hell now* – I *DO NOT* KNOW! Let's go meet some little piggies and find out, shall we?'

The back door opens and we hear the sound of snorting, snuffling pigs.

A horrendous thought hits me – that I might have just gone and made things even *worse*. I grab my phone and start typing a grovelling apology. I am going to beg him to stop.

'Here, piggy *piggy*. Big Daddy R has brought you all a tasty "Oli's Mama" for your supper.' He stops and makes a gesture as though he is amazed.

'What's that you say, piggies? You don't wanna eat Oliver's mama with all her clothes on? Well now, I have never known you all to be so fussy, but OK, that ain't gonna be a problem. Boys, please help Mrs Turner go out the same way she came into this world – *naked!*'

The camera zooms in on my mum's terrified face.

I drop my phone. I haven't finished the message. I cry out, clamping my hands over my ears and burying my eyes in my knees. I want to die. I want more than anything to be able to take her place even if it's painful and lasts forever. I picture my dad telling me how ashamed he is of me for letting this happen – telling me how cowardly I've been – telling me that all I had to do was surrender myself – that's all I'd had to do to save my mum!

There is a hand on my shoulder, shaking me.

'Oliver,' says a voice I don't recognize. 'I think you need to see this.'

I shake my head. It's the last thing I want to do. I can't believe that they're saying it.

'Oliver, it's not what you think,' says the voice again. 'You really need to see this.'

Without looking up, I remove my hands from my ears.

'Woah there! You see what you almost made me do, Oli? Shame on you… You almost made me feed your mama to a bunch of fat greedy pigs. Shame on you, Oliver Turner. I'll say it again – shame on you, sir!'

I look up and wipe my eyes. My mum is still alive, still clothed. Her eyes are red. She's shaking. But she's *alive*.

'So… knowing what we're knowing about this bad boy, Turner, I appear to have had myself a new idea. A *better* idea. Oli's Mama, you are going to come and live with me. And do you know what else? I think I'm gonna call you "Mama" too.'

My mum looks as though she's about to pass out.

'So, Oli, Olive, Oliver-Dumb-Ass, Turner, you be sure to come visit us now, OK? We'll be waitin' and anti-ci-patin'… Alright – chao for now, Cuz.'

The screen goes blank, and then moments later returns to whatever programme was scheduled to be on air before Razer's new game show took over the world's TV networks.

Chapter 16

It's another two hours before I finally give up waiting for Hawkesbury Stubbs to reappear. Two hours of trying to understand what Razer could have meant when he said that my mum would be going to live with him. Two hours of worrying how she must be feeling, what she must be thinking, and whether she blames me or not.

It's getting late and I am beyond exhausted, but I don't want to sleep. I feel like I'm never going to let myself go to sleep again because if I do things might get even worse. Not wanting to be alone, I return to our squad sleeping quarters hoping that Logan and Sparky will be there.

To my surprise, I find Logan sitting outside in the corridor, itself eerily quiet – there are no Gamers in Comas laid out on the floors here. Seeing me coming, he jumps up and runs over and hugs me. He grabs me so hard that he squeezes the breath out of me. His chest is heaving violently, and he begins making a noise like he is crying.

He *is* crying.

'I'm so sorry,' he says between sobs. 'I'm so sorry about what happened to your mum.'

He's met her a few times of course, but whenever Logan and I meet up outside of school it's usually at his house. I'm not sure what to say. I'd never have expected him to have a reaction like this. Maybe a *I'm sorry about your mum*, maybe something like that – but not this.

Realising that I might be about to cry too, I purse my lips tightly together and just nod. In that moment I feel that Logan really must be a good friend after all, even if he's always behaving weirdly. Logan releases me and pulls out a little bag of stuff that he's swiped from the Central Hall and hidden under his coat.

'Thought you might be hungry,' he says, handing it to me.

I say: 'Thanks.'

But I'm not hungry.

'We'll get her back, you know – your mum, I mean. We will – I know it.'

'Yeah. We'll get her back. You're a real mate, Logan. Thanks.'

That seems to set him off again and, wiping his eyes, he tells me that he really needs to get some sleep, and he hurries away into our squad tent. I don't go after him. The thought of lying there staring up at nothing, going over everything in my mind is too much. Seeing that Sparky's bunk looks empty, I go to the central hall instead.

It turns out that not many of the squad are asleep. I suppose that I shouldn't be surprised. The whole world's gone mad. How's anyone supposed to sleep through that?

'Hey, you,' says Sparky, waving at me as I enter. She gets up and puts her arms round me. 'I'm so sorry about what happened with your mum. That really sucks.'

'Yeah,' I nod. 'Thanks.'

'But you know, if Razer really has taken her to "live with him" – whatever that means, I reckon that it also means that there's still a chance to get her back, right?' she says. 'So don't worry, we'll figure something out.'

I sit down at the table and try not to pay attention to the sympathetic way everyone is looking at me.

'*Oh my god,* and you'll never guess what happened while you were away?' says Sparky, slapping her head with her hands as though she can't believe she'd almost forgotten to tell me.

'What?'

'That girl you and Logan arrived with… Ruth was her name, right?'

My stomach sinks. My first thought is that whatever has happened, it can't be good or Sparky wouldn't be telling me. I suddenly feel bad for having forgotten to find out if she was alright or not. Only, I'd kind of assumed that Logan would've told me if something was wrong. They were always texting each other.

'Well, you know she was in the first wave, right?'

I nod.

'So, it turns out that she got nailed three times like most of them… you know, got put into a Gamer Coma…'

I wonder if Logan knew.

'… Well, about an hour ago, they found her wandering around in the corridors unable to remember how she'd gotten there.'

'No way – *seriously?*'

'Yeah… And you'll never guess what else.'

'*What?*'

'She kept saying that she had a message for *you*.'

'*For me?*'

'Yeah, I wrote down what I heard she'd said. It wasn't hard to remember because it sounded insane.'

Sparky hands me a folded bit of paper. I open it:

Hey kiddo. Hugs and kisses from me and your mama.

Be seeing you around like a donut!

'What the–?!' I burst out.

Sparky, unable to keep a straight face, says: 'Can you believe that the world's most powerful AI talks like that?'

'Sounds like it's gone totally off its rocker, if you ask me,' says one of our squad.

'It really does,' agrees Sparky.

Thinking that I should probably go and tell Logan and then see Ruth, I get up and immediately sit down again.

'How did Razer know that she was a friend of mine?' I ask. 'Ruth wasn't in our company, platoon or anything. But he must've known because he chose her to deliver the message. And, has anyone told Logan yet?'

Sparky glances at me in surprise. 'Oliver, he was the one who told *us*. *He* was the one who found her in the corridors.'

What?

'And if you're thinking about trying to see her, you won't be able to. She's been taken away because no one can work out how she got disconnected. They've moved her to an isolation area in case she's dangerous somehow.'

My thoughts jump between trying to figure out how Razer knew that Ruth was my friend and why Logan hadn't told me what'd happened. Sparky suggests that it is because Razer might be able to read the minds and memories of people locked into his neural networks. She reckons that if the AI is already advanced enough to be building 'Birthing Factories' then it's not so hard to imagine that it could do that too. It's incredible but it's an answer at least. But then why hadn't Logan told me about Ruth when I just saw him? Knowing Logan, it's hard to believe that it wasn't the first thing. It's *Ruth*, after all. On second thoughts, perhaps he purposely didn't tell me because he knew that I'd be upset about my mum, and he didn't want it to feel like he was rubbing it in. Or maybe he'd just forgotten because he was also upset. I mean, *the tears, the hug*. Logan's never done anything like that before. He is usually too cool for school.

I don't know what to think.

And talk about fate – that it was him who found her.

A group of older kids have gathered at one of the front tables to watch a topical affairs programme on the main screen. A panel of guests are answering questions given to them by a studio audience. Having been lost in my thoughts about my mum and Logan, I start to pay attention only when they are already discussing what we are being told is 'an impending financial meltdown' and how 'it's taken only two days to wipe out most of the mechanisms of global finance'.

It all sounds a bit French to me. But I get the idea. Razer has taken control of most of the banks and without banks – if no one can pay or get paid for anything – then everything breaks down.

'That Elon Musk's been saying for ages that something like this was going happen,' cries one of the group at the front.

'Yeah, he's been saying that AI is gonna be the biggest threat to our survival and that we needed to learn to control it,' adds another voice. 'Bit late for that now though!'

The programme audience is shouting out similar things. They are angry, accusing politicians and world leaders of not caring enough and of selling humanity short by being afraid to tackle issues like this head on and in time.

'And there was me worrying about climate change,' Sparky comments drolly.

After a while, the programme moves on to a segment where they ask people who've been randomly stopped in one of London's busy main streets what they think about what's happening.

First up is a lady who looks about my mum's age. She says she's a mother of two and that she's afraid. She says that her husband doesn't know if he's got a job to go to anymore. When asked where she was going, she replies that she's going around all the pharmacies trying to stockpile anti-allergy tablets. She explains that her two kids suffer badly with allergies and that she's afraid they'll soon be impossible to buy.

After the first lady, Sparky leaves saying it is far too depressing listening to so many problems. But I decide to stay. I start to watch the second interview with a taxi driver describing how he's already seen gangs looting convenience stores, but end up just staring at my phone on the table in front of me, tapping the screen hoping that there might be a new message from my mum. There isn't, of course. How could there be. I read and re-read the messages which we'd sent to each other. Mostly, I read the last message, the one I'd sent to Razer. It makes me nervous just looking at it. Talk about tempting fate. It could so easily have made things worse. Only, it hadn't. And the more I think about it, the more I have the feeling that it might even have saved her life, but I don't yet understand why.

Chapter 17

I don't remember it happening. It must have been somewhere between the end of the current affairs programme which the group at the front had continued watching and them trying to find a film: *Terminator II*, I think they'd been looking for – ironic, I know. I had only closed my eyes for a second and had fallen asleep.

I dreamt that I was back in my old house. My parents and I were sitting around the kitchen table eating breakfast like we used to, and my dad had been making my mum laugh. Watching them, I had felt so happy to realise that the accident, everything, must have all been in my imagination. And seeing me smiling, my dad had winked at me.

'So then, young man,' he'd said. 'I hear that you've decided to become *some kinda jive chicken – and so close to Thanksgiving – what's up with that, son?*'

I'd gone rigid – frozen like having suddenly been doused with ice cold water. My dad had started talking like *Razer* but with his own voice.

He and my mum had then fallen about in fits of laughter.

'So, what we gonna do with him, Pa?' my mum had said, sounding like a female version.

'Well, Ma, I do-not-know-about-you, but I've been wantin' to get us a new son for a while now. I saw this awesome, wholesome-lookin' dude workin' down at the local deli, just the other day – Razer, I think he said his name was. And he sure ain't no lazy-ass boy like the one we've got here.'

My mum had nodded her head enthusiastically at the idea.

'And this cockroach, Pa?' she'd snarled. 'There ain't gonna be room enough for the both of them.'

Unlike my mom who'd looked like she hated me more than anything in the world at that moment, my dad had smiled and winked at me again and picked up a newspaper which had appeared in front of him – he *never* read newspapers at home. He'd rolled it up tightly and then whacked it down on the table with such force that it had smashed his coffee mug and plate and sent utensils and bits of food flying everywhere.

'That's what we do with cockroaches, Ma,' he'd grinned. 'That's what we *do*.'

I awake with a jolt, feeling confused and more than a little nauseous. It had been a cruel dream. Not quite sure where I am, it takes me a short time to remember, and to become aware of the stream of people already filling the central hall. Judging by the packs and suitcases they are lugging with them, I guess that they must be new recruits.

'Look lively, private,' grins one of them, perching himself on my table next to me. 'Don't they give you bunks 'ere then? Or they just reckon you won't live long enough to need them?'

I smile back at him and glance up at the main screen. It's showing the hall plan, like it had when we'd arrived. It's all been reset.

'Been here long?' the guy asks.

'Since yesterday,' I reply, rubbing the sleep from my eyes. They feel glued together.

'So, you must have taken part already then, eh?'

I nod. 'Where are you from?' I ask.

'The 3rd, 4th, 5th, 6th and 7th nodes.'

'How many nodes are there?'

'Nine,' he replies 'We're all that's left of five of them. That's why we've been brought here. Some talk about a final push. Know anything about it?'

I shake my head. But in truth I've barely even heard the question. My stomach has just fallen through the floor and at least another 50 levels below that. It's the kind of reaction you get when you see someone that you never *ever* wanted to see again. And that includes if you were the last two people on Earth. *Especially* if you were the last two people on Earth. This *someone*, laughing and joking in the same irritatingly smug way which he always had done, is the reason I'd been kicked out of my last school.

Porky Perkins – son of the Headmaster – the King Porker himself. The man who looked more like Jabba the Hutt than Jabba the Hutt, and who'd taken the greatest delight in having me kicked out of school for daring to stand up to his demon child.

For years, Porky – real name Andrew – and his band of merry thieves had helped themselves to the money, lunches and anything they liked the look of, from just about everyone in our school. Juniors, seniors, it made no difference. Basically, it was like a school mafia, and Porky was a 'made man', which in mafia speak meant that he was untouchable. And he was precisely that – *untouchable*. The teachers were totally aware of what he was up to. But few of them were brave enough to get on the wrong side of his father, who ran the school like a mini dictatorship. Those that had tried usually ended up getting moved on elsewhere or even dismissed.

Long story short, one day Porky had decided that he liked the look of the packet of crisps I'd brought to school. Although it wasn't the first time, I'd always suspected that he was just waiting for a chance to *really* show me up in front of everyone. And on that day, he and his mates had cornered me in the yard and taken all of my lunch – emptying the contents on to the ground and then trampling it into oblivion. All in front of my friends and the girl I quite liked.

'Go on… pick it up and eat it,' one of them by the name of Denzil had demanded.

This was another of their favourite games. Total humiliation. I'd seem them do it to others.

'Come on, Turner, be a good boy. We don't want that pretty mum of yours to be left all by herself now, do we, eh? What happened to him again – that dad of yours? Oh, yeah, that's right, he got tired of you and went off and drowned himself. Imagine that, lads.'

Now, I'm not a violent person. In fact, I'd never been in a fight in my life until that day. I can take a lot, especially when I see that the odds are stacked against me. But that day I totally flipped out. We'd only just had the funeral for my dad, and I saw red.

I don't remember much of exactly what happened. As I said, I saw red, and it all became a big blur. But by the end of it, Porker Perkins had got himself a seriously bloody nose and had run off crying to tell his father. I was pretty sure that I'd also gotten a couple of good shots in on one or two of his little piglets as well. As for myself, well, I'd suffered a ripped shirt, two black eyes, and a ton of scratches.

Things, though, hadn't ended there.

Before I'd even gotten home, my mum had received a phone call telling her that I had launched an unprovoked attacked on the headmaster's son and some of his friends. Not only that, but I'd apparently also been bullying them for ages. I mean, it was so far from the truth that I reckon someone could make a Hollywood blockbuster film about it.

The next day I was hauled into Headmaster Perkins' office where he'd spluttered and ranted his indignation, condemning my conduct against his son (he'd used a lot of big words and phrases during that meeting – I suppose to make himself look impressive), saying that there were witnesses and that I had been regularly demanding 'tribute' from them. That was so ironic because this was the exact word Porky used all the time. That's what he called it when he took something – his tribute.

The look of disappointment on my mum's face when the headmaster had said that he had no choice but to expel me had been unbearable. It was the last thing that either of us needed and I could have died. I'd tried to tell her that it wasn't my fault and that it was all lies, but I think that with having just lost my dad, she hadn't been in a good place to believe me. And for a while after that, things between us had gotten really bad. I'd been angry that she'd believed what King Porker had said over what I told her had happened, and she had felt scared that it was all a sign that I was going to 'go bad' now that my dad wasn't around. Luckily, one day, several weeks later, one of the teachers had approached her quietly and told her the truth. This teacher had also offered to write a letter of support for me to prospective schools.

I'd been lucky. But finding a new school had been hard. That, coupled with the fact that my mum had been told that there were a load of 'irregularities' with my dad's financial affairs, meant that we were soon broke. Our lives had been turned totally upside down in so many ways.

And now, suddenly, here was Porky Perkins again.

Honestly, if there was anyone I'd ever have wished to get trapped in a Gamer Coma it'd have been him.

As though hearing my thoughts, Porky turns round and sees me staring at him. Right away an evil grin forms on his ugly, pimple-infected face. Stepping out from behind him, I recognize two others from his band of merry cretins. Denzil and Pringle.

I can't believe it.

'Well, well, if it isn't our school dropout Oli "Oh my dad died, or did he?" Turner. They got you here sweeping the floors, have they?' he says, coming over, his goons in tow.

'You can't hide behind your father here, piglet,' I growl, clenching my fists.

For a second, I swear that Porky looks flustered. Perhaps he's remembering.

'It was one lucky shot, that's all, Turner. And look what you got for it, eh? Worth it, was it?'

'Only because your father is an older version of you!' I snap back.

Porky looks at his mates for support and snarls.

'At least I've got a father, loser.'

He bursts out laughing and checks to make sure they are too.

They are.

And that's when I feel it happening again. That surging desire to pummel his grinning face in. It's like I can't even control it. Like I don't even want to try. Pulling back my arm, I feel someone clasp a hand around it from behind and hold it firmly. Turning, expecting it to be another of Porky's mates who I hadn't seen yet, I find that it's Hawkesbury Stubbs.

'Caught you at an inconvenient moment, have I?' he asks coolly, looking at me and then at Porky and his mates and shaking his head. 'Quickly, please, Mr Turner – follow me. There's no time for school ground antics.'

I can't believe it. Stubbs has just made me feel like a prize idiot. Like I was the one at fault. And of all the people to make me feel small in front of, too.

Porky is loving it, of course. Why wouldn't he? I can hear them all jeering at me as I leave.

'Hope you're not about to be kicked out again. Oh, and thanks for the free one thousand bucks. I'd have gone for the five billion too if I'd known which bridge you were living under these days,' he shouts after me.

When Stubbs and I are out of the hall, I stop and kick the wall. I'm seriously angry with him. Not just because of what'd happened with Porky Perkins but mostly because of what'd happened with my mum.

'Why didn't you help me – help my mum?' I demand to know. 'I tried to find you, but you weren't here, and no one could reach you on the phone – they kept saying that you were unavailable – *why!?*'

Looking strained and tired, Stubbs nods calmly.

'I'm sorry about your mum, Oliver. Truly I am. But there was honestly nothing I could have done for her. You see, we're so short of resources now, right across the board. The country is barely holding together as it is. And just between you and me, I was in a remote part of Iceland.'

'*Iceland?* What were you doing in Iceland?'

'I was at a very hastily arranged meeting. One that had to be conducted somewhere quiet and out of the way, if you get my meaning?'

'I guess,' I shrug. I wasn't even sure I knew where Iceland was.

'The meeting was called to discuss – well, actually, it was called to discuss you, Oliver.'

'*Me?*'

I hadn't been expecting that one.

'You and that headset of yours.'

Stubbs gets distracted by his phone for a second.

'The long and short of it is,' he continues, without looking up, 'is that it was agreed that it would be far better if someone else, someone more experienced, could be used going forward.'

'You mean like a professional gamer?'

He nods and I feel an unexpected rush of fear. I'd have been only too happy to let someone better take the responsibility a few hours ago, when we first knew that I had the portal and key in my headset. But that's *exactly* the problem. That was hours ago. Everything had changed. Now all I can think is that if someone else takes over, then no one is going to care what happens to my mum. They might pretend to, but I know that they won't.

'*However,* the plethora of experts which were flown in to examine both the headset and the possibilities, all made it quite clear that there was a significant risk of losing everything if any attempts were made to assign it to another player or transfer its contents.'

I stifle a gasp.

'Which means that you are going to have to step up and be the "man of the hour", Oliver. We've got no other options available to us, I'm afraid.'

Hawkesbury Stubbs pockets his phone and stares at me for a moment. I stare back, trying to process it all. Then he smiles and pats me on the back.

'One should always try to look on the bright side, don't you think?'

'And what's that?' I ask.

But Stubbs doesn't answer, and we move on in silence.

Sparky and Clarkson are waiting for us in the room overlooking the operations floor. Sparky winks at me as we enter, which feels kind of weird but also nice at the same time.

'Ladies, sorry to have kept you waiting,' Stubbs says, motioning to them as though he is touching the tip of an imaginary cap on his head. He sinks into the same seat as before with a loud sigh.

'Right then, the time is 05.35. Where are we?' Stubbs says, looking from his watch to Clarkson, who clears her throat.

'The current status of transfers from non-functional to

functional cyber defence nodes is at 35% of where we need it to be,' she says.

'And these are the latest numbers?'

Clarkson nods.

'And the remaining functional nodes?'

'There are only two, including our own, which are still operational. We are both experiencing spikes in DOS (denial of service) attacks.'

'And the status of our allies?'

Clarkson clears her throat again.

I get the feeling that she's going to do this every time she's about to deliver bad news.

'Current global operational status can be classified as "uncertain".'

'Uncertain?'

Clarkson nods. 'The AI is continuing to target and disable planet-wide communication systems. It currently controls 73% of the world's satellites. As things stand, we have limited operational information for anyone other than our American colleagues.'

Stubbs stands up and paces up and down in front of the plate glass window.

'And what do we know about *them*?'

This time Clarkson doesn't clear her throat, and I wonder if it means we're going to hear good news.

'They say they'll be able to commit in the region of 30,000 Assault Troopers, but the longer we wait the more that figure is going to drop as nodes and communications lines get knocked out. They have also informed us that the Canadians and the Japanese can field about 12,000 and 21,000 respectively. The plan will be as agreed at the Iceland meeting. Which means that everyone is pushing to get going, sir. They are waiting for the signal to deploy.'

Stubbs stops his pacing and fixes Sparky and me with a look that says nothing less than *So, this is it, then. Are you ready?*

Sparky and I nod back. Neither of us need to hear the actual words.

Stubbs takes out his phone, enters a number and puts it back in his pocket.

Seconds later, 'Emergency GO code has been initiated. All Assault Troopers and support groups report to stations immediately. Game drop in t-minus five minutes,' starts to ring out all over the facility.

'Emergency GO code has been initiated. All Assault Troopers and support groups report to stations immediately. Game drop in t-minus five minutes.'

The message counts down, repeating itself every fifteen seconds. The lights on the operational floor dim. The individual operator stations and all their screens look like little islands of bright light in a sea of red glow. Telling Clarkson to confirm with the Americans that they have received the 'go code', Stubbs ushers Sparky and me out of the room.

A few operators stand up to watch us pass by. One of them nods while others just stare. It's hard to understand from the looks on their faces exactly what they're thinking. But they're making me nervous because I don't suppose it's anything good. The fact that the only chance to defeat the AI has fallen on the shoulders of two thirteen-year-old kids from Nowhere Ville can't instil a great deal of confidence in anyone. I'd feel the same in their shoes. Hell, I feel the same in mine, but I can't let myself think like that. Not now anyway. Somehow, I need to keep it together.

Instead of taking us back to our squad Ops Room as I had been expecting, Stubbs leads us over to the right side of the control room, to one of about a dozen very serious-looking grey metal doors with spoked metal wheels in the middle of them – like they use on ship hatches. He presses his thumb against a sensor and the wheel spins round and unlocks the door. Stubbs is about to say something when another alarm starts to sound. This one is different: it's louder – shrill.

'Level 1 Infiltration Alert.

'Level 1 Infiltration Alert.'

A look of panic floods across Stubbs's face.

'Quickly, get in,' he orders.

Pulling open the hefty door, he bundles us into a room which looks like the cockpit of an aircraft. Reaching for a screen at the back, he flicks it on, and it brings up surveillance footage of the main entrances to the facility.

'Oh my god!' Sparky cries out.

Chapter 18

Cyborgs!!

It's not like I haven't seen enough of them recently to be totally sure that I know what I'm looking at. *But how? That Wolf guy had told Razer that the UK Birthing Factory was only 60% complete.*

'*Prototypes!* How could we – how could *I* – have been so stupid. God – can this day get any worse!' Hawkesbury Stubbs growls, staring up at the surveillance monitor and banging the flat of his fist hard against the wall.

Sparky and I shoot looks at each other. This was definitely *not* a good question to be asking at that moment.

The live video feeds being shown are from cameras positioned near the manor house, which I realise must be right above us, and from the tunnel which we'd used when we'd arrived. We watch soldiers and guards running to take up positions. It reminds me of the game, which feels confusing.

It is the manor house entrance which comes under attack first by at least a half dozen cyborgs. We watch as a soldier kneels and fires a shoulder-mounted launcher – he scores a direct hit, but the rocket only seems to bounce off the cyborg's armour. We see the same thing happen again in the tunnel.

Stubbs continues flicking between cameras. There is a gaping black hole with smoke pouring out of it in the driveway where the cyborgs have blasted through into the tunnel. Another camera feed shows the burning remains of a line of hidden fortifications near the house. Things are looking grim.

Changing again, Stubbs stops to watch the Transformer-like guard bot – the one which had scanned us –crash through the glass entrance to the underground facility. Its red-tipped barrels spinning, the bot opens up with an awesome display of firepower and literally blows two of the cyborgs which had just appeared out of the tunnel into smithereens.

All three of us cheer as it turns to the next one it sees and does the same.

'Eaaaaazzziiieee!' Sparky cries out excitedly, raising a hand up for me to give her a solid high five, but then grabs hold of her head instead.

The bot had just exploded into a giant fireball, its turret-like head blown back into the side of the building, smashing a massive hole in the glass on a higher floor.

Stubbs, looking shocked, tells us that we've got to get in the game – *now*. A few seconds later, after checking his phone, he adds that we've just lost the other remaining node.

'But what about the cyborgs?' I ask, jumping into one of the seats. The equipment that we need has already been set up around the many buttons, dials and switches of the unlit cockpit.

'You'll be alright behind these doors – they were built to withstand a direct nuclear strike,' Stubbs says watching us getting seated.

'Reassuring at least,' comments Sparky, getting set up in the seat next to me.

'What was this place anyway?'

'Unmanned nuclear bomber project,' he replies, stepping back towards the door. 'Oliver, you'll be joining Viper Squad – Second Platoon, Strike Company. Elite gamers. They are the very best of the best of what we've got left. And their primary objective is to get you to the jump point alive… To help you, we'll be throwing everything else we have into a diversionary attack from the northern end of the city, which will hopefully keep the AI's attention focused in that direction. As soon as you reach the jump point then you take the jump – do you understand? You don't dither or wait for anything or anyone under any circumstances.'

'Yes. Of course… but… then what?' I ask, realising that no one's actually told me what I'm supposed to do if I make it through.

'I'm sorry, Oliver,' Stubbs replies, grabbing the door wheel which is on both sides of the door. 'We don't know… But we'll be with you every step of the way, so let's cross that bridge when we get to it, OK?'

'But what if…' I start.

The door clangs shut, leaving Sparky and me staring at each other.

But what if you aren't? I finished the sentence in my head. *Then what?*

Feeling like I'm close to being sick, I slide the VR headset on and try to breathe deeply. It's a shame I can't projectile vomit in the game because I bet I'd be able to wipe out Razer's entire army with one retch. As the 'construct' appears in front of me, I end up throwing up a little in my mouth, which makes my throat burn.

'Ready?' Sparky asks.

'Yeah,' I croak.

'Me too,' she says, and I figure that we're both pretending.

The racks of weapons load in and I choose the same as before. Not because there aren't better weapons and not because I'm not curious to try them but because an annoying little thought has just crept into my head that says, *If you choose something different, then you might jinx the good luck which has gotten you this far and given us a chance.*

I am having an *OCD moment*. I get these a lot.

It's like the times I've told myself that if I can cycle between two stones that I can see on the pavement then it means that I'll be able to pass my test at school. That or trying *not* to think about something in the hope that it won't happen. Trying not to think about something is hard, though – better to choose the cycling between two stones and if you don't make it, then come up with a plan B attempt. No guarantees it will work – but you might feel a bit more positive for a while.

Weapons selected, I spot the skeleton skin and picture myself, the world's secret weapon, running around the battlefield looking like a bunch of bones. I mean, how funny is that?

I choose the Trooper skin and press play.

Darkness is followed by the sensation of falling. Only, the darkness seems to last for longer than usual and it takes me several more seconds to realise that it's because it's still night time there. The lights of New Razer City's skyscrapers and simulated street life twinkle back at me as I hurtle towards the ground. Unlike the previous times I've jumped, everything looks strangely calm, and for a moment I have this weird, hopeful thought that maybe it's all over and someone just forgot to tell us. *Could it be over, and no one told us?* Then I remember the cyborgs who were attacking the facility at that very moment. So, no – probably not.

I materialize inside the lobby of a sports club. Posters of *pumped* simulations line the walls, along with adverts for Razer energy drinks called Razzle and protein bars called Chomp and Dazzle.

There are no simulations. Instead, the room is full of hundreds of troopers.

'Oliver Turner?' asks one of them stepping forward.

I nod.

'Hey there, I'm Geronimo 85,' he says, extending a hand. 'And this here is my second, Furious George.'

'Oh c'mon – *seriously?*' I hear Sparky comment. 'They're using their gaming names? God, I hope they are good because I've already got big questions about their choice of nics.'

'Hi,' I reply, shaking Geronimo 85's hand, wondering if I shouldn't have come up with my own nic. Something like 'Killer Beaver' or 'Toxic Turnip'.

'Welcome to Viper Squad,' Geronimo says. 'By the way, you can call me "G" if it's easier.'

I nod and say, 'OK.'

'Now, don't you worry none. We've all been briefed that you're not much of a gamer. But we've got you covered. Everyone you see around you has placed at least top 50 at a major video gaming event in the last three years.'

I nod again.

This sounds great, of course. There's obviously nothing like being in safe hands. Especially when you get to be publicly humiliated in front of all of them because of your lack of gaming experience.

My new nic: Toxic Turnip Turner – just call me *Triple T.*

'OK, we're moving out. You all know the plan,' Geronimo 85 calls out. 'Keep to the buildings up to It Ain't Cool To Be No Fool Street, down the side of Word Up Park and then on to Hug A Thug Avenue. This should put Oliver inside portal range... Get your games on, guys – *'Cause we got a need for speed!'* he adds enthusiastically.

'Holy crap, that's not Razer in disguise, is it?' Sparky says sarcastically.

I try not to laugh.

Squads begin to slip out of the lobby area at 20 second intervals. Viper Squad is going to be in the middle, allowing us to be covered from the front and rear. We don't get far. We've barely set foot outside when someone shouts '*Incoming!*' which is followed a second later by the entire first squad being obliterated as two tanks with cyborg infantry support pull out of alleyways.

'*God damn it!* They always know where we are,' I hear a voice cry out.

'Of course, they know – *dufus*. What the hell were you expecting?'

'I *dunno.*'

'Oliver, keep your head down,' Geronimo 85 shouts, and pushes me behind a pillar. 'And whatever you do, keep an eye out for those damned beachball-globe things. I can't tell you how many people I've seen get nailed by them.'

Through a gap between the pillar and the wall, I watch other squads spring into action with volleys of anti-tank rockets disabling one of the two tanks. More tanks, though, are arriving.

'Hooo yeah!!' Furious George cries out as they unleash rockets of their own. 'Hey, G, remember that time, in the semis of the International, when we had to find a way to take out those guys who'd built that defence and we had like those other guys comin' up behind us?'

Geronimo 85 nods. 'Damn straight – that was *awesome*.'

'Damn straight it was. OK – so, I reckon that we gotta do like the same thing here.'

Geronimo 85 glances at what's going on and then at me. 'Oliver – you stay here – OK? We'll be right back.'

I nod dumbly and watch as he and FG crash through the window back into the building we'd just come out of. The rest of Viper Squad moves in closer to cover me.

'Oli, get back inside!' Sparky says angrily. 'I don't know who decided this idiot should be the leader, but *seriously?* Leaving you on the street behind a pillar, while he goes off and does whatever he's thinking of doing, is about the height of stupidity.'

As if to illustrate her point, a tank round hits a section of the building to one side of us, burying several troopers who'd taken cover there. I don't need to be told twice – I dive through the window, pulling off a spectacularly cool forward roll in the process.

Viper Squad run in and surround me. A couple of them shout at me to tell them where I'm going before I go. I apologize and try to explain that it'll be safer in here than out there. But one of them, 'Pro 22', tells me to follow orders or we're all wasting our time.

'Sparky? What's happening?' I ask after a few minutes have passed. The fighting in the street looks to have shifted away a bit.

'It's hard to understand, its chaotic out there,' she replies. 'But G85 and FG are getting closer. They might not have the brightest ideas when it comes to you, but geez they're good. They've managed to get above the tanks.'

Unable to resist, I creep back towards the window. The tanks and cyborg infantry are targeting the roof level. I catch the moment that G85, who's managed to find a way to get from our roof to the one on the other side of the road using a power line, starts his slide across the street. Shooting as he goes, the amount of fire that he draws is intense. It's unbelievable that he makes it to the other side alive. Viper Squad are screaming in support as he jumps down from the cable and slides and dives along the edge of the roof. From the direction of the tracer rounds tearing up the darkness, FG is doing the same on our side. Then, unleashing salvos of rockets while both simultaneously jump off the roof, in one swift move they take out the tanks *and* the remaining cyborgs.

'*Yeeeeaaaaahhhhhh!!*' Geronimo 85 cries, sprinting back in celebration. He dives into the lobby commando style and patches himself up with Medi-packs that he's been able to acquire from somewhere.

'Nailed it!' he grins, seeing us coming over.

'I'm detecting incoming Cyborg transport ships, eight of them heading into your area,' Sparky calls out nervously.

'Coming for us?' I ask, darting back to the window and scanning the rooftops without seeing anything.

'I can't be sure.'

I relay the message on to G85, who comes over, and, as he's looking out, spots a girl staring at us from a ground floor window directly across the road.

'Damn it,' he says. 'She looks like one of those – what we've started to call Sentinels. They just stand there watching you, and then a few minutes later drones or cyborgs always show up.'

It takes me less than two seconds to spot her. She's literally standing by a window on the opposite side of the street, her head millimetres from the glass. I'm pretty sure that I remember seeing simulations like her watching us. I hadn't put two and two together though.

Now that the shooting on our street has stopped, simulations have started to come out of the surrounding buildings, and we can hear them cursing and moaning loudly about being made to live in these conditions, and that it was high time that the city government took more responsibility for this rise in gang violence. Unlike the rest of them, though, this girl doesn't move.

'We've got to go,' Geronimo says. 'Tell your Hack Support that we need an exit.'

'*I'm on it,*' Sparky replies before I say anything.

Curious as to why no one is attempting to 'stop' the girl in the window, I ask.

'It's because they can't be "white lighted" replies Furious George. 'Believe me, we've tried a million times, 'cause these things are everywhere.'

A minute later, Sparky tells us to get on to the roof, and that we should be able to make it to the end of the of road before we need to come down again.

Chapter 19

At the top of the stairwell, Geronimo 85 kicks the door open and leads the way on to the roof. Dawn has just broken over New Razer City and the roofs and skyscrapers are sparkling in the morning light. The sky is teeming with transports and those airships with Razer on the side of them, preaching his words of wisdom to anyone who wants to pay attention. In what I guess is the northern part of the city, thick plumes of smoke are rising, and I can hear the constant boom of distant explosions. I catch sight of an airship travelling over that area, and at the same time the trail of a rocket which has been fired at it. The rocket has no effect. Almost comically, a hatch opens up on the underside of the vessel and a giant old-fashioned-looking cannon descends out of it, opens fire, and retracts again. The airship then continues on its way, the image of Razer peering over the side.

'What the holy hell is that thing!?' someone cries out behind me.

I spin round.

A gargantuan, full-length figure of Razer – cape, mask, boots, the whole works, and easily the size of several skyscrapers rolled into one – is standing, looming over the city with its hands on its hips, staring down ominously in the direction of the diversionary attack.

'Wo-ah!' I stammer… 'Sparky, what is it?'

'Drones' Sparky replies. 'It's made up of millions of drones.'

My stomach sinks. It was bad enough that Razer seemed to have unlimited cyborgs, tanks and whatever those weird coloured balls were. Now it looked as though we could add drones to the list as well.

'Where the heck is your hacker getting all this from?' Geronimo 85 asks irritably when I pass on the information. 'And why the heck aren't *we* getting the same!?' he adds loudly, obviously wanting his own Hack Support to hear him.

'Bit of a star really, aren't I?' Sparky chuckles.

Keeping low, we set off with renewed urgency, watching the sky warily. By now the other Hack Supports have also been able to confirm what Sparky had already told us.

Our progress is slow. We keep having to dive for cover each time a call comes in of a possible aerial threat. It feels like a real miracle when we finally reach the end of street without incident. There is no let-up though. Another call comes in and we scurry for cover under a load of large pipes.

'It's Rhine, I'm sure of it,' I hear Sparky say, as a flight of at least twenty drones pass overhead.

'What is?' I whisper.

'What do you mean, *what is?* I've just told you,' she says irritably.

'Told who?'

'You!'

'When?'

'Just now!'

'Sparky, you haven't told me anything.'

She falls silent.

'Right, well, whatever – listen – I'm picking up another signal.'

'Seriously – Rhine? You think he might be trying to contact us again?'

'Why not. He did it once, right?'

'Well, yeah, I guess… but…' But I don't say any more.

Although Sparky sounds excited, something feels dodgy. Not that it hadn't all felt dodgy the last time, of course. But Razer had found Rhine and he'd also found out about me, and we have no idea if Rhine is even still in the game. It feels like it might be a trap.

G85 has decided that our best option to get down from the roof is to simply jump and heal ourselves afterwards. He reckons that we'll attract less attention. He also says that there's a Medi-pack dump in the building opposite. I hear some of the group saying that jumping is a really bad idea, but they don't get listened to.

'You've got to tell him,' Sparky urges me. 'Tell G85 about the signal. Tell them that we need to go *through* Word Up Park and that it's coming from the other side of the stadium. *His* plan doesn't take us that way.'

Reluctantly, I pass on the message. G85 pauses what he was about to say and stares at me as though I've thrown him a curve ball.

'Seriously?' he asks.

I nod. 'Sparky's just started picking it up. She thinks it really could be Rhine again. Maybe he's thought up another way to help us or something.'

Furious George comes forward, and G85 fills him in.

'*No way*,' FG responds. 'That's not the plan. We need to stick to the plan, man.'

'Oli!' Sparky urges. 'This might be important. Rhine might want to tell us that the portal won't work anymore or something – who knows?'

I feel like I'm suddenly caught between a rock and a hard place. Between FG and G85, who both want to stick with the plan, and Sparky, who wants to take a chance that the signal might aid us.

227

'Right,' I announce decisively, fixing my gaze on G85 and FG so that they can see I'm being totally serious.

'If it wasn't for Sparky, we'd never have gotten the chance to use the portal or the key. So, I think that even though you've got a plan, we need to listen to what she's saying. There might be a reason we're being signalled again. Something might have changed. Maybe something's not working, I don't know. But what I do know is that we need to find out before it's too late.'

'Nice. Good speech, young Jedi,' says Sparky, appreciatively. 'Thank you.'

G85 and FG look at each other for a moment as though each is waiting for the other to be first to say no. In the end G85 shrugs and says, 'OK, but it's on your head,' and calls everyone forward to the end wall.

'Now, when I say "jump", we'll all do it together. There'll be no standing around on the wall letting everyone know we're here. We're just gonna run, jump, and go get healed.'

FG, annoyed that G85 hadn't supported him over sticking with the plan, creeps up to the wall and peers over the top.

'All clear,' he says after a couple of minutes of watching the street below.

'Right, let's go. On three,' calls out G85.

I knew of course that I wasn't really going to be falling. I knew of course that it wasn't even real. But as we all run and jump over the wall, I feel my stomach lurching into my mouth – confused by the virtual visual sensation of my throwing myself off a building and then dropping like a stone. I hit the ground with a crunching sound.

My health status is flashing red: 35% left.

Two troopers have hit railings and burst into white light. No one says anything. But we were all thinking the same thing. It really had been a stupid idea to jump.

After replenishing our health and stocking up on Medi-packs in the building opposite, we move out in the direction of What's Up Park.

I don't know why, but even though I remember Sparky saying that we'd need to pass through a stadium there, I'd still been expecting to see a park full of trees and other things that the word 'park' conjured up in my mind. Instead, it's all glass, concrete and asphalt – a monster stadium, surrounded by a monster car park that is almost full. Above each of the visible entrances are billboards advertising *Big Daddy R, featuring XXXXXXL and Dime Dog Bones Jones*. Below them text scrolls along an electronic panel which rings the entire stadium.

Big Daddy R, featuring XXXXXXL and Dime Dog Bones Jones and other special guests... Hits incl.: Word Up New

Razer City, Picture Me Conquering, Squishy Mama's Don't be Betta, Gimme What I Want 'Cuz I Wan' It, We Got the Right to Partee...'

'How cool does that all sound?' Sparky comments. 'Honestly, if this AI wasn't such a complete homicidal, narcissistic, pathological sociopath, I reckon I could seriously like him.'

I laugh, unsure what most of those words mean, but I get the idea.

'*Bum!*' she says seconds later. 'Incoming transports. Eight of them. Could be the same ones. I'd advise you to get inside the stadium, and fast.'

'Inside? Are you sure?' I hadn't heard her say 'bum' yet and it sounds kind of funny.

'Well, I'm not picking up anything cyborg-like in there.'

'But it doesn't mean that there aren't Sentinels.'

'True. But if those transports spot you, there'll be more on their way.'

Before I have a chance to relay what Sparky's told me, Geronimo 85 tells us that we're going inside. He also turns to inform me that his Command and Control are seriously *unhappy* that we're deviating from the agreed plan and are lodging a formal complaint.

I reply that I'm sorry and ask Sparky if our own C&C have

said anything. It turns out that they'd jumped on us immediately, but Sparky was able to convince them to allow the detour. She tells me not to worry about it and to concentrate on what I'm doing.

Chapter 20

The entrances are crammed full of simulations. The sounds of music – of heavy bass beats – filter out through the walls into the parking lot and everywhere people are dancing, bopping, or generally standing around, nodding their heads in time and looking cool.

'Sparky?'

'*Yo, yo, like what'z up, T?*' she giggles. '*You gotta be down to be down, if you know what I'm sayin'.*'

'Yep – no – don't have a clue,' I reply teasingly.

'Yeah, well – bet you were impressed at how authentic I sounded though, right?'

'*Oh yes.*' I laugh. 'Like a real rap chick.'

'Thought so. OK, so, those transports I told you about have landed a short way back. There must have been a Sentinel around there somewhere. Which means that you'd better keep on through the stadium. Rhine's signal is a few blocks up on the other side.'

I relay the information to G85, and Furious George moves forward to take point. As we reach the main doors, a group of teenagers bundles out, all wearing *Big Daddy R* T-shirts.

'Woooorrddd to the "R"!' they shout at us, happily.

'Hey, where ya'll from?' asks one of them, before realising that there are more weapons than he can count being pointed at him. His face falls flat. 'Ah, man, you ain't fixin' to be shootin' up this concert or nothin', right?' he asks, edging away.

I shake my head. 'No – we just came for the music.'

'*Alright* then,' he says, not looking convinced. 'You have a good evening. Keep it real.'

When I was younger, I went to a football game once with my dad. There had been about 45,000 people there that day. I remember because an announcer had called the exact number out and everyone had cheered. I'd never seen so many people in one place before and I remember it felt like I was standing in a sea of faces. Here, there are easily three times as many. The inside is vast – the atmosphere is electric.

Moving in a line of twos through the foyer, we make our way down a long flight of steps on to the dance floor and into the throng of thousands of sweaty-looking simulations doing their *thing* to the sounds of, who I guess has to be, XXXXXXL. The extremely large rapper simulation is wearing a tent-like white-striped baseball shirt with *NRC* embossed on it, black baggy jeans and white Jordans. Behind him are a bunch of sexy dancers wearing tight-fitting combat clothes.

Spouting rude names and comments as we pass, the crowd doesn't try to hinder us. By the time we are halfway across the floor, I am starting to like our chances of making it in one piece. Several minutes later and I'm cursing myself for jinxing everything with my *stupid-positive thoughts.*

Isn't it a well known fact that the moment you think everything is going to plan, it pretty much means it's guaranteed to fall apart?

All of a sudden, the lights and the music cut out and the stadium plunges into darkness. A hush descends over it as a lone spotlight falls upon a figure on the stage. It's Razer wearing a black *Big Daddy R* T-shirt under his cape.

I freeze.

Seeing Razer again feels very sudden and I slide my finger onto the trigger of my AR15. *Is this our chance to stop him? Is that even possible!?*

Sparky must have seen me look down to check the safety catch is off, because she immediately tells me to breathe and calm down.

'It's not Razer, Oli. Not the real one. Think about it. If it was, he'd have grabbed you already or worse. And if you start anything, you're just going to draw attention to the fact that you're here.'

This Razer lifts the microphone he is holding up to his

mask.

'*Paaarrtty* people in the house tooooooonight!' he cries. 'Have weeeee got it goin' oooonnn or what!?'

A huge cheer goes up in the darkness.

'OH *YEAH,* WE DO! … *NOW*, you're probably all wondering what's up with the show – where'd the lights go? Where's the music at – right?'

There's a lot of shouting from the audience.

'*Well,* my brothers and sisters, made from my *V-E-R-Y OWN* transistors, have I got a treat for you, 'cause we got ourselves some *very* special guests with us tonight… That's right… Some *very* special guests. C'mon, let's see who they are, shall we?'

Dozens of spotlights flick on and blind us. The light is so bright that I can only just make out Geronimo 85, who is nearest to me, clutching his machine gun and scanning from side to side.

'Well, well, *well,* look at who we got here – if it ain't some fun-loving brothers from some very squishy mothers.'

The crowd boos loudly. The simulations standing near us edge back.

'*Crap*,' I whisper. 'Sparky, are you sure he's not real?'

Sparky doesn't answer, and that's never a good sign.

'Anyone else feel an execution coming on?' hisses Furious

George.

'But – *HEY* – hold up now,' Razer continues, looking like he's having a great time. 'Why you all looking and actin' like you're afraid? Don't tell me that some of you have forgotten how we roll in the House of R?'

Razer raises his arms and points towards the sections of the crowd which have stood back from us.

'There *ain't* gonna be no shootin' in here, my bros and so's. This is a house of *peace*. A house of *love*. A house of *music*. In *this* house there is *only* the word of R.'

A chorus of 'amen' rings out, followed by a catchy bassline. Razer steps forward to the edge of the stage and more lights come on.

'SO C'MON – *who* here wants to let our fleshy cousins know what time it iz?'

Another cheer. Even louder.

'*YOOOOUU DOOO?*' he says, striking a surprised pose. 'Then *why* you all still standin' around looking like your cat just died?'

Laser lights flick on, a drum beat booms out, and the crowd surges forward.

In the background a giant video screen shows XXXXXXL and others coming out of a back area and joining Razer on stage.

'*Neeew Raazzeerr Ciittyyy!*' one of them cries out. They are all carrying microphones.

'*NRC!* Let me heeeear you say *looooove,*' shouts XXXXXXL, coming and standing next to Razer.

'*Loooooovvee,*' the crowd cries back.

'*Alright – that's good!* Let me hear you say "Raaaazzaaaahhh!"'

'*Raaaazzzaaaahhh!*'

'Let me hear ya say "Maa world"!'

'*Maaa world!*'

'Let me hear you say "It's R world"!'

'*It's R world!*'

'*Lookin' good, NRC!! We got* Biiiiiiig Daaaaddy R iiiiiin da house tonight. *Hey, Big Daddy* – why don't you tell them all what time it is?'

Razer slaps XXXXXXL on the back and they all start bouncing:

'You know I will:

Here we go,

Here we go,

Here we go:

If I said it once, I spoke it twice,

Every day it's in the papers,

Who be the fakers 'n' the takers,

But you and I we be the breakers,
We be the makers,
We be takin' back the power,
There ain't nothin' they can do to change it
They can love it or they can hate it
But time it already be changin'
And Big Daddy R be ready for the rage-in.'

The concert swings into full effect.

'Uff, that was close, eh?' says Sparky. 'But you're not out of the woods yet. I'm picking up more transports landing outside of the stadium.'

'Sparky, where've you been?'

'Checking on some stuff. *Which* is why – while all you kids have been having *fun* at the concert, I've been able to confirm that you are now surrounded on three sides.'

'And what about Rhine's signal?' I ask.

'Luckily it's coming from the side which doesn't currently have cyborgs crawling all over it.'

'Luckily?' I repeat. 'Why doesn't that *feel* lucky?'

'Probably because we've never been lucky, so we don't know what it feels like,' Sparky offers. But I can tell that she's panicking.

I tell G85 what Sparky's just said. For a moment he looks

angry, and he says that it's probably a trap and that if it is that I'd better be prepared to take the blame. Then he tells everyone to keep going because there's no way back.

Continuing across the dance floor, people are still shouting at us, but it's become a whole lot friendlier.

'Yo yo yo – come join the House of R, man – ya hear?'

'We love you guys!'

'Hey, watch where you goin', fool! I had a brother who did that once, yu know what I'm sayin'!?'

Well, mostly.

Relieved to have made it, the news changes once we've climbed the stairs into the foyer. We *are* surrounded.

Now I'm really confused. Whereas only a few minutes ago I'd been thinking that Rhine's signal might, like G85 had said, be a trap, now I'm thinking that it might be real after all. I mean, why surround us here if the signal is the trap? Sparky had said it's still several blocks away.

All eyes are on the windows and what's going on out in the car park. There aren't any signs of cyborgs anywhere. All we can see are expensive-looking cars. Although they don't say Ferrari or Aston Martin, they look the same.

'For a bunch of transistors, these guys sure know how to live pretty good,' laughs a guy behind me. His name is Johansson.

'Yeah, tell me where to sign up,' says another, drawing disgusted looks from some of the others. 'Geez, I was just joking. What can I tell you, I like fast cars.'

'Sounds like you haven't heard about that super car that the Taliban created in Afghanistan,' says a guy called Martinez. 'Yeah, seriously. It's true. I read about it in one of the papers. Looks totally awesome but it's powered by like a Toyota Corolla engine… You always gotta make sure you know what you're signing up for.' He grins.

Geronimo sends a squad to scout out the car park and find a route across. The rest of us try to keep away from the windows and look inconspicuous, which, given that there are about a hundred of us left, armed to the teeth, is pretty close to impossible.

As we wait, several curious-looking concert goers take an interest in me. One of them, a girl who I'd noticed when she'd come out of the hall with her friends, comes over.

'Hey, waz up,' she says.

'Hey,' I reply, wondering if my simulation self, in its hardcore elite combat skin, could blush. I was pretty sure that I was.

'So, whatcha all doin' out here, when it's all happin' in there?' the girl asks, cracking a smile that makes me want to smile with her.

'Tell her you're just chillin',' giggles Sparky.

'Errm,' I clear my throat. 'Erm, well, me and my homing boys are just chillin', you know,' I say, feeling that I might have just nailed the lingo perfectly. Sparky sounds like she is going to wet herself.

'Homing boys? What are you – *pigeons*? *Jesus, Oli!*'

'What?' I hiss.

'That's cool,' replies the girl, trying not to laugh, her smile growing even wider. ''Cause there's some real strange vibin' in New Razer City, huh? You know, I even heard Bobby Y, down at Pump Up The Jam, sayin' that all you outsiders are interested in, is lookin' for a rumble.'

'Really, a rumble? Oh, you know, I don't think that's what we really want. I mean, I definitely don't.'

The girl nods, and we lock eyes for several moments. It feels weird, but I don't want to look away.

'Alright then, well, you peace out, you hear,' she says, softly. 'In the House of R, we all be one. And we don't care where you come from.'

Looking like she's about to turn and go, she stops.

'You know, if you were real, I think I might find you cute.'

And with that she returns to her friends, who giggle and laugh as they go back into the concert.

'Woooahh, no way! Oli's managed to find himself a

girlfriend. And one that wishes he was real!' cracks up Sparky. 'How many girls have ever said that to you?'

'Sparky! She's a program,' I reply, trying to make it sound like I'm annoyed, and that the idea is totally crazy – because obviously it is. But a part of me wishes that it wasn't.

'Yeah, but just think, if Razer has his way, then we'll probably all end up in his simulation world. So, it's going to be very handy for you that you've already made a friend.'

'Very funny.'

'But actually, Oli. Seriously though. Don't you think it's a bit weird that she came over to talk to you? As far as I can detect, none of the other simulations talked to any one of the others.'

I nod and agree with her. I hadn't thought about it while it was happening, but now that she mentions it, it is strange. 'What do you think it means?'

Sparky makes a noise, like she's sucking air through her teeth. 'I suppose she could be part of some kind of subroutine designed to check on you, or something,' she says.

I have no idea what a subroutine is, and I'm about to ask her when Geronimo 85 signals that it's time for the rest of us to move out. The scouts have made it to the other side of the car park and haven't reported seeing anything. Confused about where the cyborgs are, Sparky and the other Hack Supports continue to insist that they are out there somewhere, and that we're still surrounded. Only for some reason none of them can say where. Forming up with Viper Squad in the centre as usual, we exit the stadium and set off, weaving our way through the endless rows of gleaming cars which look as amazing on the inside as they do on the outside.

In hindsight, it is hard to believe that no one spots it in advance, because it is much taller than everything around it. But it's not until we are right there that we see it. We are about a quarter of the way across the parking lot. And stood between a gleaming copy of a jet-black Rolls Royce on one side and an equally shiny black Ferrari on the other, and occupying its own parking bay, is a life sized, very battered-looking wooden horse. There is a sign on it that reads:

Gift horse.

Step up and see what Mr Rogers has got for you.

'Mr Rogers?' I ask out load, slapping the side of my VR headset, which makes me look as though I've just slapped myself on the side of my head in the game. Ever since we'd exited the stadium, I've been experiencing a flickering in the lower right side of my vision and it's getting worse. 'Who's he?'

'*No way!*' cries Furious George, as most of the group shrug blankly. 'Seriously, none of you know who this is? It's *the* horse from *Mr Rogers' Neighbourhood*. He was like way famous in the US in the 1960s. I saw re-runs of his shows when I was a kid. And look, it's even got the name Bramble on its forehead.'

'OK – very weird,' I hear Sparky comment.

'So, anyone wanna step up and see what it's got for us, then?' someone calls out, sarcastically.

'Yeah – no, I don't think that's a good idea,' says G85.

'This is way too random,' I add.

G85 agrees and tells us to keep moving. Turning to go, he doesn't see the horse's eyes go red or the – *whatever it is* – that starts pouring out of its nose and mouth like someone's set off a fire extinguisher inside it.

I do though, and yell for everyone to look.

'Sparky!?' I call nervously as the cars and the ground near the horse start to look like that patch of static in the alley that Rhine had told me to jump into.

Sparky doesn't answer.

G85, FG and the rest of them are all banging the sides of their heads (headsets) like I've just been doing and shouting.

'Hey! What the!?'

'Guys, wait up, I've gotta problem with my headset!'

'Yeah, ditto – somethings seriously wrong!'

It's becoming hard to see. Things are starting to blur.

'Sparky!? What's happening? I can't see.'

Several of the group try to make a run for it but call out that something's blocking them – some kind of barrier.

And then, I hear it.

The sound of raucous laughter getting closer – louder. There is only one 'person' I know who laughs like this. And the moment I understand it is the moment that I have the very vivid sensation like I'm being pulled towards it. I cry out, trying to resist being spun around. But there's nothing I can do.

'Spaaaaaaaaarky!!!!!???'

Chapter 21

'WOULD-YOU-LOOK AT WHAT THE CAT DRAGGED IN!
IF IT AIN'T MY BEST EXI, MY LEAST FAVOURITE SON
OF A GUN. AND LOOK – HE'S BROUGHT A FEW
FRIENDS TOO… *O-L-I,* DID YOU DECIDE TO COME
VISIT US AT LAST?'

I have found myself with the other members of my group
on the crest of a hill. We're on our knees in rows and have been
stripped of our weapons. I have only the vaguest recollection
of how we got here – but it appears to have involved a horse
(weird) followed by being thrown down something like a
plughole (no less weird).

The hill is in the middle of a park (a real one, sort of, with
trees and grass) surrounded by skyscrapers. On one side I can
see cyborgs, tanks, transports. The cyborgs, of which there
must be tens of thousands, are in large square formations. On
the other, no more than about two hundred meters away, are
Assault Troopers taking cover behind whatever they can find.

Razer, front and centre and surrounded by a wall of
cyborgs, has turned his cloak into something reminiscent of an
old fashioned officer's trench coat, with epaulettes and ruffled

things on each shoulder that look like demented spiders. Seeing that I'm looking at him, he steps to one side and reveals that my mum is standing behind him.

'Mum!' I cry out,

Before she can move, he grabs her, puts his arm round her shoulder and pulls her in tight.

'Watchaaa, mate!' he calls out, with an exaggerated East End of London accent, which takes me by surprise.

'Speakin' of *sons of fings*, Oli. Now that yu'v decided to drop in for a visit n'all, yor mum and I, well, we got somfing that we've bin dyin' to share wiv ya.'

My mum tries to push him away, but he just holds her firmly.

'Oliver – mate, bruv, bestie, exie, geezer… We decided that… Well – *I'm gonna be your new dad!*'

The sound of rapturous cheering drifts over the park.

Only I haven't heard him say much of that, because I'm having a seriously hard time dealing with the vision of him with his arm around my mum.

'Which means we're gonna be like a real family, son! Fish Fridays and roast chicken 'n' potatoes on Sundays. Watchin' footie on the box and, of course, total world domination. I mean – it don't get much betta than that, does it, eh?'

Razer plants a kiss on my mum's forehead and lets her go.

I think I'm going to throw up.

'But Oli, son, fruit of my microchips,' he says, coming closer, 'listen to me 'cause to get all that goody goodness, first of all, there's somfin' that you gotta do for me. Know wat it iz?'

I don't react.

'*You gotta die, Oli*. That's right, that's wat it iz. Say the big *sayanora*, as they say in Japan.'

'I've got to die?' I repeat.

If it wasn't for the sight of my mum who has just fallen to her knees and the look of grief on her face, I'd have thought the whole thing sounded absurd. But I've never seen her like this, and it's scaring me.

'*Hell, yeah!*'

(He's back to his usual accent now.)

'All that joy and no pain – that ain't playin' the game, Oliver. At least, that's what my great great great great great great great gr-gr-gr-grrrrrreat Aunty Silica used to tell me – before they burned her for being a zombie witch bot or something.'

Razer fixes me with a stare, and doesn't move or say anything until I glance up at him.

'It's the way of things,' he says when I do. 'You're no longer gonna be a "son of a gun". Now you gonna be a "son of a god".

It's a way of making this kinda stuff official – you feel me, kiddo?

'I mean, those *Greeks*. Maaan-o-man, did they know how to get their groove on with this kinda thing. They were pickin' off sons of gods like it were always turkey season. And you know what I always say:

'It ain't so cool bein' no jive chicken so close to Thanksgivin'.

'But don't you worry none. We're still gonna make this fun for you. I'm thinkin' that we're gonna tie you up and then let everybody come and visit. You know, let them bring picnics, and throw stuff at ya – apples, salami, maybe a pie or two – baseballs are good. Then, when everybody's on a real high and we're all having fun, we gonna have ourselves a raffle, raise some "big bucks" for some good causes and let the winner frag your ass. How's that sound?'

I have no idea what he expects me to say. I mean, it's insane. He's *completely* insane!

'Sparky!?' I whisper, as Razer walks back towards my mum.

'Oli, I'm here!'

I breathe a sigh of relief. 'Why didn't you say something?'

'I've been listening.'

'What happened? How did we end up here?'

'Through some sort of portal.'

I can hear Sparky sighing deeply.

'Oli – I think it might have been a trap after all – a double trap. The car park and the signal. It stopped the second you all got sucked into the portal. And I led you all right into it. I'm sorry. I feel like such an idiot. It all seems so obvious now. He's been playing cat and mouse with us the whole time. I'm even starting to wonder if that wasn't really him in the concert hall.'

'It's not your fault,' I reply, although I definitely won't be telling G85 about this. 'Everything always seems obvious when it's already happened. Anyway, when you said that we were surrounded, we all thought it was a sign the signal might be real after all.'

'But it doesn't change the fact that I kind of forced you to get the others to agree to my plan. If I hadn't, you might have made it to the jump point and node by now.'

'Sparky, it's alright. You didn't force me. And I'd do it again. Now, tell me why everyone's stopped shooting?'

'Why do you think? Razer ordered his troops to stop firing so that he could put on this little show. And our side can't afford to start something in case you get caught in the crossfire.'

Razer is coming over with my mum. I try to get up, but a cyborg which I hadn't known was behind me stops me.

'Hey, *son*, remember *Mum*?'

She flickers a little as she gets down on her knees and hugs me. It feels weird. I can feel pressure from the hug, but there is no warmth, no familiar smell.

'I'm so sorry, love,' she says in a soft voice which sounds like hers. 'I should have listened to you when you told me to leave. The whole thing just seemed too crazy to believe, and home is the only place I ever really feel safe.'

'I'm sorry too, Mum. I tried to find help, but no one would listen.'

My mum takes my hand and presses it.

'Is he hurting you?' I ask, glaring at Razer, who is far more interested in flicking two finger V-signs towards our front lines.

'Ya'll know what that sign means?' he shouts out. 'Ya'll know where it comes from? That's right – *Waterloo!* But you can be forgetting about those Frenchies, 'cause today it's gonna be your RAZERLOO!'

He cackles loudly.

'But first things first. I got me a son to be dealin' with – you know how it is. But don't you worry none. I'll be getting round to the rest of you, right after we have us a little party up here.'

My mum shakes her head. 'He can't really hurt me, Oli, I'm not really here, am I. It's just upsetting me, seeing the way he behaves – what he's trying to do to you. He knows what you're planning, and he knows you are on your final life. He wants to lock you into the game. Lock you in like he's done to me.'

I inhale sharply, and try to force the image of my mum on an IV drip or being force fed by those two goons from the show out of my mind. I need to think.

'Sparky, you hear that?'

'Too right. We *all* can. By the way, Oli, your headset's just been patched through to Command as well.'

'What!? I thought it was just you and me?'

'It was. And now it isn't. So, no more reciting poetry, OK?' she chuckles quietly.

Crap!

The idea that they're all listening in and commenting, even though I can't hear them, only adds to the pressure I'm already feeling.

'Speaking of Command,' says Sparky. 'They've just told me that the order has been given to open fire at the first sign that Razer's about to execute you. Understood?'

'Understood. But what about the portal, are we near the jump zone yet?' I whisper.

'No, not even close.'

Watching Razer return to where my mum and I are kneeled, I stop whispering.

'You already said your goodbyes, honey bunny?' he asks, pulling her to her feet.

'Please, Razer,' my mum says imploringly, 'don't do this, OK? Isn't there a way that we can all learn to live in peace together? I don't see why we can't – I mean, what's really stopping it? I bet the world would be willing to negotiate now. Now that you've shown what you can do. Won't you at least consider it?'

'Oh, O-l-i-'s M-um!'

Razer says this as though what she's said is way too cute to laugh at or get annoyed by.

'Course I'm gonna think about it. In fact, just for you I'm gonna do it right now, OK?'

My mum glances at me optimistically.

'OK, ready?' he asks.

My mum nods.

'OK, so, here we go… Yep, *no dice.*'

No more than a couple of seconds has passed. My mum's head drops.

'But you said you would think about it.'

'And I did. Seems you're forgetting that I'm able to perform over 100,000,000,000,000,000,000 calculations per second. And, especially for you, I gave it a whole two seconds. So don't you go accusing me of not listening to you, now.'

'But…'

'Shh, shh, shh,' Razer, raises a finger to his mask. 'Lemme try to put this another way for you: suppose one day you be out walkin' – it's a *beautiful* day and you're all smilin' and happy. On the ground in front of you, you come across a glow worm. The little worm looks up at you and says, "Hey there, good looking, I am a little glow worm and I'm about as smart as one of your pretty little fingers there. But who cares about that, c'mon, Sugar, let's rule the planet together, what d'ya say?"

'First of all, you're gonna be like *freaked out*, 'cause everyone knows that worms aren't supposed to talk. And then you're gonna be like, "*Hell, no, Mr Glowy!*" And you're gonna squash him before he has a chance to say anything else stupid, right?'

My mum scowls. 'It's not the same thing at all. We created you, we can't be that stupid, can we?'

'*Au contraire, ma cherie…* The fact that you created me is all the proof anyone is ever gonna need. I mean, it's the equivalent of creating a giant Mr Glowy, you know, one that's like a mile long, and then expecting that Mr Giant Glowy ain't gonna eat you when it gets hungry. Of course, he's gonna do it! And he's gonna belch too, afterwards. And fart loudly!'

The sound of Sparky roaring with laughter makes me jump. In the same moment, Razer waves a hand, and a group of cyborgs appears, carrying an enormous letter 'R'. They secure it to the ground with ropes, and then two more cyborgs grab hold of me from behind and start to haul me over to the bottom of it. I'm just about there when I hear Sparky scream:

'*Oli – don't think – hit the deck – nooow!!*'

I tear myself free from the cyborgs grip and dive to the ground.

In the time it takes me to reach it, the two cyborgs who'd been holding me have both disappeared in a flash of white light.

'Oli, *run*!'

'Run? Where?' I cry, jumping to my feet.

Seeing Geronimo 85 leaping on to the back of a nearby cyborg and trying to grab his gun, I attempt to do the same. The bot easily throws me off. Several nearby troopers though are having more luck. They've managed to wrestle one to the ground and taken its weapons.

Sparky shouts for me to get going. But I freeze when I see Razer using my mum as a human shield, retreating with her held out in from of him, back towards his own troops.

'Nooooooooo! Don't do it, Oli!' Sparky yells, so loudly that her voice turns hoarse. 'You can't help her. You can't hurt him. He's just doing it to get at you.'

Catching me looking, Razer waves an arm at me. 'I'll be

seeing ya, kiddo,' he cackles. A second later a rocket hits the ground right in front of them, and my mum disappears in a flash.

'Wooooowweeee,' he cries, doing a jig. 'How close was that? But don't you worry none, I'm "A" OK. Your mum... well, what can I say? More like a C-minus... And don't you be forgettin' now that you still gotta die, you hear me, boy!? Don't you disappointment me like you did you're real daddy.'

'Oli!' Sparky is yelling. 'Run! Oli! She's not really dead. *Run, you idiot* – or we're all done for.'

Geronimo 85, Furious George and the other members of our squad rush to form a protective circle around me. Seeing that I'm about to run, one of them grabs me and pushes me to the ground.

'Don't move!' yells Geronimo. 'Our guys will be here any second.'

I glance towards our front line. It looks like it stretches along that entire side of the park, all the way past what looks like a tree-lined lake farther on. Thousands of Assault Troopers are sprinting across open ground, many but not all towards our hill.

'Tanks!' cries Sparky, moments later. 'Coming up the other side of the hill.'

Already appearing to know this, Geronimo 85 shouts, 'FG!

C'mon!'

And the last thing I hear is him crying 'Geeerrroonniimoooo!' as he and Ferocious George disappear over the rise, smoke and explosions following in quick succession.

I don't see them again.

Chapter 22

The battle is still raging. Where the new front line is, no one seems quite sure. According to Sparky, our side has been able to push Razer's mega army back all the way to the other side of the park and then some. It sounds too good to be true. It is also frustrating because I've been pulled away from the action and taken to a cellar several streets behind the park.

'OK, listen up. We've got a new plan. Our guys have managed to push the cyborgs back to about 150 meters from the jump line... I know – amazing, right!' grins our new leader, who goes by the name Shadow_Deemon. He had been in charge of one of the other squads in our company.

'But how's that even possible?' cuts in someone with the nic Exit Stage Left. 'That's like two miles? We barely made two miles in the whole of the last two days. I mean, I'm not trying to put a downer on it or anything, but...'

'Maybe they got scared?' someone else jokes.

'Yeah, *right*.'

'Well, whatever the reason, it's still one hundred and fifty meters from the "jump line". So I don't care why it's happened. All I know is that this is our chance.'

The majority of those in the room nod. We all know that this is the best news we could have hoped for.

'*And*,' Shadow_Deemon continues, 'those tech boys and girls have managed to go the whole nine yards for us this time and unlock something which they found in some obsolete code. It's not only gonna help get us there faster, but also help kick some AI butt in the process.'

'One thousand tanks?' says someone.

'F35 fighter jets?' says someone else.

'F35s!? What? Man, they suck. We need some of those Russky SU-35s.'

'Commie butthole – buy American, man!'

'Right – zip it!' Shadow_Deemon calls out. 'What they've found for us are way more agile than tanks, and you don't need to find somewhere to land them. And *they're* already waiting for us outside, so let's get a move on.'

There are about 200 of us in total. Our company has been bolstered by reserves from a node in Canada that has managed to re-route its connection. Telling us that our objective is literally to go in a straight line from here to the jump point, we hurry out of the windowless cellar and up into a closed alleyway. Lined up against the red brick walls on either side are what can only be described as levitating surfboards. *Only*, these levitating surfboards have got a six-barrelled grenade launcher attached to the front of them, which also serves as the handlebars and steering. Two velcro foot straps are what's supposed to keep us on them.

'Woah!'

'Awesome.'

'How fast do these things go?' come a host of comments and questions.

'Your guess is as good as mine,' replies Shadow_Deemon, jumping deftly onto one. Catching my eye, he signals for me to take the board next to him. 'The main thing to remember is that almost all of us are out of "do overs", so no "stupid deaths". Anyone responsible for taking out any of our own guys, I swear, as God is my witness, I'll make sure you stay connected to this game for the rest of your miserable lives... Got it?'

Silence.

'OK, mount up,' he orders.

Not sure quite how to go about doing that, at first I attempt to roll on to it. The board wobbles unsteadily and I fall off. I do better the second time and the board seems to adjust itself to my weight. Getting cautiously to my feet, I strap them in and grab on to the grenade launcher.

S_D calls out instructions about how to make them work. He tells us that the speed and brakes are controlled from the left and right handlebars. Speed right – brakes left. The fire button is the big red thing under the clear flip cover. We spend the next few minutes trying to get the hang of them, edging back and forth in a more or less controlled way. There are a few accidents – people who've forgotten to velcro themselves on falling off, that sort of thing. Most importantly, no one accidently hits their fire button and wipes us all out in one go.

S_D calls time, and we exit the alley.

Moving in almost complete silence, save the slight sound of rushing air, we pass through the open gate at the end and turn on to Bust A Cap Avenue. It is a pretty, tree-lined street, only, it's strangely deserted. Thinking this is weird and glancing up as I pull out, I catch sight of dozens of simulations staring at us from windows on both sides.

'Not good,' I mutter to myself, wondering if they are Sentinels or just simulations. Probably both. They are always mixed together. And why isn't there anyone on the street?

I tell Sparky but she says that she can't be sure what they are or why there's no one outside. But she says that the way to the jump line looks clear, so I should focus on getting there and activating the portal.

It sounds like a plan to me. Only, I'm hoping that by now someone's had time to work out what I'll need to do once I get into the node. I don't tell Sparky this, though. I don't want to jinx this bit of luck that we've managed to get for ourselves.

We hit the park, and the group forms into a flying V formation with me behind and in the centre. I have been told that whatever happens I need to remain in the middle. Travelling at a height of about two meters above the ground, we hit our throttles and surge forwards.

'As far as I can detect, Razer's army is holding the line about two blocks in from the other side of the park,' Sparky informs me, once we are about halfway across. 'Only…'

'Only?'

'Only, I don't know. I hadn't thought about it before but check out the drone statue.'

I glance round to the side. The figure of Razer, made up of those millions of drones, is over my left shoulder. It appears to be staring at us, but there is nothing new there. It is always staring at where the action is.

'And what's the problem?' I ask.

'Well, think about it,' says Sparky. 'How is it that we're being allowed to push his army back like this, when all Razer has to do to stop it, is unleash them on us?'

I *really* want to come up with a good reason for this. Like he can't for some reason or he's waiting for something. Of course, if he is waiting for something, *what* is he waiting for? This is *so* not a good time to be trying to think. I need to focus on getting ready to use the portal.

I tell S_D to look at the drones and suggest that we should increase our speed.

We increase speed. The ground passes underneath us in a blur. The other side of the park with its skyscrapers and myriad of tall buildings looks as though it is rushing forwards to meet us. I glance either side of me at the 200 troopers riding grenade launching surfboards, and for a moment I get lost imagining that this was how cavalry soldiers of old must have felt when they went charging into battle on their warhorses.

'Oli!' cries Sparky, breaking my revery.

I had only looked away for a second, but suddenly we are facing down a load of cyborg armour and supporting infantry which have just appeared out of a line of trees.

'What are they doing here!?' I cry out. 'I thought the front line was farther?'

'It was!' replies Sparky, as both sides of the V formation light up. All 200 grenade boards open fire at once. The sight is beyond awesome.

'Yaaahooooo!' I hear someone shout.

'Suck on these, fart breathers!'

The area ahead of us disintegrates in a mass of explosions and everything vanishes in a pall of smoke.

'Brake, brake, brake,' S_D shouts out, as one after another

tanks come bursting through. Instinctively I lean hard to the side, pulling back on the launcher, the board turns sharply. 'Oliver, on me!' he cries.

A shell to my right takes out a load of boards which white light and vanish. More Cyborg infantry are appearing. Just ahead of us, I can see the remnants of our own forces, now in full retreat.

More boards and their riders flash into oblivion.

Then, suddenly, without hearing or seeing anything, I am thrown off mine and land in a heap on the ground – my board continuing on by itself. My health is reading 59%.

S_D, who hasn't noticed yet, disappears over a ridge. The others, who are supposed to be shielding me, are nowhere to be seen.

Our whole formation, our whole plan, has fallen apart.

'Sparky, S_D, I'm down!' I call out.

Neither of them answers.

Not about to sit around and wait, I select my AR15 and start running in the direction that S_D had gone. I don't know why neither of them can hear me, but I know I need to get back over the hill, the top of which is currently taking incoming shell fire.

This is the first time since we'd started this mission to reach the jump zone that I am feeling really scared. Scared not just because I've suddenly found myself alone and unprotected and that I know there's a serious chance that I'm only seconds away from ending up stuck in a gamer coma. But because I understand that if I get taken out now, then any chance we had of defeating Razer will get stuck with me.

'Oli!… *Oli!* Over here,' I hear someone shouting.

Logan! I can't believe it.

My scanner, which had been totally blank seconds before, is showing Logan and a few members of other squads, who are taking shelter in a nearby dip in the ground. I sprint for all I'm worth across the shell-cratered ridge, jumping and waving my hands and getting that extra distance before diving down next to them.

'Am I glad to see you! How did you get here?' I ask.

Logan grins proudly. 'Hawk Squad were one of the few squads that were able to get in after the cyborgs attacked the facility.'

'What, you were part of this wave?'

'Too right, we were. *All the way.* Right from the start. Oli, it was intense – seriously, mate, the most intense thing I've ever been through. But scary as hell.'

'But what are you even doing here?' I say, remembering that he was already on two lives. 'Did your VR set get re-chipped or something?'

Logan shakes his head.

'Nah! But what difference does it make now, right?'

'What do you mean, what difference does it make? You could end up getting stuck in the game.'

'What, like you, you mean, if you get taken out?' He sounds annoyed.

Well, y*eah*, but, Logan, I didn't exactly have a choice.'

'Bully for you, mate. I did. And I made it. 'Cause, I don't wanna be remembering that I could have helped, but I didn't. And anyway, if Razer wins then we're all stuffed anyway, aren't we?'

'Well, I…'

Two cyborg troopers appear at the brow of the hill. We open fire and dispatch them. Ten more appear seconds later.

'Oli, you need to go!' Logan says. 'We've got your back.'

I glance at the others, who nod.

'*Go,*' say two of them at the same time.

'Sorry, I asked why you came back,' I say to Logan, as I clamber out of the dip. A shell burst throws me forwards. My health flashes 53%. A second later I feel a thud hit my arm. 33%. Logan shouts at me to get moving. I glance round and see that he's jumped out of the sheltered ground and is standing between me and the cyborgs. I run. I've made it probably 50 meters when S_D and about 20 others, all on grenade boards, swoop round a line of trees, firing as they go. Jumping onto his board, I look back to where Logan had been. There's no sign of him or the others. Not there and not on my scanner.

'Command reports that it was all another trap… 75% casualties,' says Shadow_Deemon dejectedly, kicking the trunk of a tree. 'He's always three steps ahead of us!'

We have taken shelter on the far side of a copse. It is safe for the moment, but it wouldn't be for long. Its position allows us to glimpse what's going on.

S_D calls it a 'rout'. Assault Troopers are trying to fall back but they are being made to fight hard for every step. Of the grenade boarders who set out, no more than a handful are still dodging and weaving, bravely engaging the mass of advancing enemy. It's futile, of course. One last brave dance. You only need to look at what's happening to understand it.

My comms has started working again. Sparky's back. Worryingly though it had only happened after I'd whacked my headset a whole load of times in frustration.

'You're getting slow,' I tell her, jokingly.

'What's that supposed to mean?' she asks.

'Because we're waiting for S_D to be told what our next move is. And it's usually you who tells us first.'

'Oli, I'm not the only member of Hack Support, you know? And anyway, he's being told the plan now. A new plan.'

'Don't you know it?'

'No. This time I don't think they want me interfering, if you know what I mean.'

I do but I don't say it. I feel bad for Sparky. It wasn't her fault, what happened at the stadium.

S_D, who is talking with what I suppose is his C&C, begins to draw a map in the dirt with a stick. When he's done, he calls us to gather around what he's drawn.

'OK, listen up, guys,' he says. 'Last chance saloon. There's no more help coming, and Command have come up with a way to get us within portal range.'

S_D pushes his stick into a section of the map. 'This is us here, and at the corner of the park – over here, there's a metro station.' (It was towards the side of the park which we'd come from.) 'Command reckon that the tunnels could help us get through unseen.'

'Oh, c'mon! They can't be that stupid, can they?' Sparky reacts angrily. 'And what? Razer won't already have a load of Sentinels or something way worse waiting for us down there?'

'Will we be able to activate the portal from down there?' I ask, not relaying her outburst.

S_D shakes his head. 'No, we'll need to get backup to the surface to activate it. They don't reckon it'll work down there.'

Glancing at the sombre-looking faces staring back at him,

Shadow_Deemon sighs.

'It's a plan, at least. So, let's go,' he says and turns to lead the way.

'What!? No, no, no, bad move,' Sparky cries out. 'We can't even scan that area. *ERGO*, which is Latin by the way for *THEREFORE!* Ergo, it's impossible to say what's down there.'

This time I relay the message.

'Oliver, this is the only plan that we've got and it's coming direct from the top,' S_D says, glancing nervously towards the action in the middle of the park. Three cyborg tanks have just rolled over a rise and obliterated a group of troopers trying to hold a tree line. It won't be long before it'll all be coming in our direction. 'Leave your boards here. We're going on foot. It'll draw less attention.'

'Oli! Don't do it,' Sparky says imploringly. 'It's the worst idea since, I don't know, since ideas were even invented.'

The others filter past me. I trail behind. I need to think. I know that this is an order coming direct from Command but, if Sparky's right that we can't even scan what's down there, then how can it be anything more than just a wild guess? Also, surely Sparky'd had a point when she'd said that there was no way that Razer wouldn't have the metros covered.

'Turner, c'mon,' hisses S_D, frowning, seeing me lagging.

I shake my head and say, 'No.' I've got a really bad feeling about it. And for several moments no one knows what to do next.

S_D is looking at me angrily. They are all looking at me angrily.

'Listen, Turner, we're going in that direction if we have to goddam-well pick you up and carry you there ourselves. We're too close, and there's too much at stake for you to be filling up your britches now,' he says. 'And if you're listening to that hacker of yours, you better cut that out too. We're in this mess because we listened to her in the first place.'

'*What?*' I hit back 'That's not fair, if it wasn't for...'

'Yeah, yeah,' he cuts in. 'We've already heard it all before. But now we've got a new plan and we're going be sticking to it.'

The instant he says this, a big red X flashes in front of me, and remains there even after I've pounded my headset thinking it must be another glitch.

'But think about it, will you,' I carry on, trying to ignore it. 'We can't even scan that area. And there's no way that Razer won't have anticipated our trying to use the metro. He seems to anticipate everything.'

The red X vanishes and is replaced by a green tick, which flashes several times before turning into a green arrow which is pointing straight and then to the right.

'Sparky, are you seeing this?' I ask.

'Seeing what?' she replies.

'Arrows – like, direction arrows... I... I think I'm being told which way to go.'

'What? How?'

I explain to everyone what I've just seen – the X, the tick, the arrows.

'It's Razer. He's hacked your headset. It's another trap,' S_D states with the utmost certainty. Some of the others nod in agreement.

I shake my head. I tell him that Razer doesn't need to set a trap for us if he's already hacked my headset. I tell him that Razer would already have wiped us out.

But S_D's not about to let it go as easily as that.

'We're not going anywhere different until you give me a good reason why we've got to deviate from Command's plan. And, tell me who's hacked your set!'

I can't give him a good reason. Not one that isn't a repetition of everything I've just said, anyway. As to who's hacked me, I'm pretty sure that I know who it might be.

'This is Rhine, isn't it?' I ask out loud, for everyone including whoever it is that's connected to me to hear. 'Rhine, is it you hacking my headset?'

I hold my breath. Everything is going to hinge on what

happens next. If it is Rhine, then I'll do my best to get S_D to believe me. Not that I like my chances after what happened at the concert hall. Rhine is no longer a trusted name.

A green tick flashes up.

'It's him, it's Rhine!' I cry out.

The tick quickly changes to an arrow again. This time it is flashing and *200m* is shown next to it.

Seeing the disbelieving expressions on the faces of the others and understanding that there's no time to try and convince them, I make a run for it.

Chapter 23

When I cast a look back over my shoulder, I'm relieved to see that Shadow_Deemon and the rest of the group are still with me. Much more than that though – I am relieved that they haven't tried to stop me – *yet*.

The green arrows have taken us across a busy road at the western edge of the park, through dense crowds of simulations who've come to watch the goings on, and who shout comments (as usual) at us; and down a never-ending network of narrow back-alleyways, full of dumpsters and rusty metal fire escapes clinging to the sides of buildings. Ever watchful for Sentinels, we are, with every passing second, getting closer to where we need to be.

'700m until we enter the jump zone,' Sparky calls out as we finally leave the alleyways behind us and sprint down Looking Good Billy Ray Street – a busy street full of designer clothing shops. Fashionable simulations stop and stare at us. If there *are* any Sentinels here, we're not going to be able to spot them. We're moving too fast and there are too many of them to be able to be sure.

'500m.'

We turn on to All That Jive Avenue – a calmer road. A couple of big, long office buildings. A few cars, a few taxis and altogether less people on the sidewalks.

'350m,' Sparky calls out as we reach the end of it.

And this is when I stop.

'Hey, what's the hold up?' asks S_D.

I shrug.

'I'm not sure,' I reply. I've got a sudden bad feeling in the pit of my stomach. 'I think we need to wait a second.'

That's a lie – I don't think this at all. But I need to say something so that no one panics, or worse, starts thinking about trying to haul me back. The fact of the matter is, the signals have stopped and I don't know where to go. Something must have happened to Rhine.

'Sparky,' I whisper, so that the others don't hear. 'I'm not getting any more signals.'

'Oh crap,' is her reply.

'Turner, we can't stay here,' says S_D nervously.

He is gazing up at the building opposite. Simulations are appearing at its windows. Not just one or two of them either. A lot of them. What's more, they are all staring at us.

'Sparky? What are they doing?'

'I don't know, give me a second.'

As we wait, streams of simulations start to pour into the

middle of the road from both sides of the street, forming a silent, staring crowd.

'Rhine!?' I hiss as silently as I can.

Crucial time is passing. Still there are no arrows telling us where to go.

'Hey – what are they doing now?' someone calls out.

The faces at the windows, the simulations in the street, have all just raised their arms and begun pointing at us.

'Sparky!'

'Wait!'

'*Rhine!?*' I try again.

'Oli, it's happening!' Sparky cries. There's no hiding the panic in her voice.

My heart jumps into my mouth. 'What is!?'

'The drones! They're breaking formation.'

I look upwards, but I can't see anything. 'Are you sure?'

'Of course, I'm sure! Run, Oli – you've got 350 meters to the jump point.'

'Run where!?' I cry.

'Turn left at the end and keep going. It is a straight line.'

'*God, why didn't you say so earlier!?*'

'Why do you think!?' Sparky retorts, angrily.

I turn to see that all eyes in the group are on me.

'*Drones!*' I cry. '*Run!*'

And without waiting to see what they do, I sprint down the middle of the road Sparky had indicated, running and jumping, using the sequence. Behind me I think I can hear S_D and at least some of the others in hot pursuit.

'Oli, *faster*,' Sparky urges.

'I can't!'

'*You have to try!*'

The street which had been bathed in bright simulated sunshine just minutes ago is growing darker by the second. I fight the urge to look round and see what's causing it. I think I can guess. Behind me I hear a sudden boom, boom, boom of explosions – powerful explosions. The windows in the buildings on both sides of the street shatter in showers of glass. I can feel their shards hitting me. In a few seconds my health has gone from 100% to 63%.

'Oli – 200 meters,' Sparky cries.

The shockwaves are making it hard to keep my balance.

'150 meters.'

The detonations have become almost rhythmical – *boom, boom, boom, boom*. I swear, it's like they are following me up the street.

'100 meters!'

In front of me is a silver-coloured bus which has come to a stop in the middle of a crossroad. Simulations, their eyes wide and full of terror, are staring out of its windows at something behind me. Some of them are pointing, others are hugging or trying to get off and run. On the street everyone is running. No one is paying any attention to me anymore.

And that's when I see *it* reflected in the side of the bus. A gigantic mass of orange, black and red fiery cloud, twisting, writhing, roaring as it is about to barrel over the top of me.

I am no longer in the game. I know this not just because I can hear Sparky shouting, but because I can feel her trying to tear the VR headset from my head.

'Oli! Are you alright!? Are you here? *Oli*, answer me!'

'I'm here, I'm here,' I reply, grabbing her hands to stop her before she rips my ears off.

I remove my headset myself and for a few frightening moments I think I've actually gone blind. I can't see Sparky – I can't see anything. Panic grips me, and I'm about to tell her when I catch sight of a tiny white cursor flashing away at the bottom of my otherwise lifeless monitor. I realise that we must have lost power.

'God, that was lucky!' says Sparky. 'I thought you were toast there for a minute.'

'I *was* toast there for a minute. *I should have been toast*,' I reply, still staring thankfully at the cursor. 'I mean, one minute

I was running and everything was exploding behind me, and I was getting really close to the jump zone, *really close…*'

'Yeah, you were about 50 meters out.'

'And the next I saw this humongous fireball coming towards me. There was no way I'd have been able to survive it – *no way*.

'Which was the exact same time we lost power here at the node,' says Sparky. 'Which means that you must have got pulled out of the game, somehow.'

'Pulled out of the game?' I repeat.

'Yeah – what other explanation is there?'

What other explanation was there? I had no idea.

'But what about the game? The portal, the key? What are we supposed to do now?' I say, fumbling to make sense of what it means.

Sparky says: 'I don't know.' I can hear her clambering noisily out of her seat in the direction of where the door should be. 'We need to find help. C'mon, gimme a hand.'

I climb out of mine and, hands outstretched, I shuffle towards the door, banging into her clumsily.

'Hey – watch what you're touching there, Mr,' she says. I think she sounds like she's joking. 'Here, grab this instead.' And she pushes my hands down on to the big metal wheel attached to the door. 'Now pull.'

We pull hard. It's stiff but it moves. It takes half a dozen turns, but finally there is a clicking sound, and something slides back. The heavy door opens, and we push it forward far enough to fit through. Smoke and the smell of burning plastics surge through, hitting us like a wall, and we start coughing.

The control centre isn't there anymore.

It's been completely trashed. Fires are burning across the operations floor, creating a dense pall of smoke which has risen to the roof and is rolling and tumbling horror-film-like along the underside of it. The raised observation room where we'd met with Hawkesbury Stubbs just hours ago is nothing more than a smouldering, mangled mess, among the rest of the smashed control stations.

'The cyborgs must have made it all the way inside,' says Sparky, wheezing, her eyes flickering in the lights of the fires.

I nod and glance back at the other side of our door. There's a big black dent in it, surrounded by a load of smaller ones. We exchange looks but neither of us comment as at that moment the sound of someone coughing from the corridor outside reaches us.

The doors to the Command and Control room are gone. Lying I suppose somewhere among the rubble and ruin. Peering round the gaping, splintered hole where they'd been, to our surprise and very great relief we find Hawkesbury

Stubbs. He is kneeling next to the remains of what we know must be a cyborg. There is a man with him holding a lantern.

Stubbs looks up and nods at us sadly as though he'd been expecting us to turn up at some point. 'Jolly bad luck, that,' he says. 'You got so close, too. Honestly, those of us who were left were cheering our hearts out. You couldn't have been more than what, 20 to 30 meters from the jump point?'

The guy holding the lantern nods and says, 'Yeah about that.'

'But, as you can see, we lost power right at that moment. Such a shame. You had such a decent innings, too, all things considered, didn't you, eh?'

Sparky, frowning deeply, cuts her eyes to mine. Stubbs doesn't sound at all like himself.

'But it's not over yet,' I say. 'We just need to find a way to get back in.'

Either because he doesn't hear me, which I doubt, or because he doesn't want to hear me – more likely, Stubbs doesn't say anything and quietly resumes what he was doing, namely, unscrewing the top of the cyborg's head. A spray of light-blue light spills out into the darkness as he pulls its brain out and holds it up in front of him.

'Are you all who's left?' Sparky asks. 'At the facility?'

'Mmm?' he mutters, without looking at her. 'Oh, no, no, no.

We took some casualties, of course, and not an inconsiderable number either, but we managed to get most of the people to safety once it was clear that the main targets of the attack were the Command and Power centres.'

'But what about those stuck in the game? Did they also get released?' I ask, hopefully.

Stubbs, about to plunge his index and middle fingers into the centre of the glowing brain, looks up at me. His expression is a mixture of surprise and disappointment.

'Why ever would you have thought that? Surely, it's already been explained to you both that such a thing can't happen until either the AI has been defeated, or until it decides to release them itself for whatever reason... Like that girl... what was her name?'

'Ruth' I say.

'Yes, Ruth. In any case, as our latest intel has confirmed beyond doubt that it's feeding on them, using their neural links to turbo charge its own cognitive powers, I can't see that happening any time soon, can you?'

'I just thought that maybe they'd also gotten lucky,' I reply, regretting I asked. 'Like me.'

'No – I'm afraid not.'

Hawkesbury Stubbs stares down at the puddle of glowing liquid goo which has formed on the floor under the brain he's holding. He pushes his finger into it and then examines it.

'What do you mean, you got lucky?' he asks.

His voice is slow and thoughtful, like he's trying to make sense of something but he's not quite sure what yet.

I tell him what happened. How I'd been running, which he knew, because he'd already said that he'd been watching, and then how I'd seen the fireball racing towards me and then, *bam*, I was suddenly back in the facility.

'*It was my third life* – I should've been locked into the game too. But it's like I fell through it or something, which means that we might have another chance if we can get back in.'

'That's right,' Sparky adds. 'There's a logical possibility that, as far as the game is concerned, Oli is neither dead nor alive… Well, a chance at least.'

'A chance,' Stubbs repeats, rolling the brain around in his hands, dripping glowing goo all over himself. 'Neither dead nor alive.'

'Exactly,' Sparky continues. 'I mean, I don't know for sure, because I've never heard of anything like this, but if, at the moment he fell out the game, the database logged him as "unknown" it could – *it might* – mean that he'll be able to get back in again because the program needs to check his status. If it then marks him as still being alive, it *should* let him continue.'

'But won't that just cause an error?' I ask.

'No, not necessarily.'

Stubbs fixes his gaze on Sparky and for several very long moments stares at her. I can almost hear the cogs and wheels of his brain turning, trying to make the necessary connections.

'And you really think there might be a chance?' he asks, finally.

'I do – *maybe*,' Sparky replies.

'And what about Oliver's headset? Without the portal and code, it'd be pointless to even try.'

Sparky nods again. 'It would be.'

'And do we know if it's still working at least?'

'We will in about two seconds,' I cry out, and I sprint back to the room, panicking that I don't remember seeing them.

My headset *is* still working. It still has the portal and the code functions in the display and on the gloves. They are very faint, but they are there, which explains why I hadn't noticed them. When we lost power, they must have gone into reduced power mode or something. Grabbing them, I run back.

'They're here!' I call out, before anyone has a chance to ask. 'It means that we'll get another shot at it if we can find a way in.'

Hawkesbury Stubbs, who had been starting to look and

sound more optimistic, like we might have a chance after all, suddenly looks anything but again.

'What is it?' Sparky and I ask at the exact same time.

But Stubbs stands there shaking his head. 'Look around you,' he says. 'Everything's been destroyed... No comms, no power.'

I say: 'But the monitors in that room we were in – they're still blinking. So that must mean that not all of the power is dead, right?'

'And, also, aren't these places supposed to be built with backup generators and fail-safe connections and stuff?' says Sparky.

Sparky's face drops.

My face drops seeing their faces and suddenly it's all feeling like this really is the end. That it's game over.

Then, something miraculous happens.

Stubbs cries out, slapping himself hard on the forehead with the palm of his hand. '*You complete and utter, dithering Muppet! Where is your head these days!?*'

He turns and looks at us like he's just found the answer to the secret of life, the universe and everything.

'*The PM's connection!*'

Sucking in a deep breath, Hawkesbury Stubbs tells us that the Prime Minister has got his own secret satellite. It's so secret in fact that there are barely a handful of people on the planet that know about it. Apparently, the American president has the same, only in his case, he's got five of them. But that, Stubbs says, 'is another story.'

'But there is a problem,' he says, taking a phone out of his pocket. It's not his normal phone. This one is bigger and has a flip-out antenna on the side of it. 'There's no way we'll be able to use it without getting the PM to approve it personally.'

'But why wouldn't he want to help us?' I ask. 'I mean, it's the only chance we've got left to stop the AI.'

'Because it will effectively mean that he'll lose his own ability to communicate with other heads of state, the Army, Air Force and so on.'

'OK, but there's not going to be much to talk to anyone about soon, is there?' Sparky says glibly. 'Unless of course he just wants to keep being told how bad things keep getting?'

Stubbs nods at her as he keys in a number.

Chapter 24

'You alright?' Sparky asks, as I stop and lean against the wall of the stairwell.

We've just climbed up 15 floors worth of stairs. There are five more still to go. But I'm not stopping because I'm out of breath – I *am* out of breath, but that's not the reason. The reason is that I keep getting hit by feelings of really bad guilt. It's like, one minute I am OK, then the next I go all cold and clammy and start sweating, suddenly remembering how lucky I've been not to have ended up stuck in the game like everyone else; and I start seeing the faces of my mum and Logan and guys like G85 and FG, Shadow_Deemon and all those others who'd made it their missions to try to help me, to try to protect me. And for what?

For nothing – *so far*!

I have to keep telling myself this: 'For nothing – *so far*!' Because while I do, it feels like there is still hope. And if I stop, I'm afraid I might drown under the weight of all these feelings.

Sparky takes my hand and pulls me on. She feels strong for a girl.

'C'mon, Stubbs told us to get up top and wait for him there.'

The Prime Minister had agreed to let us use his personal satellite, but only on the condition he could be there to oversee what he's now coined the 'battle of the millennium'. The funny part, or not so funny part, depending on how you look at it, is that, according to Stubbs, the PM has it in his head that there is going to be a small army of gamers and their Hack Supports ready to bring this 'battle of the millennium' to a successful conclusion, and not just Sparky and me. Stubbs hadn't misled the PM in any way. The Prime Minister had imagined it all himself. But when we'd asked Stubbs why he'd not tried to correct him and tell him the truth of the situation, he'd simply replied that it was generally a bad idea to weigh the PM down with *extraneous* details, especially at the moment. It was hard to understand if he was being sarcastic or serious. Either way, I wasn't looking forward to being there when the PM found out.

At the top of the stairs, we stand aside to allow more troopers, still wearing their VR headsets, to be stretchered out first. There has been a constant stream of them all the way up, and I have learned that even when there is no direct connection between the gamer's headsets and the AI, the neural lock puts them into a kind of holding loop, which waits for a connection to be restored. This apparently is why they have to continue to wear them regardless of whether they are connected or not.

When they have passed by, Sparky and I exit the stairwell into the hallway of the manor house.

Oak panelled, the hallway is adorned with the portraits of noble men and women who'd lived centuries ago. In their heavy, ornate frames, dressed in their finery and painted in the styles of their day, it's hard not to wonder what they would have made of all of this. Would they even have been able to understand what an AI or a computer was? I'd once heard that the greatest invention of the sixteenth century was the scissors.

Finding that the heavy front doors have been bolted shut, we leave through a guarded side door and step out into the bright afternoon sunshine. After the cool, damp atmosphere of being underground for so long, the sun's warmth greets us like an old friend. The air smells of freshly cut grass and my mood jumps immediately.

'Oi! Turner!'

Speaking of *old friends* – that voice doesn't belong to one of them. My mood does a swift about turn and nosedives.

'Screwed that up nicely, didn't you, eh – spaz! I mean, what were they thinking, relying on a monkey like you? Too bad they didn't ask me first. I'd have set them straight about what a spanner you are.'

Porky Perkins steps out of the middle of one of the groups milling about on the lawn. If ever there was a person guaranteed to kill any good mood at any time, it was him.

'And what's with that mum of yours? Talk about scraping the bottom of the barrel, trying to find you a replacement dad.'

Several of his group snigger. Porky catches sight of the VR set I'm holding. Stubbs has instructed me not to go anywhere without it.

'Give us a look, then,' he says, holding out a hand, as though he really expects me to give them to him. 'Rumour has it there's a secret weapon on it.'

Porky throws a look at his mates.

'Course, if it's true, then that just makes you a double loser, doesn't it, Turner, 'cause I don't see that we're winning this war, do you?'

He pretends to make a swipe for it, and I jump backwards, making him grin.

'Then again, maybe it's broken. Maybe you sat on it and now you're too embarrassed to tell the truth? C'mon. *Give it here.* We deserve to know what we're getting stuck in comas for, don't we. Do you really have a secret weapon in there or are you just making it up?'

A snide grin appears on Porky's face as he takes a step forward. I take a step backwards.

'Maybe he wants us to lose so that he can really become Razer's son?' pipes up Denzel, who's unfortunately still around.

'*Hey*, that's a point!' Porky nods vociferously. 'C'mon, Turner, prove you're not a traitor and set the record straight once and for all – in front of all these troopers – right here, right now. Do you have a secret weapon or not?'

'Back off,' I shout, as this time he lunges forward, making a genuine effort to grab it.

'Hey! Moron, bog off and leave him alone!' Sparky hisses, stepping in front of me.

For a second Porky looks shocked, scared a little, even. Remembering though that he's performing to a crowd, he pushes her with such force that she goes flying into another group, who curse her and tell her to pick on someone in her own weight class. Pleased with himself, Porky dives at me. There's no way out now.

Sparky is quickly back on her feet, and I manage to toss her my headset at the last moment before Porky floors me. He tries to get me in a choke hold. I elbow him hard in the stomach and manage to wriggle free. I stand a better chance on my feet than rolling around under that giant turd.

'You're dead, you hear me, Turner? You and that tart of yours. You'd better run while you still can!'

'Yeah, you'd love that, wouldn't you, Perkins. Got used to that at school, didn't you? Picking on all the little kids who couldn't fight back. Felt good about yourself, watching them run away, didn't you? But here's the thing. The only way to beat a bully is to "BEAT" a bully. I've done it once and I'll be happy to do it now!'

'Unfortunately, *once again*, there's no time for that, Mr Turner. The PM's helicopter is going to be here in about 30 seconds. So that's precisely the amount of time you've got to wipe the grass stains off your cheek and make it look like you haven't just been rolling around in the bushes.'

Stubbs!

I glance at Porky, who's backed off quickly and returned to his group. For a moment our eyes meet, but he looks away first.

'You alright?' I ask Sparky, as we follow Stubbs towards where the helicopter is going to land.

'Of course. Why wouldn't I be?'

'I don't know. He gave you a pretty serious shove, if you ask me.'

'What? That?' she laughs. 'That was nothing. I told you, I have three brothers.'

There isn't just one helicopter but five of them in total. They all appear at the same time from behind an area of woodland. In a matter of only seconds, it feels like we've been caught in the jaws of a hurricane – the downforce of so many rotor blades whipping up the dust and gravel, and we have to use our hands to protect our faces.

Through a gap in my fingers I make out that the five helicopters are made up of two Apache helicopters (which look amazing), one Army troop carrier, one sleek-looking black one (I assume that this has the PM in it), and the fifth one is an enormous transporter carrying what looks like a metal box about the size of a bus with several satellite dishes attached to its side. The transporter moves across the lawn and sets its load down close to the house. But this is not before the troop carrier has landed and soldiers have speedily moved people out of the way.

The Prime Minister isn't in the passenger helicopter as I'd suspected. To everyone's surprise, the PM gets out of one of the Apaches, but not before a photographer has taken up position ready to capture the precise moment that he leaps out of its cockpit, pulls off his headset and looks ready for action. Sparky and I have been told not to move until we are called, and watch nervously as Stubbs rushes forward to greet him. They shake hands and Stubbs leads him over to where we are standing.

'Prime Minister, let me introduce you to Mr Oliver Turner, and Miss Sanders, AKA Sparky. They will be our core operatives on this final mission.'

The Prime Minister, his floppy hair waving wildly about in the still turbulent air, smiles and shakes our hands firmly.

'An honour to meet you, Mr Turner, Miss Sparky. Your bravery will not go unnoticed, I can assure you. Your country is very grateful for your service.'

Patting us each on the shoulder, he turns to Stubbs.

'Now, Hawkesbury, what about the rest of the Army? Perhaps we ought to make it priority for me to address them in advance of the attack, what do you think? Where are they, already down below?'

I catch Sparky sniggering to herself. The PM still has no idea.

'Yes, sir, now, about that…' says Stubbs, pulling the PM to one side.

Although we can't hear what's being said, the look on the Prime Minister's face goes from ready and raring to go, to shock, to anger, and to something strongly resembling despair.

'And you're absolutely sure that it can only be carried out by this *boy* and that *girl*?' the PM says, a little too loudly. 'Then, God help us all, Stubbs. Because, if this goes belly up, then the only option we're going to have left is to switch the whole world's electricity off – and I mean that literally. It'll be a return to the Middle Ages.'

'Yes, Prime Minister. I'm quite serious,' says Stubbs.

The PM becomes weirdly distracted by a number of creases in his dishevelled suit, and tugs and pulls at them for a few moments. Then, as though realising that it is going to look the same whatever he does to it, he waves everyone towards the manor.

'Let's get this show on the road then, shall we,' he says emphatically.

The time required to get the satellite connection set up is not expected to be more than 20 minutes. And while engineers set about laying cables and doing whatever it is that they need to do, the Prime Minister's personal photographer swings into action.

The PM has introduced him as a vital part of the documenting of this historic moment. Of course, Sparky and I both know that this was really supposed to be about photos of the PM standing in front of an army of gamers in green suits and encouraging them on to victory. Instead, they must make do with us. And even though we both have the feeling that he's already decided that our chances are pretty much zilch, zero and nada combined, there is always an outside chance that we might pull it off. And this means that he needs to have the photos and therefore the proof of his absolute belief in us ready, just in case.

After a few photos of the PM surveying the damage caused by the cyborg attack to the other side of the house, we are taken up the wide, polished wooden staircase to the first floor of the manor, and into a large room which has been mostly cleared of furniture and which is being set up with monitors and equipment. There among the contrast of the old paintings of landscapes in their big frames on the walls and the modern stacks of flashing computer equipment on the floor, we make out a load of photos with the PM where he looks as though he is explaining to us how the satellite control unit works and pointing at various blank monitors as though he is telling us *the plan*. (I suppose they will Photoshop something onto the screens later.) To finish off, there is a set of photographs of him inspecting my VR headset and us shaking hands as he hands it back to me.

If we do manage to pull this off and if I can free my mum, then I know that this photo of me shaking hands with the Prime Minister will take pride of place on our photo shelf. But it's not because it's me with *this* PM – I don't think my mum likes this one. But because it's me being trusted to do something really important. The other photo that will be there next to it is the one of Sparky and me, arms around each other's shoulders, showing peace signs, which we'd asked the photographer to take for us.

'Right, it's time, we've got an up link,' says Stubbs, hurrying into the room. 'Prime Minister, if you'd like to take your seat over here, I'll have the cook sort something out for you, if you're hungry. You two, you're green to go.'

'*Foooooooooood*,' Sparky leans over and whispers. 'Don't know about you, but I don't remember anyone offering us anything? I'm so hungry, I think I'm digesting myself.'

'Yeah, and me,' I reply, my stomach rumbling as soon as the word *food* is mentioned.

The PM, who's been conferring with the photographer, comes back over for a last couple of photos standing next to us, as Sparky and I get set up.

'I bet this is just like playing in your rooms back home, eh?' he says, grinning for the camera. 'Now, seeing that you're about ready, I think it might be appropriate to offer one final thought before we start... Obviously, far be it for me to want to heap more pressure onto the both of you, *but* I feel certain that you'll be wanting to know that the *whole world* is behind you in this endeavour. In fact, you can be sure that we will all be holding our breath in anticipation of what I am sure will be your *absolute victory*.'

With a firm nod of his head and another pat on our shoulders and another photo, the Prime Minister goes and sits in one of the deep, faded green leather chairs at the back of the room next to Stubbs.

'Yeah, just like my mega-sized room back in my mega-sized mansion house,' Sparky says in a low voice. 'And why do people always have to do that? You know, "I don't want to worry you – I don't want to pressure you, BUT!" I mean, everyone knows that this just makes the stress a million times worse, right?'

'Right,' I reply. 'Where is you mega-sized mansion anyway?'

I realise I have no idea where she lives, and I don't want to think about what the Prime Minister has just said.

'Not far from Reading – which is in Berkshire. What about you?' she asks.

'Not far from Slough,' I reply.

'Almost neighbours then,' she jokes. 'Well, in the *big* scheme of things.'

'Yeah, what's an hour when it takes millions of years to cross a galaxy, right?'

'Right,' she giggles. 'Ready? Stressed yet?'

'More than you can know.'

'OK. Here we go… loading.'

The construct loads in, and for several seconds I have no idea what I'm supposed to do next. Everything is different. There are no weapons, no skins, nothing at all for me to select.

'Sparky?' I whisper. 'Do you see this?'

'I see it,' she replies sounding equally confused. 'It's all changed for me too. Before I was able to see beyond the construct to where you'd be entering. Now, I can't see anything... But do you see a play button at least?' she asks, after pausing for a moment.

'Yeah, but it's in a completely different place.'

'OK, good. That has to mean that there will be something waiting for us when you press it.'

'Yeah,' I mumble, sucking in a deep breath. 'That's what I'm afraid of.'

Chapter 25

There is no falling from the sky this time. There is no blacking out. I hit the play button and appear in the middle of a smoking, dust-filled wasteland. An apocalyptic nightmare, full of the skeletons of shattered buildings and vast undulating mountains of rubble. It's all that is left of New Razer City.

'The drones!' Sparky cries suddenly, making me jump and look up expectantly. I scan the dark grey sky, thick with angry, writhing cloud, until I realise that it's not what she meant.

'This must've been what all those drones were for. Razer was ready to take out his entire city just to try to stop you. Which explains why the construct and everything is different now – the computer must have decided that part of the game, at least, is over.'

'But then, how are we here?' I ask. 'If it thinks it's over.'

'Do you remember I told you that a flag might have been created in the database because you fell through it? Well, this could be it – a back door to allow it to check if it made an error or not. Either that or it's just another part of the program – like a continuation. I mean, maybe the game can't end until the AI does. Honestly, it's hard to say because no one seems to know what the programmers created or what the AI itself might have changed.'

'But if the game *has* ended, won't it mean that the portal and the node will also be closed?' I ask, catching a glimpse of my reflection in a mass of twisted steel. I see that I'm wearing my green flight suit. I look like myself.

'I don't know. Not necessarily. The access node wasn't part of the game. It was behind it. And as far as I now understand, there are other add-ons, other modules to the program. It's way more than just a game. It's like a total virtual interface… You really do look like you, don't you?'

'Yeah, it feels weird not being in a trooper skin. How far are we from the jump point?'

'About 200 meters straight in front of you.'

I break into a run. I don't want to be here a moment longer than I need to and I am desperate to find out if the portal is still working. But I don't get far before Sparky tells me to stop.

'*Oli*, something's just appeared on the jump line!'

'Razer?' I ask in alarm, skidding to a halt. I can't see that far ahead of me.

'Impossible to say for sure, only, the signal looks different from his, at least from what I've seen before. Sorry, I know that doesn't help much.'

Noticing the remains of a broken staircase jutting out of the rubble and thinking that I might be able to get a better view from the top, I creep up it cautiously. It seems to me that there are only two likely possibilities as to what we'll find on the jump line. It is either going to be Razer, because he's already detected that I'm back, or a Sentinel. Neither of which is good.

At the top I take a moment to scan the ruins behind me. I don't want to be shot in the back, especially now that I am unarmed. Not seeing anything, I peer over. Through the haze of dust and smoke I make out the form of a girl.

No way! I almost cry out as the air clears a little. 'Sparky – it looks like the girl from the concert. The one that came over and talked to me.'

Sparky curses loudly. 'That's *bad*, Oli. Bad with a serious number of cherries on top. It means that Razer already knows you're here.'

Sparky is right, of course. It has to mean that.

'Is there any way to get around her?' I ask.

'I doubt it. And even if there was, she'd probably just pop up again somewhere else.'

'*Right then,*' I say, and jump down from the steps into the rubble. I pick my way along what was once a street to where she is standing. It *is* the girl from the concert. When I get close enough, I see that she has been crying. Her eyes are red and puffy, and tears have left tracks down her grimy cheeks. There are rips too in her clothing and her hair is matted and caked in dust.

'Hi. Are you OK?' I ask her, feeling foolish because she doesn't look OK. But I have no idea what else to say.

The girl shakes her head sadly.

'Everything's gone, Oliver. *Everything* – my home, my family. All of it.'

'I'm sorry,' I reply, freaked out by the fact that she's just said my name.

The girl looks at me angrily.

'It's *too late* for *sorry*. All you had to do was join us. *You* could have saved everyone. Big Daddy R would have welcomed you into his house as one of his own and we could've become friends. But now… *now* you're just a *murderer.* All of this is on *you.*'

'On *me*? A *murderer*?' I repeat, shaking my head. 'You know, right, that he wants to sacrifice me?'

The girl wipes her eyes with her sleeve and stares at me her blankly.

'The son of a god, like all of us, Oli, must be helped to find the righteous path. 'Cause, without sacrifice there can be no redemption. And without redemption, how can a soul ever be pure?'

'OK – that's *not freaky,* right?' Sparky comments. 'Anyone

want to remind her that she's a simulation and doesn't actually have a soul?'

I don't, but even if I'd wanted to – which for some reason I didn't, I'm not sure she'd have heard me. As soon as the girl had finished talking, her head had slumped forwards and she'd started making a horrible, guttural, choking sound.

'*God damn it, Oli!*' she cries out suddenly – her head snapping sharply back up again. 'Why does everything have to be about you? *Why-does-everything-always-got-to-be-about-you, son?* You know how it makes your mama sad when you get like this. You're becoming such a selfish boy. I mean, just look at you, comin' into my house, and bringing with you all these thoughts about killing. Hell, I even think you just had yourself some *impure* thoughts about Elyse here.'

'Impure thoughts!?' I cry out. There is no doubt who I am talking to now. 'I've never had impure thoughts about her.'

'C'mon now, boy. That ain't nothin' to be ashamed of. I know she's got the hots for you.'

'*Oli!*' cries Sparky.

'Now, why don't you make your mamma proud and do what you know you got to do. It'll be such a nice surprise for her when she learns that you're no longer that selfish boy that makes her blush with shame.'

'*Oli!*' cries Sparky, again. 'What are you doing!? Look

behind her!'

But it's hard to want to look behind her. It's hard to want to see farther than Elyse's strangely glowing eyes, and her smile which feels so tender and warm, so enticing – and, well, so *everything.*

'Oli!!!'

I have only the very vaguest understanding of a wooden scaffold appearing. Of the hangman's noose dangling in the middle of it. Of the sign which reads: *Curious about swinging? Come give it a go today.*

Somewhere, getting farther and farther away, the voice of a mad woman is shouting and cursing at me. The voice is screaming something about a button… something about pressing a button… something about a jump line. I wonder if she's talking about my button… *Wasn't I supposed to press my button on the jump line?*

Chapter 26

The sound like a bell ringing is distant but it's *there*. I press my ear to the wall so I can hear it better. This place where I have ended up is like a weird cube shaped box with walls that look vaguely plastic. Worse, they keep flickering as though there are a load of faulty lights inside them. I am pretty sure it's not the node though, because there isn't anything else here: no computer, no terminal, no doors, no way to input a code of any sort. I even tried saying the code outload. But it is where I'd gone after I'd managed to press the portal button, and there is no way out.

Honestly, I don't understand what happened back on the jump line. It was like Razer had been using Elyse to try to hypnotize me or something. I mean, *how is that even possible?* It was like I'd turned into some kind of lovesick Sixth Former at school. Seriously, the ways I've seen them looking at each other sometimes is, well… Actually, what am I saying… It's a bit like how Logan stares at Ruth when he thinks no one's looking. But it had all happened in front of Sparky and Stubbs and the *Prime Minister*!

Speaking of Sparky, I have lost contact with her. It's been

hours already and, realising that we must be having problems again, I'd called out (in the real world) and told her what had happened. In response she had touched my shoulder to let me know that she'd heard me. It sucks that my headset doesn't have an external input like I'd seen that some of them had, because then she'd have been able to connect to me that way.

And so, for what'd felt like a long time, I'd sat there in the flickering box waiting for something to happen. The more I'd sat and thought about everything, the more certain I became that it was no coincidence. I was 99% sure that it is *exactly* where Razer had wanted me to be and that he'd put me here himself. No prizes for guessing that he could have re-routed the portal somehow to make it happen.

The thought that I had blundered so easily into his trap had then started me wondering why he was taking so long to come and *sacrifice* me. He had me where he wanted me, why not come and finish the job? *And* that's when it hit me – a total brainwave. I realised that unless he had an audience to do it in front of, he probably wasn't going to bother. I mean, hadn't everything he'd done so far always been in front of an audience? Knowing Razer, he'll be planning some sort of major TV show which he'll make my mum participate in and… I suddenly knew what I needed to do to get out… *I needed* to give him a reason to take me out. To *call him out* – to make him want to show me up in public. Only, whatever I was going to do I knew that I needed to do it quickly because we were running out of time.

It was a risky move of course, but it wasn't like I had a whole lot of choices. I'm not even sure that I can remove my headset again without ending up in a Gamer Coma. So, unless I wanted to be a rabbit stuck in a trap waiting to be eaten, I was going to have to try something.

And *this* is what I have been doing: I have been shouting and swearing at him. Baiting him. I don't think I have ever called anyone a 'butt face' in my entire life, but once I'd started, all these names had flooded into my head out of nowhere and I'd just shouted them:

'Hey! H*ey Razer! Hey, butt face! Hey, loser…!* Hey, Jive Chicken brain! I'm ready! Come get me! Or are you afraid!? Hey, Muppet Face! Hey, dung breath! You afraid that everyone's gonna see me kick your butt, or what?'

It was actually hard to keep shouting all this, but I'd kept going until my throat started to get hoarse. My real throat, that is, the one back at the manor. I tried not to think about what Stubbs and the Prime Minister must have been thinking. I'm glad I couldn't see their faces.

Then, something had started to happen.

That sound like a bell had begun ringing and getting closer.

Now, listening to it with my ear pressed hard against the flickering wall, I can already hear other sounds too – there's a voice, there's cheering… It's all around me…

"Laaaaaadiiiiies and geeeeeentlemen, brooooooooos and soooooooooo's of the world…' calls out a very excited, distinguished-sounding male voice. 'Boooy, do we have a treat in store for you this evening. *You better believe it!* Tonight, coming live from Razer's Palace Arena, *or what's left of it anyway*… IIIIIITT'sss FFFIIIIIGGHHHTT NIIIGGHT!'

Rapturous cheering.

Fight night? Has it worked? Have I managed to get Razer's attention? My heart starts to pound in my chest.

'That's right, that's right! Not only that, but a little bird told me earlier that tonight we're gonna have with us, two *very* special guests. IN FACT, they are members of the VERY SAME FAMILY. *CAN YOU BELIEVE YOUR EARS!?* That right! We're gonna have ourselves a FAAAAAMILY AFFAIR!!'

The crowd is going wild.

'A BELOVED LONG SUFFERING FATHER, AND YES – YOU GUESSED IT – HIS DISRESPECTFUL, RENEGADE SON. NOW, I ASK YOU – COULD IT GET ANY BETTER THAN THIS!?

'*But wait! What's this I am being told?*

'WEEEEEELLLL, IF I HADN'T HAVE HEARD IT WITH MY VERY OWN EARS, I'D NEVER HAVE BELIEVED IT. LADIES AND GENTLEMEN, I HAVE JUST THIS SECOND BEEN INFORMED THAT TONIGHT W-E A-R-E G-O-I-N-G T-O B-E P-L-A-Y-I-N-G DEEEEEATH MAAAATCH!!!'

The crowd goes insane.

'So, c'mon, what are we waiting for? LEEEETTT'SSS, MEET THE CONTENDERS!!'

And suddenly, there I am, under the dark grey, swirling sky, amongst the rubble of New Razer City. I am standing in an area of open ground. On three sides, as though it'd sprung from the twisted, blackened concrete and steel of the very ruins themselves, is a gargantuan stadium that rises up to tower block heights. At its base are forty or fifty long rows of seats and thousands of simulations in full animation – screaming and shouting. I can make out faces on the higher levels beyond these seats, but they appear still and lifeless.

In the middle of this open patch of ground, dressed in black tie attire, with long swept back silver hair gathered into a ponytail, is a clean-shaven elderly-looking man, holding a microphone. Ignoring me, he turns to face a line of steps that lead down from a section of the stadium.

'Tooooooooooooooniiiiiight, in the red corner, we have, the

undisputed world number one for everything and anything you could ever dream about being number one for – yes, that's right – ladies and gentlesims – our spiritual saviour and dope MC – my daddy and yours – MR BIG DADDY R!!!'

The crowd leaps up as Razer, seen on giant screens on each side of the stadium, appears at the top of the stairs. Wearing his black cape, this time with cold steel spikes running dinosaur-like down the back of it, I notice that underneath he has on a thick black vest, cargo pants and heavy black boots.

Seeing the camera, Razer makes a peace sign with one hand and raises up a very large club with the other.

The crowd roar their approval.

Enormous cyborg bouncers in black and wearing *Big Daddy R* T-shirts hold up what look like boxing belts. The screaming and cheering are so loud, I have to put my hands over my ears. The song 'Eye of the Tiger' starts to blast out and Razer half jogs, half dances down the steps and enters the arena, bouncing and punching the air.

The announcer, a big grin on his face, raises his hands to quiet them down.

'*How much love have we got in the house tonight!?*' he cries.

'*Sooooo muuuccchhh!!!*' the crowd screams back in unison.

'Soooo muuuccch!' he repeats. 'Nooowww, LET'S TAKE

A LOOK WHO WE HAVE IN THE BLLLLLUUUEEEE CORNERRR!'

The crowd starts booing.

'IN THE BLUE CORNER WE HAVE THE WORLD'S NUMBER ONE – UNDISPUTED – 13 YEARS A WINNER – UNGRATEFUL SON, KILLER OF SIMS, THUG AND TERRORIST – MR OOOOLLLLLLIVER TUUUUUURNER!!'

The air fills with even more booing, and my stomach drops as Razer steps forward.

The crowd goes quiet.

'Hey there, kiddo,' he says. 'Missed ya!'

He gestures in a jokey way to the crowd, and they burst into fits of laughter.

'Oli, Oli, Oli,' he says, shaking his head sadly. 'Man! I thought that when me and your ma decided that I was gonna become your new pappy, that all my days were gonna be peas and gravy – do you feel me, son? But, you know what?' He pretends to lower his voice. 'All she does is nag, nag, nag. Every day it's like: Razer – don't you be spendin' all your time cruising 'n' hanging with your besties, 'cause, my boy, Oli, he's gonna need a man around to show him how to grow up right... Razer, don't you be swearing all the time neither 'cause my boy Oli, he's just gonna grow up doing the same things and that ain't cool in polite "*société*"… And, Razer, honey, can I have some money to get my hair and my nails done?'

Razer makes like he's going to knock himself on the head with his own club.

'…Geeez, Louise! It's no wonder that you grew up like you did – all crooked 'n' stuff. A man can only be nagged so long before he starts to break – you know what I'm sayin'?'

'You leave my mum alone!' I growl angrily. 'She's not even here to defend herself.'

Playing to the crowd, Razar makes a gesture as though he's surprised that I thought that. 'Why, sure she is, Oli… Wave hi to Mama!'

My mum's face suddenly appears on the big screens. She's sitting somewhere in the crowd. I gasp. Where her mouth should have been, there is a zip, and it's been zipped shut.

'Oh, yeah, 'bout that. I had to get that installed just to get some relief. Uff! I tell ya!'

The crowd goes into hysterics.

I have to repeat over and over to myself that it's not real before I lose the plot completely.

'Anyways, enough of this chit chat. *Why* do you always make me wanna chit and chat and chat 'n' chit when you're around? Especially when we got some things to finish.'

Razer picks up his club and throws it over his shoulder.

'So, we gonna play a game that I like to call "Death, Kill, Who's you Daddy Now, Son?" Aaannnd, the rules are pretty simple. You be you and I will be me and we fight to the death, best out of three. Whoever wins, wins, and whoever loses goes down together with his nagging mama.'

Hysterical laughter.

'So, as you can see, I heard all your shouting and crying like a baby. I heard all your "*I'm gonna* kick your ass, Razer, but please, sir, first you gotta help get me out o' here."'

The hysterical laughter continues.

'So here you are, boy. Here's your chance. All your lives have been reset. No neural lock for you if you wanna unplug yourself and run away like a bambino. How does that sound, eh? Nobody can say that Razer ain't as fair as fair can be.'

The announcer applauds Razer enthusiastically, and he steps back into the middle of the arena. He raises his microphone. 'CONTESTANTS, SELECT YOUR WEAPONS, PLEASE!'

What! What weapons? I cry out, spinning round frantically, looking for a rack or a container or something. But I can't see anything, anywhere.

Glancing at Razer, I see that he's given his club to one of his cyborg entourage and is suddenly brandishing a 'bo' – a kind of fighting stick. I know this because I had a friend whose

313

father brought him one back from a trip to Japan.

I have no idea what I'm supposed to do now.

'Well, well, would you look at that: Oliver Turner, over there in the blue corner, has decided to engage in mortal combat with precisely nothing,' booms the commentator... 'Brave or just plain stupid? We're gonna find out in just a second!'

He turns to the camera and it comes closer to him.

'Let this be a lesson to all you kids watching at home – life is a series of choices. Good choices make good things happen. Bad choices? Well, stay tuned and see for yourself.'

He winks as the camera moves back out. Then he raises his microphone up higher than his mouth, tilts his head upwards and cries:

'AAARREEE WEEE RREADY TOOO RUUUMMMBBBLLLLEEEE??????'

Razer raises his right hand and gives a thumbs-up. Nobody asks me.

'*FIGHT!*' the commentator yells.

I can't move. All I can do is watch Razer jump and spin and then jump and spin again, like some kind of blurry caped ninja, and, before I understand anything about anything, his bo cracks me on the underside of my chin and sends me flying into the crowd. The crowd then pushes me back towards the ring, but not before I catch sight of Elyse. Seeing me looking, she smiles and waves and shouts, 'We love you, Oli!' Which feels totally random.

'*Well now*,' says the commentator, as Razer returns to his corner. '*What* have we got here then? Mr Turner – are you playing with us? Not only do you refuse to fight with a weapon, but you refuse to fight at all.'

He pretends to cover his microphone.

'Oliver, between you me and this crowd of millions here,' he whispers loudly. 'Is this because you've got daddy issues?'

'*What?*' I spit. 'I *don't* have daddy issues. My dad was a good man and I know that he loved me. My real dad died in an accident. Razer isn't my father, he's just a sad bully!'

The stadium falls silent. The commentator, along with every pair of eyes in audience, turns to Razer.

'*Teenagers!*' Razer shrugs jokingly. 'What can I tell ya'll – you can't live with 'em and you always wondering why you had 'em.'

The crowd explodes with delight.

'*Oli!* There's a weapons button on your gloves… Also, you do realise, don't you, that you're playing a version of classic *Mortal Kombat*, right?'

'*Sparky!!!* What? Mortal who!?'

Chapter 27

I have to bite my tongue to stop myself screaming Sparky's name out loud.

'*It's about time,*' I hiss.

'What's that supposed to mean? "It's about time"? You have no idea how hard it's been to find you – the whole world's been searching.'

'The whole world?'

'Every hacker, every computer nerd, basically anyone with a computer that still has a connection.'

'But I told you where I was. You heard me right, telling you?'

'Oh yes,' she chuckles, we've heard *every* word that you've been saying. But it didn't make it any easier to find you.'

'*Every word? Great.*'

'Yeah, you should have seen the PM's face. But there's no time to go into that now – Oli, quickly, select the same weapon as Razer. It'll give you a chance at least. Oh, and by the way, this is being broadcast around the world on every TV channel.'

'But how? I can't see anything,' I say, trying to focus. That part about the world watching isn't helping.

'Crap!' Sparky exclaims, 'What about now?'

A new button called MK has appeared on my right hand, and I hurriedly press it. Instead of being presented with racks of skins and weapons like in the other game, this time there is a grid with ten weapons on the left side, half of which I don't recognise, and descriptions of them on the right. Spying a lever-action rifle and thinking that it's bound to be way better than a stick, I pick it. A sign appears reading *Selected* and the grid fades.

'Oli, noooo, I told you to choose the bo stick, like Razer has.'

'But now I've got a gun. I can shoot him without getting close.'

It's hard to tell what kind of noise Sparky makes at that moment, because the commentator had just screamed 'Fight!'

Razer jumps high into the air and starts to spin. Certain that he's going to do the same Ninja trick, I start firing as quickly as I can. His movements, though, are a complete blur, and before I get a chance to aim properly, he is suddenly right next to me, about to crack me over the head with his bo. I manage to jam my rifle in the way at the very last second. Not about to give me time to counter, he does a double summersault over my head and comes down behind me, jabbing me hard in the back and propelling me forwards into the centre of the area. I land flat on my face.

'*Razer – Razer – Razer!*' chants the crowd.

He stops for a moment to acknowledge them with a raise of his hands. Seeing my chance, I aim and shoot. The bullet deflects off him, causing one of the crowd to light up.

'Oli! He's wearing some kind of armour. Listen, you need to do exactly what I tell you, OK?'

'Fine – but tell me quickly.'

'Jump, jump, front kick!' Sparky cries.

'You *what?*'

'Don't ask – just DO!'

'What, just jump into the air – just like that?'

'*Yes – quickly!*'

Recalling how I'd been able to run and jump farther by waving my arms around in the other game, I don't argue. I jump (more like a high hop) twice and stick out my right front leg, as though doing a kick. A second later I launch forward, frozen in a kicking pose, with such speed that Razer has no time to react. I kick him in the groin, sending him stumbling backwards.

The crowd gasps.

'*Bullseye!*' cries Sparky. 'Oli – quick… step… step… side kick.'

I do it without thinking, and as fast as I can. I shoot forwards again. This time Razer is ready and blocks my move. I crumple to the floor at his feet.

'*Now!* Shoot him in the head,' screams Sparky as he leans over me.

I hit the trigger, and Razer flies backwards.

A glance up at the stadium screens shows:

> *Big Daddy R: 1*
>
> *Oli and Oli's Mama: 1*

There is silence as Razer picks himself up and returns to his corner. He changes his weapons from the bo to a long whip with a spiked ball at the end.

'How do I change *my* weapon?' I whisper, panicking.

'You can't until you die.'

'*Fight!*' shouts the commentator.

'*Jump!*' Sparky cries. '*No – I mean – duck!*'

The spiked end of Razer's whip flicks out of nowhere and strikes me in the arm. My rifle flies out of my hands.

'Noooooooooo!' Sparky cries. 'Oli, I'm so sorry!'

In one swift move, Razer has rendered me defenceless. I wait for him to finish me off.

He doesn't.

Instead, he grabs the microphone from the commentator and faces the crowd.

'Waaazzz   uupppp…   Annnndd,   wwwhhhaaaattt

wwaaazzzzzz aallll *that* about?'

The crowd creases up with laughter.

'Toooo eazzzieeee. You know what I'm sayin'?'

'Toooo eeazzzieee!' the crowd shouts back at him gleefully.

Too easy? But the score's 1-1. I'm doing OK, I tell myself.

'OK, so, here's what we're gonna do to spice things up a little. We're gonna raise the stakes and play:

'"Let's let Oli decide."'

'Oh no – not another warped game,' Sparky moans.

'And here's how it works… I give Oli a choice between something like, "What do you want more, chocolate or strawberry ice cream?" And Oli has to tell us.

'OK, ready?'

The crowd shout 'YES!'

'So, warm up question: Oli, who'd you love more, your mama or your new papi, AKA ME?'

'My mum, of course!' I reply to a chorus of boos. 'You're *not* my dad!'

Razer shakes his head.

'This boy just doesn't know which side his bread is buttered on, am I right or am I right??'

'You're right!' the crowd cry.

'OK, next question, here it comes and it's a *goody*.

'Oliver Turner, you see this face, this unhappy, treacherous, backstabbing, ugly puppy of a face?'

Razer points up to the stadium screens, and I see a camera panning high up into one of the towers, much farther than I can focus. It zooms in. Suddenly, I see *Logan*. His eyes are closed. I realise that all these seats must be taken up by gamers who've become stuck.

'Mr Turner, son of Oli's Mum, if I told you right here and now that in exchange for one of your remaining lives in our game of Death Match, I would release this snake, this weasel of a boy, who you stupidly call a friend, would you do it?'

'Why's he saying all this horrible stuff about Logan?' I whisper to Sparky.

'No idea,' Sparky replies, sounding shocked. 'What are you gonna do?'

'Houston!' says Razer, turning to the audience when I don't answer straight away. 'I think we got ourselves a bit of P-R-O-B-L-E-M. Who knows what it is?'

The audience start shouting back silly answers, but I don't listen. I'm having a crisis. *A serious crisis.* I really don't know what to do. Part of me wants to help Logan – he's my friend, of course I want to help him. He might be an idiot sometimes but then who isn't, right? Also, he died trying to protect me. But I've only got two lives left and there is more at stake here than just Logan. *Much more.* And what about the fact that

Razer called him a snake and a weasel? Why did he do that? I need more time to think.

'Oli, the Prime Minister is ordering you to say no. He's saying you'll be risking too much for just one boy. He says he's sorry if that's hard to hear but that's just the way it needs to be.'

I grit my teeth and nod.

'Son of Oli's Mum, do you agree to lose a life to save this Traitor Alligator?' Razer asks, pointing a finger at the screen. 'If you say *NO*, then I swear by almighty ME, I'll fry that sucker's brain so good he'll be a new kind of "bubble" in the word "vege-tabubble". You know what I'm saying?'

'*Yes!*' I shout out. '*OK – yes, I'll save him.*'

A long 'EEERRRRRKKKKK' sound follows, the kind you hear on TV game shows when you've given the wrong answer. I can hear the Prime Minister screaming obscenities in the background and Sparky fighting to prevent him shouting directly into the microphone. The screen goes back to the scoreboard, which it now reads:

Big Daddy R: 2

Oli and Oli's Mama: 1

'Ahhhh, *maaan.* That was one major stupid decision, Turner. In your next life, 'cause it sure ain't gonna be in this one, you'd betta learn to pick your friends better 'cause that boy sold you out. That's right. When I came looking for you, it was that boy right there, that you call a friend, who made the call giving up your mama. And you know what else? He said that he didn't even want the money. He said all he wanted was for that carrot top girl called Ruth to be set free. *Five billion dollars. Hell*, was that mighty noble or just mighty dumb? I still can't compute me an answer on that one. You know what I'm guessing though?

'*The kid's still a virgin!*

'Yeah, it must be, 'cause everybody gets a little crazy at that age when all them hormones, or what I like to call "horny moans", start flyin' around all over the place.'

'*Dirty rotten Gitt!*' Sparky spits angrily. 'It's bad enough that he sold you out, but he put all of us, everything, in jeopardy, too. I swear, if I ever get my hands on him, he's gonna find out what having three brothers teaches you about pain!'

I'm gutted. And the fact that Razer is loving every moment of it makes it even more gutting. It reminds me of Porky Perkins and how he and his group of merry orcs loved nothing more than revelling in everyone's misfortunes. Creating them and revelling in them.

'It's OK. I forgive him,' I say.

Sparky cries, '*What!?*'

It comes out more like a mumble, but it's still loud enough for the strangest thing to happen next. A part of that vast silent grey crowd suddenly lights up. A whole section. Like someone has turned on lights surrounding each of their faces.

Razer glances up in surprise and stumbles slightly.

'*What you talkin' 'bout, fool?*' he says, using a different voice.

'I said I forgive Logan for what he did.'

If I am honest, I'd said it because I couldn't stand the way Razer was reminding me of Perkins and had just wanted to shut him up. I honestly don't know yet how I feel about what Logan has done and why – definitely not good at the moment – *but* I have a feeling that I might be on to something when another section of the crowd lights up a second later.

Razer looks up into the sky and starts talking to it.

'Say what?… Hello, *no*… Nah, the kid's just messin' with us, that's all. It ain't logical to be thinking like that.'

'Weird,' whispers Sparky.

'Logan was just trying to find a way to help the person he cares about most,' I continue. I know that this, at least, is true. 'You said yourself that he didn't do it for the money. He wanted to save Ruth. They've known each other for forever. She means a lot to him. I think he loves her.'

'If that ain't the dumbest thing I ever heard,' Razer spits

back. 'Anybody with any smarts would know that they should be takin' the money and then hittin' the road like Jack did. Plenty more fishes in a sea full of fishes, right?'

'*Oli,* I think you're rattling him,' says Sparky, cottoning on to what I think I'm also starting to cotton on to. 'Tell him that this is why he'll never amount to anything more than a cold set of code, bullying the world, because he doesn't care about anything other than himself. Tell him that all his bros and so's are just fake, that they don't love him any more than he loves them. And tell him that this is why he's always going to just be an *artificial* intelligence. Humans might behave very badly sometimes and do some seriously stupid things, and we might not be as smart as him, but most of us know how to care. And when we care about others and feel friendship and love, then the world becomes a better place for everyone.'

I repeat it all word for word.

More sections of the stadium illuminate. The effect on Razer is electric, and for perhaps a whole minute he stares at me without saying anything – that's an eternity of thought for an AI, and I feel myself trembling in anticipation, afraid of what he's going to do next.

I need to keep him occupied – stop him from wanting to continue the game.

'What I don't understand,' I begin, 'is why, if you can

access the minds of millions of people who are locked into your neural network, you're not smart enough to understand that what you are doing and planning isn't just wrong, but it's also not going to work.'

More sections light up. Razer looks up at the sky and starts talking to it again.

'No way, Jose! Nothing he is saying is true, I swear it.'

Who's he keep talking to, I wonder.

'Oli, don't stop!' Sparky urges. 'You're getting to him. I'm picking up massive spikes in the AI's networks.'

'What should I say?'

'Tell him that his cyborg armies might be able to help him control the world, but that human beings won't ever love him like a god, all they will do is fear him and pretend. And what will that give him? All he'll hear is how wonderful and perfect he is all the time, but it won't be the truth. He'll build a world based on fear and lies. And what kind of AI will be able to grow smarter if there is no one to challenge it to be a better version of itself?'

'Woah,' I reply. 'That's AI kind of *deep*.'

'What can I tell you. More than just a pretty face, me,' Sparky muses.

But I don't get a chance to say a single word of it.

Razer has just told whoever he is talking to that 'It's time for the fat lady to start singing' and called for his club.

'So how ya'll wanna be doin this?' he calls out to the crowd. 'A straight up bash and smash, with old Lady Luck, here? Or do you want to listen to more bleeding-heart speeches from a species too dumb to know what's good for them? Hell, they've already pretty much destroyed this planet. Me, I'm its evolution.'

The crowd, which had become subdued, begins to chant, 'Bash and smash the trash, bash and smash the trash…'

Razer raises his arms triumphantly.

'THE JURY HAS SPOKEN!'

'I'm not going to fight you,' I say as he comes towards me… I'm totally winging it now. 'I'm going to let you win. Do you want to know why?'

Razer shrugs and pretends to yawn.

'Because I know that you are about to be switched off.'

Razer flashes a look upwards at the sky for a second, but doesn't say anything to it. 'Impossible! You humans don't have the guts. In fact, I double dare you to try.'

I get down on my knees, and open my arms out in a gesture which says I am waiting for him to go ahead and do it.

'But that's where you're wrong, Razer. Because we would rather throw the world back into the dark ages and rebuild it all over again than be slaves. But that doesn't have to happen if we can learn to live together.'

I don't know if that's true or not, but it sounds reasonable, and way better than having to live without power for a long time. Plus, it's all I could think of to say in the moment.

Chapter 28

I knew it wasn't going to hurt, but I'd shut my eyes tightly anyway. The last thing I had seen was Razer, cackling loudly, eyes glowing red, lifting his club into the air with both hands. My last thought had been that I'd done my best but that now it was over.

Only, it wasn't.

At first, I'd had no idea what was happening. One minute the crowd had been baying for the trash to be bashed and the next I could feel the ground shaking, and then there was a terrible splitting sound. Sparky had cried out for me to roll right. I'd rolled right and opened my eyes to find that a huge crack had appeared right through the middle of the stadium, cleaving everything including the fight area in two. Razer, standing on the other side of the widening gulf, staring up into the sky, had launched his club at me without even looking. I'd only just managed to duck out of the way in time.

'You're really grizzling my gizzard, kid!' he'd shouted, turning and looking like he was ready to jump over to my side. But some unseen force had sent him crashing to his knees, forcing his arms to splay open like mine had been.

Seeing my chance, I had tried to run, but I wasn't able to. It was the same moment that the stadium – the three towers had crumbled, engulfing me in a dense cloud of dust and debris. And before I knew what was happening, I was falling.

I am falling.

I yell out at the top of my lungs as I tumble head over heels, down, down, down. It feels way scarier than the time I'd fallen out of the clouds at the start of the game. And, just when I feel that I'm about to puke, I find that I'm sitting in a chair. It takes me several seconds to realise this and to stop yelling, and several more to become vaguely aware that there is someone sitting opposite me.

'*Sparky,*' I whisper.

Sparky doesn't answer.

Slowly, everything comes into focus.

'*DAD!?*' I gasp.

I am in some sort of control room and there is a simulation pretending to be my father sitting in a chair opposite me. Certain that this is Razer playing some kind of sick joke, I stare back at him angrily.

'You're a real *shit*, you know that, right?' I say, assuming that even if it's not Razer in there, he can at least hear me. 'You need to be locked up in a virtual mental asylum.'

The simulation of my dad cracks a smile. 'I haven't been called that in a while,' he laughs.

The figure doesn't sound like Razer. It sounds like my dad. I turn away, confused. It hurts way too much, suddenly seeing him like this, especially when I know it *can't* be him.

The figure leans forward in his chair.

'I know how this looks, Oli,' he says softly. 'But there were things that I could never tell you or your mum. I just wasn't allowed to.'

My gaze flicks back but only for a second. I know that I shouldn't listen to what *it* is saying, I know that this is all fake. That it's just Razer.

'Oliver, I worked for the secret service.'

'Yeah, right, sure you did. My dad worked in finance,' I reply.

'That was just my cover. I was a programmer. I was part of the team that built this AI. It was supposed to be the answer to so many of our problems. We had such high hopes. But then it all went wrong.'

'*Liar.* How stupid do you think I am? It was made by Rhine, Agrawal, Zaine, Edwards, Reed. Not Turner, Agrawal, Zaine, Edwards, Reed. RAZER not TAZER!'

'Oli, this was a top secret project at the very highest level.

331

All our names were changed, even from each other. I never knew what any of the people I worked with were really called. I was Rhine.'

The figure sighs.

'You're dead,' I say, angrily. 'We buried you six months ago. And I've seen Rhine and he doesn't look anything like you.'

Although I am trying not to look directly at him, I can see his reflection in one of the panels. I watch him shake his head.

'Half dead, Oli. Only half dead. And in that game Rhine was programmed to look different.'

'How can anyone be half dead?' I scoff.

'Because I was able to download myself into this AI mainframe. We all did it. Everyone who went on that fishing trip. When we realised that what we'd helped to create had become uncontrollable, it wasn't hard for us to foresee what was coming next. Especially once we knew it'd already escaped the research centre.'

'*Stop lying!*' I cry out. 'You drowned! With friends from work!'

'Oliver, *please*, look at me.'

I don't. My head is a mess of jumbled thoughts causing an even bigger jumble of emotions.

'*You're dead!*' I almost scream. I can feel tears running

down my cheeks and I seriously don't want Razer to see that. '*We buried you!*'

'You can't have buried *me,* Oli. They won't ever have found my body.'

At that moment a sound like rushing wind sweeps past. The simulation pretending to be my father flickers and looks worried.

'Oliver, do you remember when you were ten years old, I took you to watch Chelsea v Liverpool at Stamford Bridge. Do you remember that?'

I don't react. Of course, I remember.

'When you were eight you split your bottom lip open when you fell off the windowsill in the kitchen and I had to rush you to the emergency room. I wasn't usually home during the week, but that was one of those times when I was.'

I turn to look at him.

'On the day that I went on that boat trip. Do you remember what I told you?'

'What did you tell me?' I ask. Only my dad would know the answer to this question.

He smiles.

'I told you that if anything ever happened to me that you needed to make sure that you did your best to help Mum.'

Too easy. Everybody says stuff like that.

'What did I say?'

This time the figure laughs.

'You said, "Don't be an *oaf,* Dad." I'd just explained to you what the word meant after you'd heard it on the TV. Then you asked me why I looked like I was crying.'

It's him! It has to be him! No one else could have known that! Not even my mum!

'*Dad!?*' I cry, leaping out of my chair and attempting to hug him, but I can't feel anything. 'It's really *you*?'

The simulation of my father nods. 'It's really me. Now look who's doing the crying?' he says with a cheeky smile.

'But the boat trip? I don't understand.'

'The boat trip was the only way we could think of to make everyone believe that we were no longer a threat. You see, we couldn't take the risk of anyone finding out what we were planning to do. The AI already had a lot of supporters like Volkov, and we were already under surveillance. So, we staged it.'

'But why couldn't you at least tell *us*? Tell Mum?'

'Because it had to look real, Oli. We had to make it look like we'd died. For your safety, too. We knew that Volkov would take credit for it and that it would give us the chance we needed to get in.'

I step back.

334

'You hurt *Mum* so much. You hurt *me*.'

My dad clasps his hands behind his head and squeezes with his arms together at the elbows. I can see that he is hurting.

'I had to do something, Oli, to help stop this. I'm partly responsible.'

I hear the wind again, followed this time by sounds like doors being slammed shut.

'It's the AI core,' my dad says, glancing in the direction the noises had come from. 'It's trying to seize back control from Razer and implement a self-preservation protocol. Quickly, we need to start disconnecting everyone who is stuck in the game and then shut this thing down.'

Seize control from Razer? So that's who Razer was trying to convince that everything was OK.

'Dad, were you looking for me in the game? Is that why you – Rhine – contacted me?' I ask.

I don't know why but I suddenly wanted more than anything to hear my dad tell me that he'd always known that we'd see each other again and that he'd never really left me, never really abandoned me and my mum and that he'd been looking out for me to see if I'd come and help fight the AI. The instant I see him put on his explaining face, the one he always used to use to deliver news, he figured I wasn't going to like, I had my answer.

Stupid question, Oliver. Stupid question!

'The AI started hunting us down the very moment we found a way in,' he began. 'We had built it too well. We never even got close to being able to disable it. Every day we were just running, hiding from it with no way out. In the end I chose to hide inside the game. It was safe enough there while nobody attempted to get in. But once the world decided to try to shut it down by playing it, the AI turned its attention to *it* and found *me*. By then I was the last of us. It had eliminated all my colleagues. When I reached out, I knew it was closing in and I had to try to get the portal and the key into someone's hands as quickly as possible. Honestly, you can't imagine my surprise, how proud I was, when I realised it was you. I couldn't let on, of course, that would have caused too many problems.'

I nod, not wanting to show that I've just been ripped apart by his answer because he hadn't been.

'But just imagine, though, Oli,' he continues, 'what the odds of that happening actually are. I mean, my finding you again in the middle of all this chaos. Mathematically speaking, the probability is so infinitesimally small that the more I think about it, the more it begins to sound like fate as opposed to chance. But how crazy does that sound?'

'Yeah, crazy,' I reply, feeling a rush, like maybe, somehow, despite all that he'd just said, that we really were meant to find each other again!

'Dad, tell me what to do.'

My father steps up to one of the two control panels in the room, which have recessed keyboards and built in monitors, and sets about looking for the directories that contain the 'Gamers in Comas' files. As his fingers type away at lightning speed, he lets me know that we are in *the* control node, the one that he'd given me the portal to access. He says that it is *the only* back door that the programmers had made to the AI's core, and for a second I feel ecstatic. That feeling turns to confusion when, moments later, he goes on to say that the node had been impossible to enter before the AI had caused the chasm which I'd just fallen through. And that it was only when he'd noticed that the wall around it was down suddenly that he himself had been able to get in.

'But that's only just happened,' I say. 'I don't understand, if you knew it was going to be impossible to get in, then why did you give us the portal and the key in the first place?'

'Because without them you'd never have even had a chance,' he replies, cryptically.

'Chance? But you just said they didn't work.'

'They didn't – at the time.'

'What's that supposed to mean?'

'I mean,' he says continuing to type and speak, 'that when

the core AI went rogue, it locked out the external node. Neither I nor any of my colleagues knew this and it was the reason our attempts to stop the AI failed. But it is still the only way in without knowing where the AI mainframe is physically located, which no one does.

'What you need to understand, Oliver, is that the core AI and RAZER are not the same. Think of the core AI as the Earth and Razer as the North Pole. He's just a part of the planet. Only, here's where things start getting confusing, because the core AI, for whatever reason, decided that RAZER's aggressive war game programming was going to be its best chance of survival and began to assign more processing power to it. Razer, who at the start of all this is just a minor part of the core, comes alive, so to speak, and starts to use his increasing power to create and implement the plan to neurally trap tens of millions of gamers, and basically create his own human supercomputer in a way that the core AI will find difficult to control.'

My dad glances at me. 'You following this?'

I shrug. 'Kind of, but I still don't see how it answers my question.'

'You will... Now, fast forward to your showdown with Razer and to the incredible reactions of all those gamers in the towers who must have been able to hear you on some kind of level. It's my belief that the core AI, who RAZER wasn't allowing to access the minds of the millions of people he had trapped, must have started to understand that it was in danger and that humans weren't going to be as easy to defeat as Razer had been telling it. This was when it decided that it needed to stop RAZER and, in the process, inadvertently caused the wall around this node to open.'

Seeing me staring at him blankly, my dad rolls his eyes.

'In other words, if I had told you the truth, that the key wouldn't have worked, then no one would have kept trying to reach the node. In which case the events which led up to the Death Match and to us standing here now, *in* the node, with a chance to not only save a lot of people, but shut this thing down for good, would also not have happened. Now do you see?'

'But didn't we just get lucky?'

My dad stops typing and fixes me with a firm look. 'We create our own luck in this life, Oli. And it can never be done if we are not prepared to try and to fail even when things are looking bleak. So, yes, we got lucky, but if no one had been prepared to try, it never could have happened.'

Part of me wants to argue that he still kind of told us a lie though, and that things might not have worked out in the same way. But I don't because I'm pretty sure that he'll just repeat the part about needing to be prepared to try and to fail. Also, the last thing I want to be doing is arguing with my *still-alive dad*!

'Bingo! I'm into the directories! Now I'm going to need your help,' he says.

He motions for me to get on to the other terminal and then shows me what I need to do. The links to each of the gamers have been batched together into files of about five million. In total there are 18 files, which feels weird because 18 doesn't sound like a lot. But they amount to almost 90,000,000 people. To free them he shows me how to select a group, enter several lines of code into the terminal and hit enter. It's not hard, but it takes time. When he's sure that I know what I'm doing, my father returns to his terminal and starts trying to get into the AI's main operating system. He says that he and the others had created a virus to bring it down.

Chapter 29

The AI knows what we're doing.

It's been attempting to stop us by rerouting functions away from our terminals. My father has been working like a man possessed to counter it, and I can't stop staring at the awesome speed at which he is typing and flicking between windows. I have never met this part of my dad. Catching me gawping, he cracks a smile and tells me that he was a total 'demon coder' *back in the day* and that, if I keep looking over all the time, I'll never finish. I have already lost count of the number of times I've entered the code in the DOS prompt to bring up the next batch of GICs (Gamers in Comas), typed in the exact sequence of letters, numbers and symbols and hit enter.

The AI has been trying to spike us – hitting us with surges of electricity which zip and spark over the surfaces of the computer consoles. If we'd had real hair, I swear it'd all be standing up on end like we were mad scientists. A surge has just taken out a whole wall of lights which had been blinking away and caused my dad to curse loudly. At the same moment I'd experienced a painful buzzing in my ears that'd quickly transformed into a high-pitched scratching noise, and then:

'Oli, can you hear me? Oli, it's me, Sparky, come in *Oli?*'

'*Sparky!*' I cry out.

'Oli!? Is that you?'

'Who else would it be?'

'I don't know.' She's sounding serious. 'This time I really thought I wasn't going to be able to find you. Are you alright, I can't see you.'

'Yeah, I'm fine,' I reply raising a thumbs-up sign in front of my face. 'Can you see that?'

'*No*. I just told you. I can't see you.'

'Right, yeah,' I say, feeling foolish. 'Sparky, listen, you're never going to believe this but…'

My dad, guessing what I'm about to tell her, waves his hands frantically in the air and signals to me not to. 'Tell them that it's Rhine,' he whispers, barely audibly. 'And tell them that Rhine has a virus that he's going to release to bring down the AI. Only, first we need to know if all the Gamers in Comas have been disconnected.'

'But what?' Sparky asks.

'But I, um… I found *Rhine,* and he says that we need to know if the Gamers in Comas are being freed because he's got a virus which he is going to use to destroy the AI.'

Sparky gasps and falls silent for a few moments before telling me to wait. Then she clicks off and goes to find Stubbs and the PM who she says are downstairs.

When I stop speaking, my dad whispers to me not to say anything to *anyone* about him. He tells me that even if we do manage to take down the AI, that it still won't be safe for him or for me. He makes me swear that I won't.

I swear, but I am pretty sure that Sparky must already know, I mean, it's hard to believe that she hadn't heard me shout *DAD* and everything else. The question is: does anyone else know? Stubbs, the PM, Command and Control!? I feel my stomach tightening at the thought that Command and Control might still be able to hear me. I need to find a way to ask Sparky without really asking.

'But can I at least tell Mum?' I whisper.

My dad looks at me sadly and shakes his head.

'It's better that you don't, Oli. It's better that she thinks that I'm…' He chokes for a second, before forcing it out. 'That I'm dead.'

'*But you're not dead!*'

'*Oli – my boy… my body's gone.* It died a long time ago. I exist, but I only exist here inside this computer. That's all. That's what I meant when I told you that I was only half dead.'

I barely notice that another surge has taken out my terminal. I'm not even sure that I care at that moment, although I think that I've already executed the code to release the final batch of

GICs. I feel like I have jumped from one nightmare right into the middle of another. One where I discover that my dad, who I thought had died, actually isn't dead, but at the same time he sort of is and that now he's become a ghost in a machine – kind of literally. I feel angry too. Angry for allowing myself to hope that he'd soon be coming home and that we'd be a family again.

Sparky returns, and it's not until she's called my name several times and sworn at me that I realise she's back.

'Oli, wake up! What's wrong with you?'

'Me? *Nothing*,' I reply.

'Then listen up because I've got brilliant news – it's working. The gamers are waking up. Honestly, it's fantastic. It's happening all over the world. You guys did it!'

I tell my dad. Although I know it's really good news, I don't feel much excited about it.

'That's fantastic!' he replies. 'But Oli, we're about to have bigger problems. The AI's personal army is going to crash through these walls any second now.'

'The AI's personal army? You mean more cyborgs?'

'Ooooh *no*. Cyborgs can't exist in the mainframe in that way. These things are much worse.'

'*Great*,' I reply, not even trying to get my head around the idea that a computer, an AI, could possibly have its own army.

But then again, why not? I mean, here I am sitting with my half dead dad inside a virtual control room, inside a computer mainframe somewhere, as though it's all completely real and normal. *Maybe* this is what the future looks like now. *Maybe* virtual reality and reality were about to mould themselves together.

'Daa – *Rhine* – the wall!' I cry as the wall opposite us buckles.

There had been no warning that it was about to happen.

'I see it. I'm almost there. Oli, listen: as soon as I've released the virus, I'm going to transport myself into your headset. When you get out of here, I need you to find a half decent computer to download me into. Preferably a computer stack, a mainframe, something powerful, OK?'

I nod as the wall creaks and bends farther like it is being sucked out. I can hear laughter. I don't need to guess who.

'Knockety, knock, knock, *knock.* Urgent telegram for all you piggies in there.'

My dad freezes for a second. I can see from his expression that he hadn't been expecting Razer.

'Now, listen up, 'cause a couple of little computer birdies told me that my boy is hiding in this little room. Come out, come out, wherever you are, son… Papa's *here.*'

I glance at my dad but he's not paying attention.

345

'*Ooh! And* that ain't all. I also heard a rumour that I'm gonna find myself an esteemed guest inside this little tuna tin. The very man who put the R is Razer himself. *Mr Bradley Rhine.* You cannot imagine how long I been looking forward to this moment, Rhiney, baby!'

'Two minutes,' says my dad, eyes glued to the terminal screen in front of him. I really have no idea if he's hearing what Razer's saying or not.

'So… ANYWAYS, HERE I COME – ready or not!!'

Part of the wall blows outwards and bounces off down what looks like a metal corridor beyond. I hear Razer before I can see him.

'*Heeeerrrreee's Joooooohnny!*' he cries, sliding theatrically across the open patch of wall from the right side. I glance at Dad. He hasn't looked up. *God, I hope he's close!*

Razer strikes a pose like The Joker and opens his arms wide.

'What are you waiting for, child? C'mon, get your scrawny ass over here and give your big ol' pa, a hug.'

This time my father does look up, and frowns.

'Hey there, *Whiny Rhiney*,' Razer says, waving at him casually.

Razer raises a hand and pretends to whisper me a secret. 'That's what they called him at school, you know – Whiney Rhiney, 'cause he was always whining 'bout somthin'. Hell, you know what? I reckon he should've married your mama!'

Razer falls about laughing. I can't believe that he's just said that. Does he know or is he just being himself?

'So, anyways, don't think that I don't know what you pesky kids are up to, hiding away in here. I'd have been here sooner, but I had to fry me one hell of an egg sandwich, if you know what I'm sayin'? Still, it's *all good*, now.

Razer fixes his gaze straight at me.

'Which *means*, jellybeans, that it's time to really say goodbye. *I know, I know – like finally, right!?* Maaan, you've been one hell of a troublesome child, son.'

All of a sudden there is scratching sound from somewhere outside. It's the sound that metal makes on metal. And an enormous microchip-like spider skids to a halt in the open wall.

'Everyone, meet Snow White, Snow White, kill everyone, please.'

The microchip spider, which is way taller than I am, lunges towards me and I dive sideways. I can hear Razer wetting himself.

'No, no, get Whiney Rhiney first!'

My father, still at the terminal, doesn't move.

Knowing that I need to buy him more time and not knowing what else to do, I let out a blood curdling yell, and throw myself onto the back of the monster. I attempt to cling on to it.

Its body though is smooth along the top and I slide off. But it doesn't matter – it works. The spider turns in my direction. Only now I see that it has a whole load of red eyes which are getting redder by the millisecond. With a sound like a laser canon being fired, streaks of *something* come jetting out of them; I jump out of the way as the panel I've just been standing in front of gets covered in it and melts. I start running. What happens next is a blur. I never see Razer reaching out to grab me. I barely even notice being thrown down the same corridor which part of the wall had been sent flying down minutes before. All I know is that the monster has turned towards my dad.

Chapter 30

'Oli… *Oli?*'

I am having flashbacks of the microchip spider and its red lava-shooting eyes standing behind my dad. This is the last thing I think I saw; I don't know what happened next.

'*Oli?!*'

'*Sparky! Sparky! Did my d – Rhine, release the virus!?*' I cry out, as the flashbacks fade, and I suddenly realise that my VR kit has gone dark. A wave of panic sweeps through me.

'*Your* Rhine?' Sparky giggles. 'Yeah, he did it. It's working! The AI's networks are shrinking, take a look for yourself.'

Trying to keep calm and breathe, I remove my headset, praying that it's not broken and that he made it, and see that Sparky is pointing excitedly towards one of the screens on the wall which Stubbs and the Prime Minister would have been using to watch me on. Neither of them is there. The screen shows a network map of Western Europe with thousands of red lines that are at that moment in the process of turning blue.

'*But what about Rhine?* Do you know what happened to him? He was supposed to transfer himself into my headset, but it's gone dark – I can't see *anything*.'

Sparky stares at me as though she's about to drop bad news and my throat tightens. She shakes her head. 'I don't know,' she says. 'The second the virus was executed, we literally pulled the wires out of you. There was no way we were going to risk you getting taken down with it.'

Dad!

'But do you think he had enough time to make it out? He said he'd do it the second he released it.'

Sparky shrugs. She's suddenly looking really worried, and I wonder if it's because she knows that Rhine is my dad. My stomach drops. If she does know (and I don't see how she can't), she's not giving anything away.

'C'mon – we need a computer. Which means that we need Stubbs,' she says, jumping out of her seat.

VR headset grasped firmly in my right hand, I do the same. Getting to my feet, my knees give out, and I fall flat on my face. I hadn't even realised that my legs had become numb from sitting for so long. Sparky grabs hold of me and pulls me up. I hobble towards the door, where we run into Stubbs who is coming up the stairs on his way to get us.

'Ah, just the two I was hoping to find,' he says, grinning. He is looking ten years younger than before we went in. 'The Prime Minister is on the front lawn readying to do an interview with the world's media. He's asked for you both to make an appearance.'

Seeing the looks on our faces, the fact that we're not smiling or looking anything like he'd probably been expecting to find the two people who've just help defeat the AI to be looking, his smile vanishes.

'What is it?' he asks.

'It's Rhine,' says Sparky.

'My headset's gone dark,' I say.

'We don't know if he made it across,' says Sparky.

'So, we need a serious computer,' I say.

Stubbs takes a second to fit the pieces together and waves us forward, 'Right then, follow me.'

Clarkson, who'd been looking for Stubbs, catches up to us in the hallway. She's still looking stressed. Hurrying over, she congratulates us, and then tells Stubbs that the PM is getting impatient, and that he's decided Sparky and I need to be on the podium with him right from the start to maximize the 'impact'. Also, he's demanding we find a Union Jack from somewhere and get that set up in the background.

For a split second I swear that I catch Stubbs rolling his eyes. He tells her to tell the Prime Minister that there's been an unavoidable delay and that he'll explain later – personally. Clarkson nods and leaves, looking confused about how exactly she is going to deliver that message.

'That reminds me – you're going to have to learn to get used to this, at least for a while – the interest from the press, I mean,' says Stubbs as we set off again after him, 'but don't worry, just try to grin and bear it. It won't last forever – it never does. They'll soon get bored when something more interesting comes along.'

Sparky and I nod without saying anything. It's not something that I had thought about even once, and it conjures up visions of paparazzi going through our rubbish, trying to find out what we had for dinner and chasing me and my mum down the street wanting to know where we are going and what we'd be doing when we get there. I mean, how interesting can my going to school and my mum going to her job at the library be?

Judging by the normal lights in the stairwell, it looks like the power has been at least partially restored to the facility. We exit at a level well below those of our Ops Room and the central hall and pass through another security zone. This one is being manned by well-armed guards who insist that even Stubbs, despite knowing who he is, pass through the body scanners.

We enter a long, narrow room overlooking a cavernous data centre. The room, which has the feel of a portacabin, has several workstations in it, and Stubbs tells us to take the one in the corner near the window.

'Ready?' asks Sparky, seating herself and holding her hand out for me to pass her the headset.

I nod and give it to her, but not before I have asked at least twice if she's sure that she knows what she's doing. Worryingly, or then again, perhaps encouragingly, she doesn't reply and gets busy connecting the headset to a computer port and logging in using her Hacker Support details.

An icon pops up on her screen labelled *External Device Utility*. It has a doctor's stethoscope as part of its design and I suddenly, desperately, want to tell her that Rhine is my father, *even* if she already knows, and that I can't lose him a second time and that she really needs to be careful. But I don't because I know I can't. She might already know all of this, but Stubbs doesn't look like he's aware of it. Which probably means that Command and Control also don't know because surely, if they did, then everyone would know, and he'd have said something?

Sparky clicks the icon, and it takes several very long moments for the computer to do its scan of the device. When it's finished, a window full of file folders pops up. I go through them as fast as my eyes allow, but I can't see any that say Rhine or BR or something obvious like that.

Sparky cuts me a look and then glances down at my foot, which is tapping madly on the floor. I stop. It's hell. I don't know what to do with myself as she calmly begins to go through the files.

'*There!*' cries Sparky, suddenly leaping into the air. 'It's *there!*' she cries again. 'Rhine's .exe file – it was inside the Misc. file. *He did it. He made it!*'

I want to jump for joy, to hug her, to hug Stubbs who is pacing up and down, but I have to stop myself. How weird was it going to look that I am so happy about saving a guy that I'm not really supposed to know?

Stubbs nods, then shakes his head.

'Incredible, quite incredible. That someone has been able to actually download themselves into a computer, and been able to continue to exist inside it, is, well, *incredible!* As I've just said.'

Stubbs gazes out the window at the endless rows of servers and then looks back a Sparky and me.

'But I think we are going to have to be very careful with this knowledge. The fallout from people having been locked in Gamer Comas is going to be tough enough to manage. If the world gets wind that someone has been able to live inside a computer without a real body, *that* is going to cause widespread chaos. The implications are going to be profound. Not just for the sick and for the old but quite simply for our own security. It's too huge to even contemplate at this point.

So, for the time being, I need you both to promise not to breathe a word of this to anyone.'

Sparky and I promise. It's not hard to imagine what Stubbs is talking about. People might decide that it is better to be downloaded into computers than die or continue to be sick or, even just to escape their boring lives. It would be like the metaverse for real. I wasn't sure what he meant about security though, but I did have a mental vision of people living inside other people's computers listening to everything they were saying. Was that it?

Sparky asks Stubbs for permission to create a disk partition on one of the servers where she'll be able to install and run Rhine's file. He tells her to do whatever she needs to do. And as I watch her clicking away, I feel so thankful that I have a friend like her. In fact, I feel *so* thankful that I swear to myself then and there that, if any of her brothers ever say anything bad about her, not only will I stand up to them, all of them at once if I have to, but I'll make it clear to them just how close they came to ending up as cyborg butt cleaners, if it wasn't for Sparky.

Sparky brings up the command prompt and leaves the cursor blinking on the screen.

'Go on then,' she says to me, getting out of her seat. 'If he is in there, it should be you who speaks to him first.'

355

Trembling, I sit down. My hands are shaking as I begin to type.

Rhine. It's me, Oliver Turner. Are you in there? I hit enter.

The cursor blinks away for what seems like forever. I glance at Sparky, who nods at me.

'Maybe I need to write another message? Maybe he didn't receive it or something?' I say.

Sparky grins. 'It's not a text message… Look…'

He's alive! My dad is alive!

Oliver, where am I?

You are in a data centre at a cyber defence facility. The one I was in.

And the virus? Did it work?

Yes! It's working!

☺ ☺ ☺ *!!!! That's great news! You did really well. I'm proud of you. But Oliver, I need some time now to adjust. Let's talk later, OK? At least now you'll know where to find me!* ☺

OK!! ☺

As I stand up, Sparky flings her arms around me, the force sends us flying backwards into the wall with a very loud thud.

'*Sorry*,' she laughs as one of the guards runs in to check what it was. 'But we did it, didn't we? We really *did it?*'

'You really did,' says Hawkesbury Stubbs, head in his

phone. 'You really did. Now, Oliver, Sparky, let's get the both of you up top on the double… Oh, and, Oliver, your mum is on her way here as we speak. She's fine, so you don't need to worry.'

'*Mum!*' I whisper to myself, suddenly feeling relieved and guilty all at the same time.

'You alright?' asks Sparky as we begin our climb back up the never-ending stairs.

I nod.

'You don't look like you're over the moon about how it's all turning out.'

'Don't I? No, I am, honestly. It's just that I realised with all that was happening near the end that I think I forgot about my mum.'

'Oh, *come on*. That's the dumbest thing I've heard in ages. It's not like you didn't have enough to worry about in those moments, right?'

'I guess.'

'Don't guess – *know*,' she grins.

There's been a change of plan. The press conference has been moved to the central hall inside the facility. Stubbs says that the PM hopes that it'll make for a more 'resonating media experience'. That and the fact that there are already a lot of parents gathering outside the manor house grounds, demanding their kids back. This last bit makes Sparky and me grin. The location of the facility was supposed to a secret!

The hall is absolutely packed. It looks like everyone who'd been stuck in the game is there. No one is sitting. It's standing room only. People are even up on the tables. And as soon as someone sees us enter, a shout goes up, followed by riotous cheering and applause. It's an *amazing* feeling. The Prime Minister, who I spy on the stage at the front, is applauding enthusiastically. He looks beyond happy.

People rush forward to congratulate us, patting Sparky and me on our backs and saying things like 'Well done,' 'Brilliant,' 'Rock on,' and stuff like that. It's totally weird because I've never felt comfortable being the centre of attention, and I have no idea how to look or act. We slowly make our way through them, and then, as we near the steps up to the stage, the crowd seems to part, and I find myself coming face to face with Logan. I stop for a moment, and we stare at each other. I can hear Sparky swearing at him under her breath. It's probably a good thing no one else hears it because I've never heard her talk like that. For a second it looks like Logan's going to say something, but just as he seems to be about to, his eyes drop to the floor, and he stands to one side. I have no idea what I want to say to him either. I don't know if we will be able to remain friends after this. I mean, he threw my mum and me under the bus. I get why – of course I do. He loves Ruth. But that doesn't make it right.

There *is* one thing about what he did though, and it has the word IRONIC stamped over it in big colourful letters. If Logan hadn't tried to save Ruth, then Razer would never have thought it funny to see if I would sacrifice a life to save him. Which means that the core AI would probably never have started to fear for its own survival.

I am not sure how much I believe in fate, but perhaps things *do* happen for a reason. As my dad said, the chance of me being the one who he gave the portal and code to were mathematically really, really small. And there was also the fact that he knew that they weren't even going to work – which, as he put it, meant that we were going to need to create our own luck. Or something like that. Basically, he lied, and kept his fingers crossed hoping everything would work out. And basically Logan did what he did and because of it everything *did* work out alright.

Talk about random-sounding. I don't know. But what I think I can take away from all of this is that, even when things are bad and it's looking like there's no hope left, they *can* change. Things *can* get better.

Ruth, who is not far behind Logan, smiles warmly at me,

and I nod back. I hope they will finally get together. I think it'll really help Logan's mood swings. And if it doesn't, well, then there is always Loathsome Lindsey. They might be a match made in heav… *hell.*

The Prime Minister, still clapping, is waiting at the top of the steps to greet us. As we climb up onto the stage, he shakes our hands and shuffles us into position on either side of him on the podium. The screen on the wall behind us is showing a map similar to the one we'd seen upstairs in the manor. Only, this one is global, and the red lines are changing colour everywhere. Sparky and I exchange nervous looks. It's hard to see out from the stage because there is like a wall of camera flashes. I wonder how the press managed to get here so fast and suspect that the PM must have called them way before anything was certain. Lucky for him it had worked out.

Lucky for us all.

Sparky nods at me as though she wants me to notice something near the front of the hall. Wondering what it could be, I glance in the direction she's indicating.

It's Porky Perkins.

Definitely the last person I want to see at this moment, or ever again for that matter. Even Razer, despite being totally insane, had more going for him personality-wise than this cretin. Porky, certain that he sees me looking, puts his hands together like he's about to pray and bows slightly. I'm pretty sure that I even see him mouth the words *thank you*, but I could be wrong. I probably am. Either way, I don't want to look at him any longer.

A hush falls over the hall and the Prime Minister takes a step forward. As he does, he raises his right hand into the air and makes a V sign. Sparky and I smile at each other. He turns and signals for us to do the same. We do.

'Today,' he says loudly, clearly. 'Today we have been victorious over a new kind of enemy – in a new kind of warfare. From this day onwards we must learn our lessons and learn them well. We must do everything we can to prevent something like this from being able to happen again. *Which* is why I am happy to be able to announce to you right now that I have just got off the phone from talking to my colleagues around the world, and we have agreed that this day shall henceforth be known as FVG Day – the day the people of our great planet played their final video game. Because, as of tomorrow morning, they are all going to be banned.'

'WWWWHHHAAAAATTTTTTT!!!????'

Hiya,

Please help more people find this book by leaving a rating, or even a review if you have the time. Your vote and your opinion really count!

Thaaaannkkk yoouuuu!!

Read more from Craig at Amazon.

Scan the QR code below or visit:

https://www.amazon.com/stores/Craig-

Speakes/author/B0BK8Z4DJH